key (Bour
f ice.
h sweet cider.

cocktail glass.

(From a recipe in the possession of Charles G. Leland, Esq.)

oint of lemon juice.

CKTAILS

...ara bitters
...uracao
Piece of cut loaf sugar
Dissolve in two spoonfuls of water
100% liquor as desired
1 piece
Stir w...
of lemo...
serve.

uice.
hisky.
randy.
ermouth.
d strain into
glass.

, mettre quelqu
orange bitter.

½ Calvados, or Apple Brandy.
½ Dubonnet.
Shake well and strain into cocktail glass.

PORT WINE NEGUS.

In making port wine Negus, merely o... the jelly; for when port wine comes in c... tact with calves-feet jelly, it immediat... assumes a disagreeable muddy appearan...

continually on ice, as, by doing ... will be saved; mix as follows:
1 fresh egg (the white only);
¾ table-spoonful of sugar;
1 or 2 dashes of lemon juice;
2 or 3 dashes of lime juice;
3 or 4 dashes of absinthe, dissolve well with a little water or selters;
¾ glass filled with fine-shaved ice;
1 wine-glass of Scotch whiskey.
Shake up well with a shaker; strain it into a good-sized bar glass; fill up the balance with syphon selters or vichy water, and serve.
The above drink must be drank as soon as prepared, so as not to lose the effect and flavor. The author respectfully recommends the above drink as an excel-

MORNING GLORY FIZZ.

inger Ale.

ull of ice,
ktail.
brandy
lass, and

SAZERAC COCKTAIL.

A LA ARMAND REGNIER, NEW ORLEANS, LA.

...full of cracked ice place about a small ba... of Selner bitters and a jigger of Saze... em cocktail-glass which has been rinsed... a piece of lemon peel over the top an...

OLD FASHIONED COCKTAIL

...oned Cocktail glass.
½ piece Domino Sugar
2 dashes Angostura Bitters
1 drink El Bart Gin
1 slice Orange Peel
1 slice Lemon Peel

TUXEDO COCKTAIL.

(Use a large bar glass.)

¾ glass full of fine-shaved ice;
1 or 2 dashes of maraschino;
1 dash of absinthe;
2 or 3 dashes of orange bitters;
½ wine glass of French vermouth;
½ wine glass Sir Burnett's Tom gin;
Stir up well with a spoon, strain into a cocktail glass, putting in cherry, squeeze a piece of lemon peel on top and serve.

PEGU CLUB

4 parts Dry Gin
1 part Curacao
1 part Lime Juice
1 dash Angostura Bitter...

OLD FASHIONED COCKTA...

A LA OSCAR OBERSTALLER, NEW YOR...

Into an old-fashioned, heavy-bottomed bar glass ... sugar and enough water to dissolve the same; muddle ... until the sugar is dissolved; add a large piece of ice, ... bitters, a jigger of the desired brand of liquor and a ... peel. About two dashes of Boker's bitters should be us... are not obtainable, two drops of Angostura bitters wi... Stir thoroughly and serve in the same glass with ice

½ Gin.
¼ Lemon Juice.
¼ Kummel.
Shake well and strain into cocktail glass.

Juice
y Gin.
into

...ab, Burma,
...ed, and is asked for, round
...he world.

1 dash oran...
6 dashes cu...
¾ jigger rye whiskey.
2 dashes grenadine syrup.
1 white of egg.
Stir well. Serve in claret glass.

Metrop...
(A sm...
½ pony brandy.
1 " French verm...

Old-Fashioned Whiskey Cocktail.

Dissolve a small lump of sugar with a little water in a whiskey-glass; add two dashes Angostura bitters, a small piece ice, a piece lemon-peel, one jigger whiskey. Mix with small bar-spoon and serve, leaving spoon in the glass.

...om and Jerry.
...-bowl for the mixture.)

Made sa...

SOUTH SIDE FIZZ

BEE'S KNEES

Gin	½ jigger	Orange	1 spoon
Lemon	1 spoon	Honey	1 spoon

Shake well with ice, strain into chilled cocktail glass and serve.

...of Lemon Peel on top of gl...

Juice of ½ Lemon.
...espoonful of Powdered Sugar.
...gs Fresh Mint.
...s Dry Gin.
...ell and strain into ...ize glass. Add dash of ...on soda water.

RATTLE-SNAKE COCKTAIL.* (6 people)

4 Glasses Rye Wh...
The Whites of 2...
1 Glass Sweetene...
Juice.
A Few Dashes Absinthe.
Shake very thorough... by straining it thr... sieve.

* So called because it will either cure R... bite, or kill Rattlesnakes, or make you ...

...egus is a modern beverage...

BEES' KNEES

1/6 jus de citron
1/6 Miel
faire ce mélange avant
2/3 Gordon's dry Gin
Frapper le tout

FRANK MEIER, *Bar du « Ritz ».*

CORP... REVIV...

...gger Brandy.
...gger Creme de Menthe White.
...non Peel.
...e, strain into Cocktail Glass.

...the bar, ...
...xture of ½ brandy, ½ Jamai...
...m, inste...
...y mixed a...
is used to each tu...
N. B.—A tea-...
much carbonate ...
vent the sugar fr...
This drink is sometimes called Cop...

¼ Italian Vermouth.
¼ Apple Brandy or Calvados.
½ Brandy.
Shake well and strain into cocktail glass.

CORPSE REVIVER. (No. 1.)

To be taken before 11 a.m., or whenever steam and energy are needed.

(No. 2.)

½ Dry G...
½ French...
Shake well ... tail glass. Squeeze le...

155.

...ixing-glass ⅔ full of ic...
3 dashes of ...

Neg...

...of ten ... orange using ... and stir u... can be mad... Rum, etc., i...

...ktail g...
, twist a piece

CO-SPECS

CAS OH

rader Vic's
artender's
uide
Revised
THE FINE ART OF
MIXING
DRINKS
DAVID A. EMBURY
OFFICIAL MIXER'S MANUAL
GAVIN DUFFY
COCKTAILS
MORNING GLORY FIZZ
MANHATTAN COCKTAIL
KING'S PEG or BRANDY AND CHAMPAGNE
MAMY TAYLOR
KOLDKURE
MIMOSA or CHAMPAGNE ORANGE
Cocktails
ALEXANDER COCKTAIL
ALICE COCKTAIL
ALLIES COCKTAIL
ATTENTION COCKTAIL
AVIATION COCKTAIL

GIN COCKTAILS
MOJITO
GIN RICKEY
1 Lemon.
1 Part of Gin.
Seltzer water.
Serve in a High Ball glass, with ice.
— 14 —
TOM COLLINS
SLOE GIN RICKEY
The juice of a Lemon.
1 Part of Sloe Gin.
Seltzer water.
— 15 —
HERE'S HOW
HANDBOOK FOR HOSTS
GUINNESS'S
EXTRA STOUT
IMPORTED DIRECT FROM DUBLIN
E. GILLET
QUEEN'S PEG
or GIN & CHAMPAGNE
116. Soda Cocktail.
116. Brandy Crusta.
119. MULLS AND SANGAREES.
DEEP SEA COCKTAIL.
DRY MANHATTAN COCKTAIL.
DRY MARTINI COCKTAIL.

Book Design
by United Creatives Ltd.

Photos
by Debbie Bragg

Copy Editing
by Sophie Cross

ISBN
978-1-9162-1550-4
Hardcover Edition

Printed & Bound in Turkey
First Published in 2020

Contact
Cazerac Ltd.
Suite 213
28 Old Brompton Road
South Kensington
London SW7 3SS
United Kingdom

Email
contact@cazerac.com

Online
www.cospecs.com

A catalogue record for this book is available from the British Library.

CO-SPECS

CAS OH

PREFACE

CAS OH

Five years ago I threw away my cocktail specs.

By that time I'd already been bartending for well over a decade, and from the moment of my first entrée into the bar world I was fascinated with cocktails, and with how to make them.

That first gig wasn't the kind of venue that required me to be making drinks at the highest level – it was a turn and burn bar, where Sea Breezes and vodka Red Bulls were about the extent of the 'cocktails' demanded – but I was hooked on learning, creating and improving my drink-making skills nonetheless. Over the years, I got my hands on every book I could find, old and new, as well as the specs used by various bars and bartenders.

But, I *still* didn't feel like the specs I had for the classic cocktails were definitive, despite being accumulated and tweaked over many years. So I (perhaps foolishly; certainly naively) decided to begin from scratch, taking one cocktail at a time and starting with a clean slate.

If I had known then how long-winded the journey would be, and what a total time suck, I would never have embarked on it. But standing on the other side, I'm glad I did, and hopefully, this book will be useful to anyone interested in classic cocktails.

THE PEOPLE WHOSE SHOULDERS I STAND ON

Thanks to my friends and family for their patience and support, and for putting up with me during this time.

Also, a special thanks to those, without whose tireless research and resources, this book would not have been possible, people such as David Wondrich, Simon Difford, Greg Boehm, Jared Brown and Anistatia Miller, Jeff Berry, Martin Doudoroff, Jim Meehan, Ted Haigh, Gary Regan, Dale Degroff, Robert Simonson, Martin Cate, and many, many others.

I would implore anyone interested in this topic to seek out the books and articles written by these talented and dedicated authors, you won't regret it.

Cas Oh

HOW TO USE THIS BOOK

INTRODUCTION

I HAVE SPLIT EACH DRINK INTO TWO COMPONENTS: INFORMATIONAL AND PRACTICAL.

INFORMATIONAL

From the *informational* perspective, my aim was to find out everything I could about each classic – the history, provenance, any points of interest (or of contention). This would be distilled down to the main details; the things I would have wanted to know. To do this I pored through every book on the topic, along with scouring the deepest recesses of the internet.

PRACTICAL

On the *practical* side, I wanted to be certain that the final recipe was the version I felt was best balanced, whilst staying as true as possible to its origin. Each cocktail was made in all its iterations; balancing some were straight forward, whilst others required endless experimentation and ratio tweaking, to get to the 'Goldilocks' moment. I tried on every pair of jeans in the store, so to speak, to ensure there was no buyer's remorse!

This whole process took goddam forever. I essentially went into hibernation, and upon my emergence years later I was three shades paler from lack of sun, and certainly warranted the salty looks from family and friends given how insufferable I was during this period.

At the genesis of this project, I was too far down the rabbit hole to see that what I was working on was essentially a book. It's not until I had near finished the research that I looked at what I'd amassed and realised the shape it had taken.

These were just my own specs for my own interest, and for training my staff. But as the number of drinks increased and the folder thickened, it became logical to turn it into an A to Z of essential classics *(full disclosure, there are three distinctly non-classic, author's own cocktails scattered into the mix).*

The way the book is laid out conforms to how I want cocktail information presented to me. Each classic cocktail contains the recipe, first and/or key appearances in print, the credited invention (if known) and any important information or interesting trivia. I don't go into techniques, like how to stir or shake a drink, nor do I wade into explanations of equipment or other ins-and-outs of bartending. There are already plenty of great books out there covering these topics, written by bartenders and historians more knowledgeable and talented than me.

Rather, I'll assume that you already know how to shake and stir a cocktail, whether from working behind a bar or making drinks at home.

A NOTE ABOUT FUTURE EDITIONS

Origin stories can often be apocryphal, or just hearsay, with new details and information, discovered laying waste to previously thought truths. As and when new information comes to light, I will endeavour to update any future editions of this book to present the most accurate and up to date data available to us.

A FEW NOTES ON

SYRUPS

SUGAR SYRUP

I generally use a 2:1 ratio for sugar syrup or rich simple syrup as it's referred.

LEMON SHERBET

The first step is to make oleo-saccharum. Using a peeler, remove the skin from 12 lemons. Remove all the white pith without pressing too hard as we want to retain all the oils in the skin. Add two cups of caster sugar to the peels and gently muddle the mixture until all the oils have been expressed into the sugar. Leave for an hour. To this oleo-saccharum, add two cups of strained lemon juice, stir thoroughly, then strain out the lemon peels with a chinois, bottle and refrigerate. It will keep for two weeks refrigerated.

GRENADINE

Add one part fresh pomegranate juice to one part caster sugar, heat in a pan on a low/medium heat, stir until the sugar is dissolved, then remove immediately from heat, bottle and refrigerate. You can optionally add a tiny splash of vodka as a preservative. It will keep for around two weeks refrigerated.

RASPBERRY SYRUP

Macerate one part crushed raspberries with one part caster sugar with a ½ part hot water. Cover and leave for an hour, then strain the raspberry curds out, bottle and refrigerate. You can optionally add a tiny splash of vodka as a preservative. It will keep for two weeks refrigerated.

A FEW NOTES ON

MEASURES

MEASURES

Every ingredient should be measured, and whichever jigger you use, pour exactly to the line as if you were measuring for a science experiment.

For 1 tsp *(5ml)* and ½ tsp *(2.5ml)*, use cooking measuring spoons. Again, pour flat to the line; the liquid should neither be concave or convex. Same applies when using a spoon for sugar. Avoid using a bar spoon, as the amount you scoop will vary every time; instead use cooking spoon measures, and again flat to the line.

CONVERSION TO OUNCES

Converting from ml to ounces and vice versa poses the conundrum that when done directly it produces some arbitrary numbers. 25ml cannot be converted to ounces in any practical way, and conversely, ¼ oz is equal to 7.5ml, ¾ oz is equal to 22.5ml, both of which aren't compatible when using metric jiggers. Therefore, in my conversions, I've tried to match the proportions as best I can, that can be measured with common jiggers, whether you live in a place that uses metric or imperial. Some convert tidily when they are simple ratio based recipe like a 2:1:1 cocktail, but for others, I've adjusted the spec to approximate the best fit.

LIST OF

COCKTAILS

A

B

C

D

E

F

G

H

I

J

K

L

M

N

O

P Q

R

S

T

V

W-Z

ABSINTHE FRAPPÉ

TO

AVIATION

CO-SPECS

CAS OH

T H E

ABSINTHE FRAPPÉ

A GREAT INTRODUCTION TO ABSINTHE FOR THE UNINITIATED.

The ***Absinthe Frappé*** was created by *Cayetano Ferrer*, a Spaniard from Barcelona. He invented the drink whilst working at *Aleix's Coffee House* in New Orleans in 1874. His recipe was such an instant and enduring hit that the venue changed its name to *The Absinthe Room*, and twenty years later it was rechristened the *Old Absinthe House* – a name it still bears today.

Fast forward thirty years and the drink was popular enough that the hit 1904 Broadway musical *It Happened in Norland* name-checked the ***Absinthe Frappé*** repeatedly in the chorus of its titular song.

Whenever I mention absinthe as an ingredient throughout this book there's one brand I recommend above all others: Jade. The man behind Jade, *Theodore A. Breaux*, might look like a jacked, retired UFC fighter – one who quit the game to preserve his brain cells – but what he's done for the absinthe category cannot be overstated.

Breaux managed to reverse-engineer *actual* absinthes from the Belle Époque era so we can finally taste a convincing replica version from the spirit's heyday and see what all the fuss was about. In doing so he dispelled the fallacious myth of absinthe's drug-like effect and shows that the real reason for its success is that it was just so goddam tasty.

A

ABSINTHE FRAPPÉ

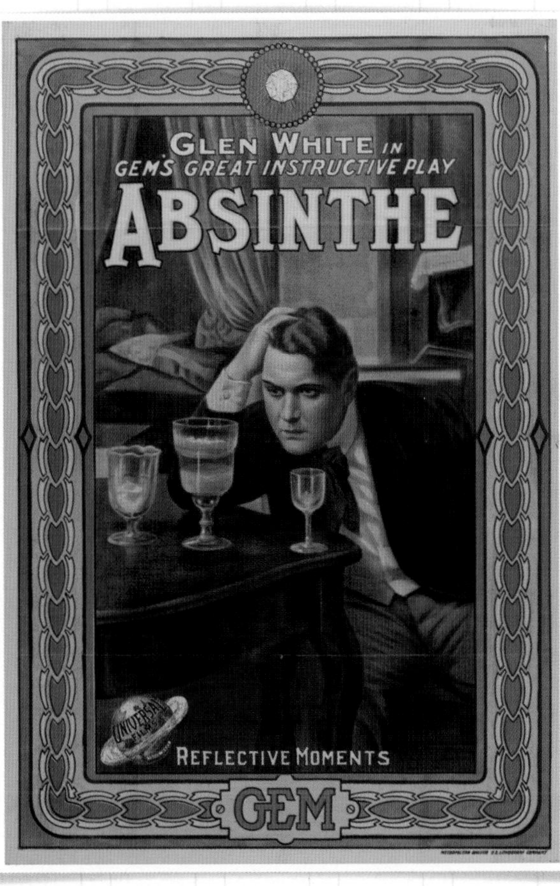

Thinking About Monday Like...

An absinthe addict eyeing three glasses on a table; advertisement for film "Absinthe" by the Gem Motion Picture Company.' by Gem Motion Picture Company. Credit: Wellcome Collection.

SPECS

ABSINTHE
50ML (1 ½ OZ)

SUGAR SYRUP (2:1)
5ML (1 TSP)

SODA WATER
50ML (1 ½ OZ)

METHOD

1. Pour absinthe and sugar into a rocks glass over crushed ice.

2. Churn gently with a spoon.

3. Add soda; top up with more crushed ice.

NOTES

Anisette is also added in some recipes. This drink can be shaken, however building it will chill the drink sufficiently, and provide adequate dilution.

THE

ADONIS

THE DRIER THE SHERRY THE BETTER FOR THIS DRINK. A FINO SUCH AS TIO PEPE, OR A BONE DRY MANZANILLA IS THE TICKET.

ADONIS COCKTAIL.

1 Dash Orange Bitters.
1/3 Italian Vermouth.
2/3 Dry Sherry.
Stir well and strain into cocktail glass.

ADONIS COCKTAIL

2 Dashes Orange Bitters.
1/3 Jigger Sherry.
2/3 Jigger Italian Vermouth.
Stir.

The Savoy Cocktail Book, *Harry Craddock, 1930*
Straub's Manual of Mixed Drinks, *Jacques Straub, 1913*

The ***Adonis*** is one of the best sherry-based cocktails and is often thought of in conjunction with the ***Bamboo***, its dry vermouth sibling. This wonderfully dry, low-alcohol cocktail was named after *Adonis (1884)*, which is believed to have been the first Broadway musical. It starred Henry E. Dixey in the eponymous role and ran for more than 600 performances.

Note: Crockett notes under the recipe "Named in honor of a theatrical offering which first made Henry E. Dixey and Fanny Ward famous." In fact, some say the Adonis was invented at the Waldorf Astoria Hotel, although that's hard to substantiate.

A ADONIS

Game... Blouses

The ratio of sherry to sweet vermouth in the *Adonis* cocktail varies depending on the publication. Here are the ratios for the three most noteworthy cocktail book recipes:

- Jacque Straub *Manual of Mixed Drinks (1913)* – two parts sweet vermouth to one part sherry.
Note: This is the first cocktail book appearance of the Adonis.

- Harry Craddock *The Savoy Cocktail Book (1930)* – two parts sherry to one part sweet vermouth.

- Albert Stevens Crockett *The Old Waldorf-Astoria Bar Book (1935)* – equal parts sherry and sweet vermouth.

SPECS

DRY SHERRY
FINO OR MANZANILLA
50ML (2 OZ)

SWEET VERMOUTH
25ml (1 oz)

ORANGE BITTERS
2 dashes

METHOD

1. Stir and strain into a cocktail glass.

2. Garnish with an orange twist.

THE

AFFINITY

A 'SCOTCH PERFECT MANHATTAN'.

AFFINITY COCKTAIL
⅓ French Vermouth
⅓ Italian Vermouth
⅓ Scotch Whiskey
2 dashes Aromatic Bitters.
Stir well in a mixing glass with cracked ice, strain and serve with a cherry and a twist of lemon peel over top of glass.

Recipes for Mixed Drinks, *Hugo R. Ensslin, 1917 2nd Edition*

"To My Dear Affinity" was a common Victorian-era phrase that featured heavily in Valentine's cards of the time; ubiquitous enough to be a sensible explanation for the cocktail's name.

The *Affinity* first appeared in print in 1907 in *The New York Sun* newspaper which speaks of a new cocktail on Broadway and gives the recipe as: *"One medium teaspoonful of powdered sugar, one dash of orange bitters, one jigger of Scotch whisky and a half jigger of Italian vermouth."*

But the definitive recipe for the *Affinity* is found in its first cocktail book appearance in Hugo R. Ensslin's *Recipes for Mixed Drinks (1917)* as shown.

A

AFFINITY

There is also a hit song, released in 1907 by composer John W. Bratton, titled *'Molly McGinnity, You're My Affinity'* – given the timing, that's another plausible explanation for the cocktail's unusual moniker. Apparently, the song was more popular than its clunky title might suggest.

The *Affinity* is often described as a *'Scotch Perfect Manhattan'* and these days it's usually made with a 2:1:1 scotch to vermouth ratio, however in my view the equal-parts recipe produces a more interesting drink.

SPECS

SCOTCH
30ML (1 OZ)

SWEET VERMOUTH
30ML (1 OZ)

DRY VERMOUTH
30ML (1 OZ)

ANGOSTURA BITTERS
2 DASHES

METHOD

1. Stir and strain into a cocktail glass.

2. Garnish with a lemon twist.

"I'll play it first and tell you what it is later."

– *Miles Davis*

THE

AIRMAIL

"IT OUGHT TO MAKE YOU FLY HIGH."

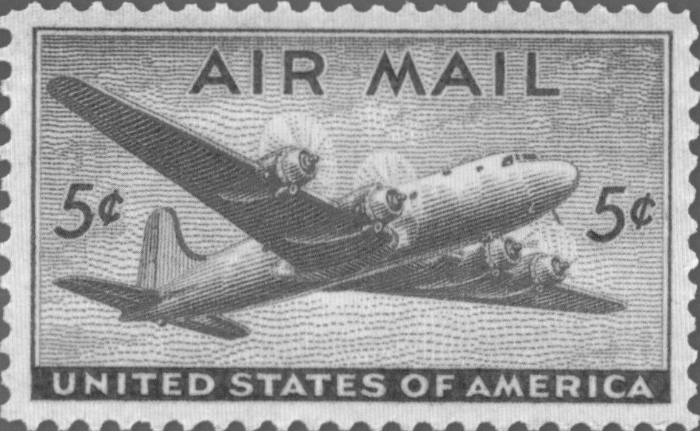

The origins of this drink are unclear, but we do know that it appears in *W.C.Whitfield's Here's How (1941)* and then again eight years later in *Esquire's Handbook for Hosts (1949)*, where the recipe is listed as:

1 jigger gold rum, 1 teaspoon of honey, Juice of half a lime, served in a highball glass.

However, the first record of this drink was in a recipe pamphlet produced by Bacardi in the 1930s, found by drinks writer and historian Greg Boehm.

A
AIRMAIL

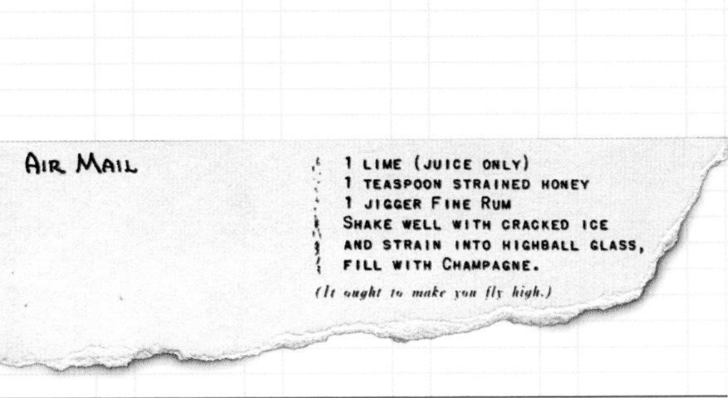
AIR MAIL

1 LIME (JUICE ONLY)
1 TEASPOON STRAINED HONEY
1 JIGGER FINE RUM
SHAKE WELL WITH CRACKED ICE
AND STRAIN INTO HIGHBALL GLASS,
FILL WITH CHAMPAGNE.
(It ought to make you fly high.)

Here's How, *W.C.Whitfield, 1941*

GOING POSTAL

The introduction of airmail revolutionised the postal service, radically taking over as the quickest way to get something from A to B. Aptly named, this drink will certainly get you from sober to lit in no time – as Whitfield writes – "It ought to make you fly high."

SPECS

GOLD RUM
45ML (1 ½ OZ)

LIME JUICE
15ML (½ OZ)

HONEY WATER (2:1)
15ML (½ OZ)

CHAMPAGNE
TO TOP

METHOD

1. Shake rum, lime and honey.

2. Pour over cubed ice in a highball. Top with champagne.

3. No garnish.

NOTES

These days, the Airmail is often served straight up in a flute, though it was originally intended to be served in a highball.

THE

ALASKA

I CAN SEE RUSSIA FROM MY HOUSE.

ALASKA COCKTAIL.

¾ Dry Gin.
¼ Yellow Chartreuse.
Shake well and strain into cocktail glass.

So far as can be ascertained this delectable potion is NOT the staple diet of the Esquimaux. It was probably first thought of in South Carolina—hence its name.

The Savoy Cocktail Book, *Harry Craddock, 1930*

The *Alaska* cocktail made its debut in *Jacque Straub's Manual of Mixed Drinks (1913)*. Harry Craddock included it some years later in *The Savoy Cocktail Book (1930)* although he omitted the orange bitters and changed the gin from Old Tom to London Dry, as well as rebalancing the ratio from 2:1 to 3:1.

A

ALASKA

ALASKA COCKTAIL
1 Dash Orange Bitters.
⅓ Jigger Yellow Chartreuse.
⅔ Jigger Tom Gin.
Shake.

Straub's Manual of Mixed Drinks, *Jacques Straub, 1913*

The name is a bit of a mystery: Craddock states that the cocktail probably has nothing to do with the state of Alaska, the most obvious reference and that it possibly originated in South Carolina.

Note: A slight variation appears in David Embury's The Fine Art of Mixing Drinks (1948) as the Nome Cocktail, and has the addition of dry sherry.

SPECS

GIN
45ML (1 ½ OZ)

YELLOW CHARTREUSE
15ML (½ OZ)

ORANGE BITTERS
1 DASH

METHOD

1. Stir and strain into a cocktail glass.

2. No garnish.

THE

ALBEMARLE FIZZ

A FRUITY VARIANT OF A GIN FIZZ.

ALBEMARLE FIZZ

Made same as plain Gin Fizz, adding Raspberry Syrup.

GIN FIZZ

Juice of ½ Lime
Juice ½ Lemon
1 tablespoonful Powdered Sugar
1 drink Dry Gin

Shake well in a mixing glass with cracked ice, strain into fizz glass, fill up with carbonated or any sparkling water desired.

The World's Drinks and How to Mix Them,
William Boothby, 1908

The *Albemarle Fizz* makes its first book appearance in Hugo R. Ensslin's *Recipe for Mixed Drinks (1916)*, and then later in Harry Craddock's *The Savoy Cocktail Book (1930)*.

A

ALBEMARLE FIZZ

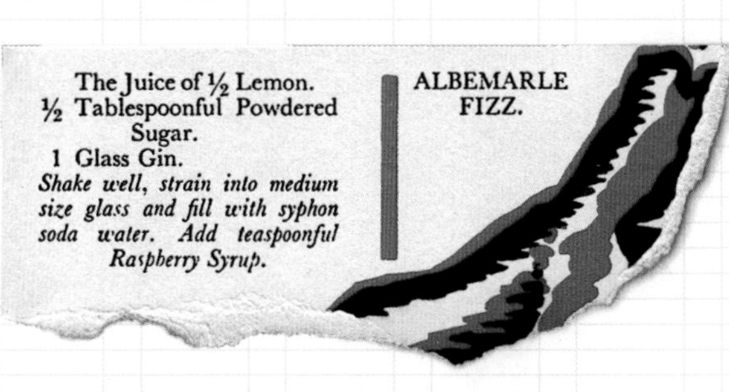
The Juice of ½ Lemon.
½ Tablespoonful Powdered Sugar.
1 Glass Gin.
Shake well, strain into medium size glass and fill with syphon soda water. Add teaspoonful Raspberry Syrup.

ALBEMARLE FIZZ.

The Savoy Cocktail Book, *Harry Craddock, 1930*

The *Albemarle Fizz* is a variant of the classic *Gin Fizz,* with the addition of raspberry syrup.

Traditionally, Fizzes were served without ice in a small highball, between 6-8 oz in size. Nowadays most bars serve it with ice, and in a larger highball glass. Tastes great both ways - dealer's choice.

SPECS

GIN
50ML (2 OZ)

LEMON JUICE
25ML (¾ OZ)

SUGAR SYRUP
10ML (2 TSP)

RASPBERRY SYRUP
5ML (1 TSP)

SODA
TOP WITH SODA

METHOD

1. Shake and strain into a small highball (6-8 oz) without ice; top up with soda and pour the raspberry syrup over the top.

2. No garnish.

NOTES

If you add a dash of maraschino to this drink it becomes a Bayard Fizz.

THE

ALFONSO

AN UNDERAPPRECIATED CHAMPAGNE COCKTAIL NAMED AFTER THE DEPOSED KING OF SPAIN.

The *Alfonso* takes its name from Alfonso XIII, the deposed King of Spain. It's often mistakenly said to have been invented in 1931 (the date of Alfonso's exile) or shortly afterwards, in France.

However, we know this can't be true, as the drink features in two of Harry MacElhone's books dated from before Alfonso's departure from Spain: *Harry's ABC of Mixing Cocktails (1922)*, as well as *Barflies and Cocktails (1927)*.

MacElhone's recipe is: *"...one lump of sugar in a medium-sized wineglass, 2 dashes of Secrestat Bitters poured on to the sugar, one lump of ice, one quarter of the glass Dubonnet, and fill remainder with Champagne, and squeeze lemon peel on top, and stir slightly."* He adds an interesting note underneath saying: *"The [above] cocktail was very popular at Deauville in 1922, during his Majesty the King of Spain's stay at that popular Normandy resort."*

Born alone, die alone, no crew to keep my crown or throne.

This very quote may be the culprit for the creation-date confusion, as France was indeed one of the countries he took up residence as an exile (the others being London and Rome), but MacElhone clearly states he's referring to the King's visit in 1922, not his later period of French exile.

Alfonso XIII's place in history may be ignominious, but his namesake cocktail is exquisite.

A ALFONSO

SPECS

DUBONNET
30ML (1 OZ)

ANGOSTURA BITTERS SOAKED SUGAR CUBE
1

CHAMPAGNE
TO TOP

METHOD

1. Place a sugar cube soaked in Angostura bitters into a flute glass. Add Dubonnet and top up with champagne.

2. Garnish with a lemon twist.

"I like to have a martini,
two at the very most.
After three I'm under
the table, after four
I'm under my host."

– *Dorothy Parker*

"Why don't you get out
of that wet coat and into
a dry martini?"

– *Robert Benchley*

THE

ALGONQUIN

A

ALGONQUIN

"ALL THE THINGS I REALLY LIKE TO DO ARE EITHER IMMORAL, ILLEGAL OR FATTENING."
– *ALEXANDER WOOLLCOTT*

The *Algonquin* is named for New York's Algonquin Hotel, home of the famed 'Algonquin Round Table' – a group of celebrated critics, writers and artsy types, who met almost daily for lunch, sharing their razor-sharp wisecracks and witticisms from 1919 through to 1929.

The gregarious group was comprised of such venerable members as the playwright George S. Kaufman, humorist Robert Benchley, *New Yorker* magazine founder Harold Ross, Alexander Woollcott, Harpo Marx and famously witty poet and critic Dorothy Parker. Despite its name, this drink was probably never consumed at the Round Table, as they famously drank *Highballs* and *Martinis.*

It's also worth bearing in mind that it was Prohibition at the time, so the hotel was technically dry. It was most likely invented some years later, as the first known print appearance seems to be from 1935: G.Selmer Fougner's *Along The Wine Trail.*

SPECS

RYE WHISKEY
50ML (1 ½ OZ)

DRY VERMOUTH
25ML (¾ OZ)

PINEAPPLE JUICE
25ML (¾ OZ)

METHOD

1. Stir and strain into a cocktail glass.
2. No garnish.

NOTES

The Algonquin is usually stirred though it can also be shaken, which produces a drink with a foamy head.

There is another obscure drink sharing the Algonquin name made with rum, blackberry brandy and Benedictine.

BITTER
CAMPARI
LITOGRAFIA GALILEO · MILANO
A Hohenstein
MILANO

THE AMERICANO

A SPIN-OFF OF THE MILANO TORINO; A COCKTAIL INVENTED IN 1860S MILAN AT CAFFE CAMPARINO, A CAFE OWNED BY GASPARE CAMPARI (OF CAMPARI FAME).

The name *Milano Torino* came from the drink's ingredients which comprise of equal parts Campari from Milan, and sweet vermouth from Turin (the traditional home of sweet vermouth). This would have been served on the rocks, in a tumbler.

During the early 1900s, it was so popular with visiting Americans that they redubbed it the *Americano.* This new version called for the addition of a splash of soda, although some say the soda was already present in the *Milano Torino* and it was merely a change of name, not ingredients.

AMERICANO

SPECS

CAMPARI
45ML (1 ½ OZ)

SWEET VERMOUTH
45ML (1 ½ OZ)

SODA
TOP WITH

METHOD

1. Build over ice in a highball.
2. Garnish with an orange slice.

TRIVIA

The Americano is the first drink James Bond orders in the original Ian Fleming novels.

“It wasn’t until late in life that I discovered how easy it is to say ‘I don’t know’.”

– *Somerset Maugham*

THE

AMPERSAND

AN OBLIQUE NOD TO THE AMPERSAND IN MARTINI & ROSSI.

A

AMPERSAND

SPECS

OLD TOM GIN
30ML (1 OZ)

COGNAC
30ML (1 OZ)

SWEET VERMOUTH
30ML (1 OZ)

ORANGE BITTERS
2 DASHES

PIERRE FERRAND ORANGE CURAÇAO
5ML (1 TSP)

METHOD

1. Stir and strain into a cocktail glass.

2. Add orange curaçao on top to finish.

3. No garnish.

The drink's name is most likely an oblique nod to the ampersand in Martini & Rossi, the brand of sweet vermouth that would have been used.

First printed in Albert Stevens Crockett's *Old Waldorf Bar Days (1931)* as one-thirds brandy, Tom Gin and Italian vermouth, with two dashes of orange bitters and another two of curaçao on top (after it's been stirred and strained).

THE

APEROL SPRITZ

IT'S EVERYWHERE YOU LOOK.

Sometimes called a ***Venetian Spritz***, the popularity and proliferation of the ***Aperol Spritz*** in recent times is a modern-day phenomenon. It is now, by far, the most popular aperitivo in Italy, as well as being consumed by the river load globally.

The *'Spritz'* found its genesis in the Veneto region of Italy, in the early 19th century; this was after the period of the Napoleonic wars when the Austro-Hungarian Empire took over the region. The occupying soldiers found the native Northern Italian wine a touch too strong, so they would ask for a splash ('spritz' in German) of water to be added – which later became carbonated water. In time, aperitifs and other fortified wines were added to the mix.

APEROL

The Barbieri brothers launched Aperol in the Venetian city of Padua in 1919. Shortly afterwards, in the 1920s, they began their first marketing campaign (in the form of posters) aiming their product at sporting types. Aperol had a lower alcohol percentage than existing competitors, and as such was presented as a healthier choice. Later, in the 1930s, the targeted demographic in advertising campaigns widened, extending to women also, and extolling similar supposed health-related virtues.

APEROL SPRITZ

The *Aperol Spritz,* alongside other Spritzes such as Campari and Cynar, enjoyed consistent popularity over the years, but the real boom happened for Aperol after the brand was bought out by Gruppo Campari in 2003.

Through some very savvy and wide-reaching marketing and TV campaigns, they heavily promoted the *Aperol Spritz;* the success of their PR efforts is plain to see.

The ***Aperol Spritz*** is the Dwayne *'The Rock'* Johnson of cocktails – it's everywhere you look, and everyone likes it.

SPECS

PROSECCO
3 PARTS

APEROL
2 PARTS

SODA
1 PART

METHOD

1. Build over ice in a rocks glass beginning with prosecco, then Aperol, followed by soda.

2. Give a quick stir prior to serving. Alternatively, this drink may be served in a wine glass.

3. Garnish with a slice of orange or olive on a stick.

NOTES

Some people (like me) choose to leave the soda out.

APPLEJACK RABBIT

A

THE

APPLEJACK RABBIT

ONE OF THE FEW OLD DRINKS (AND THE ONLY ONE YOU COULD DEEM A CLASSIC) THAT INCLUDES MAPLE SYRUP AS AN INGREDIENT.

SPECS

LAIRD'S STRAIGHT APPLE BRANDY (BOTTLED IN BOND) 60ML (2OZ)

LEMON JUICE 15ML (½ OZ)

ORANGE JUICE 15ML (½ OZ)

MAPLE SYRUP (GRADE B) 15ML (½ OZ)

METHOD

1. Shake and strain into a cocktail glass.

NOTES

In terms of the maple syrup, quality also matters – a high quality 'grade B' syrup is the one you'll want.

THE APPLE JACK RABBIT COCKTAIL.

1 Hooker of Applejack.
The Juice of 1 Lemon.
The Juice of 1 Orange.
1 Hooker of Maple Syrup.
Shake well and strain into cocktail glass.

The Savoy Cocktail Book, *Harry Craddock, 1930*

It first appears in Harry Craddock's *The Savoy Cocktail Book (1930)* however his version many will find a touch too sweet. A much drier recipe is detailed in David Embury's *The Fine Art of Mixing Drinks (1948): six parts apple brandy to one part orange juice, lemon juice and maple syrup, shaken with cracked ice.* My preferred ratio is 4:1:1:1 as shown.

Try to get a hold of Laird's straight apple brandy (bottled in bond) which is fantastic. But if you can't, you can substitute in Somerset cider brandy or calvados.

THE ARMY AND NAVY

NOT DAVID EMBURY'S FAVOURITE DRINK.

Information on this drink is scant, but thanks to David Wondrich we know that it was created by New York adman and occasional *New Yorker* contributor Carroll Van Ark.

Van Ark submitted it to G. Selmer Fougner's *Along the Wine Trail* (a drinks column in the *New York Sun*) in 1934, and this is the first record of the drink in print.

The next notable appearance is in David Embury's *The Fine Art of Mixing Drinks (1948)* where Embury calls for a simple 2:1:1 recipe comprising two parts gin, one part lemon juice and one part orgeat. He throws shade on the original formula calling it *"horrible"*, adding that: *"If made to my 1:2:8 formula, it is merely the Gin Sour with orgeat used in place of sugar syrup."*

SPECS

GIN
50ML (2 OZ)

LEMON JUICE
25ML (¾ OZ)

ORGEAT
15ML (½ OZ)

METHOD

1. Shake and strain into a cocktail glass.
2. No garnish.

NOTES

Some modern interpretations add dashes of Angostura bitters, as well as a lemon twist garnish.

ARNAUD'S SPECIAL

A

THE

ARNAUD'S SPECIAL

NAMED AFTER THE LARGEST RESTAURANT IN NEW ORLEANS.

SPECS

SCOTCH
50ML (2 OZ)

DUBONNET
25ML (1 OZ)

ORANGE BITTERS
1 DASH

METHOD

1. Shake and strain into a cocktail glass.
2. Garnish with a lemon twist.

Named after the famous Arnaud's restaurant in New Orleans, opened in 1918 by French wine salesman Arnaud Cazenave and still the biggest restaurant in NOLA.

During the 1940s and 50s, this was the restaurant's signature drink. They've had several over the years, the most recent being the *Arnaud's French 75* – which is a cognac version of the classic, and can be ordered at the restaurant bar, which just so happens to be called the *'French 75 Bar'*.

The recipe first appeared in print in Ted Saucier's *Bottom's Up! (1951)* listed as:
⅔ Scotch, ⅓ Dubonnet, Dash orange bitters. Shaken and served in a cocktail glass with a lemon peel garnish.

THE

AVENUE

A COCKTAIL FROM THE CAFÉ ROYAL COCKTAIL BOOK WITH ONE AMBIGUOUS INGREDIENT.

What we know of the *Avenue* cocktail comes from W.J. Tarling's *Café Royal Cocktail Book (1937).*

Tarling says it was invented by a W.G. Crompton and is made up of a third each of bourbon, calvados and passion fruit juice, along with a dash of grenadine and orange flower water.

The difficult thing about this drink is trying to figure out quite what he meant by passion fruit juice. Did he mean freshly squeezed juice from the pulp or the heavily sweetened synthetic versions that can be found in cartons? Hard to say, but the best bet is to use a quality passion fruit puree (one comprised of 100% fruit) and balance that with real pomegranate grenadine.

SPECS

BOURBON
30ML (1 OZ)

CALVADOS
30ML (1 OZ)

PASSION FRUIT PUREE
30ML (1 OZ)

GRENADINE
10ML (2 TSP)

ORANGE FLOWER WATER
DASH

METHOD

1. Shake and strain into a cocktail glass.
2. No garnish.

THE

AVIATION

A TRIBUTE TO THE DAWN OF COMMERCIAL AVIATION.

THE DAYTON WRIGHT AIRPLANE, SOUTH FIELD-MAY 14-18.

Quick, take a pic for Instagram!

Although it's not clear who invented it, the first ***Aviation*** appeared in Hugo Ensslin's *Recipes for Mixed Drinks* in 1916, and as such he is often cited as it's likely creator.

Hugo Ensslin, born in Germany, was the 30-year-old head bartender of the Wallick House Hotel in Times Square, New York. Other than those scant details very little is known about him.

AVIATION COCKTAIL
⅓ Lemon Juice
⅔ El Bart Gin
2 dashes Maraschino
2 dashes Crême de Violette
Shake well in a mixing glass with cracked ice, strain and serve.

Recipes for Mixed Drinks,
Hugo R. Ensslin, 1917 2nd Edition

A AVIATION

SPECS

GIN
50ML (2 OZ)

LEMON JUICE
15ML (½ OZ)

MARASCHINO
10ML (2 TSP)

CRÈME DE VIOLETTE
5ML (1 TSP)

METHOD

1. Shake and strain into a cocktail glass.
2. No garnish.

His book, however, was hugely influential and was an important source for Harry Craddock's *The Savoy Cocktail Book* which followed in 1930. For years the *Aviation's* first appearance was thought to have been in Craddock's book and possibly invented by him. Only when drinks historian David Wondrich found an old copy of Ensslin's work did everyone discover differently – and begin adding crème de violette as standard; something missing in the later Savoy recipe.

The early twentieth century was the dawn of commercial aviation, and as such, it was much in the news as an exciting developing technology of that time. This drink is thought to have been a tribute; the sky blue tint from the crème de violette adding further credence to this theory around its name. Another cocktail which appears in Ensslin's book and is often talked of as being similar to the *Aviation* is the *Blue Moon:* gin, dry vermouth, Crème Yvette, orange bitters, and a splash of red wine. You might see the link due to the use of Crème Yvette, another violet liqueur. However, there is a key difference between the two: crème de violette is only made with violets, whereas Yvette typically has the additions of berries, orange peel, and sometimes honey.

BACARDI COCKTAIL

TO

BUCK'S FIZZ & MIMOSA

B

CAS OH

THE

BACARDI COCKTAIL

IT'S VERY POSSIBLE THAT THE BACARDI COCKTAIL BEGAN ITS LIFE AS A PLAIN OLD BACARDI DAIQUIRI, WITH THE GRENADINE COMING ALONG LATER. INVENTED BEFORE PROHIBITION, IT CONTINUED TO BE POPULAR FOR MANY YEARS AFTERWARDS.

Bacardi Cocktail
½ pony grenadine syrup.
⅔ jigger Bacardi rum.
Juice of half a lime.
Shake well. Strain. Serve.

Daiguiri Cocktail
⅔ jigger lime juice.
⅓ jigger rum.
1 barspoon powdered sugar.
Shake well in fine ice; strain into cocktail glass.

Drinks, *Jacques Straub, 1914*

The first cocktail book appearance is in Jacques Straub's *Drinks (1914)*, however, there is an earlier print reference – the *Oakland Tribune (13th November 1913)* speaks of a cocktail with the same ingredients called a Rum and Grenadine.

The article describes a new cocktail from New York, made up of *Porto [sic] Rican rum, lime juice and a squirt of grenadine, – an uncanny resemblance.*

B

BACARDI COCKTAIL

SPECS

BACARDI
45ML (1 ½ OZ)

LIME JUICE
15ML (½ OZ)

GRENADINE
10ML (2 TSP)

METHOD

1. Shake and strain into a cocktail glass.

2. No garnish.

Next, we see it appear in Hugo Ensslin's *Recipes for Mixed Drinks (1916)*. He lists a *Bacardi Cocktail* and a *Cuban Cocktail* both with identical ingredients – but both are just *Daiquiris,* not a hint of the crucial ingredient: grenadine.

Tom Bullock later lists two versions in *The Ideal Bartender (1917)*: one called *Bacardi Cocktail - Country Club Style* consisting of *"1 jigger Bacardi, 2 dashes Imported Grenadine & ½ lime juice"*; and then another known simply as *Bacardi Cocktail* with the same ingredients, minus the lime juice. There is a cocktail in J.A. Grohusko's *Jack's Manual (1910)* called a *Bagardie* (which kind of sounds like a drunk person trying to say Bacardi), but alas is an entirely different drink, which calls for *Bagardie [sic] rum with Italian and French vermouth.*

As it grew in popularity after Prohibition, some establishments started to use different rums to make it. As a result, in 1936, Bacardi took a couple of venues *(Barbizon Plaza Hotel* and *Wivel Restaurant)* all the way to New York's Supreme Court to make sure that only Bacardi rum could be used in their namesake.

THE

BAMBOO

"A NEW AND INSIDIOUS DRINK".

31 **BAMBOO COCKTAIL.**

ORIGINATED AND NAMED BY MR. LOUIS EPPINGER, YOKOHAMA, JAPAN.

Into a mixing-glass of cracked ice place half a jiggerful of French vermouth, half a jiggerful of sherry, two dashes of Orange bitters and two drops of Angostura bitters; stir thoroughly and strain into a stem cocktail-glass; squeeze and twist a piece of lemon peel over the top and serve with a pimola or an olive.

The World's Drinks and How to Mix Them, *William Boothby, 1908*

The ***Bamboo*** makes its first cocktail book appearance in Thomas Stuart's cocktail manual, *Stuart's Fancy Drinks and How to Mix Them (1904): Bamboo Cocktail:*

⅔ Sherry, ⅓ Italian vermouth,
1 dash of orange bitters.

Stuart's recipe uses sweet vermouth *(making it identical to the Adonis)*, which is not how the drink is usually made today. The definitive recipe for the ***Bamboo*** can be found in William Boothby's *The World's Drinks and How to Mix Them (1908)*, where he uses the now standard option of dry vermouth and adds Angostura bitters.

Boothby's writing states that it was *"originated and named by Mr. Louis Eppinger, Yokohama, Japan"*. But was it?

The first known mention of a ***Bamboo*** cocktail appears in the Western Kansas World newspaper published on September 11, 1886. It contradicts Boothby's claim: *"A new and insidious drink has been introduced by some Englishman, and is becoming popular in New York barrooms. It consists of three parts sherry and one part vermouth, and is called 'bamboo'."*

B

BAMBOO

Interestingly, here it is an Englishman being credited as the creator of the ***Bamboo*** (whereas Louis Eppinger was German), alongside the note that it was popular in New York.

The article was published three years prior to Eppinger arriving in Japan, so if it was he who created this drink he must have done so while working in San Francisco, at the Grand Hotel.

Whether or not Eppinger was the originator, he can certainly take credit for helping spread and promote the drink - by the last decade of the 19th century, it was popular right across America.

*Note: The **Bamboo** works perfectly fine with most dry vermouths, although it can lack a little bit of depth. My personal preference would be to use the equal parts ratio as Boothby suggests, but using Dolin Blanc vermouth – the additional sweetness really elevates the drink.*

SPECS

TIO PEPE FINO SHERRY
45ML (1 ½ OZ)

DOLIN BLANC
45ML (1 ½ OZ)

ANGOSTURA BITTERS
2 DASHES

ORANGE BITTERS
2 DASHES

METHOD

1. Stir and strain into a cocktail glass.
2. Garnish with a lemon twist.

NOTES

Palo cortado or amontillado sherry also work great.

“The first principle is that you must not fool yourself – and you are the easiest person to fool”.

– *Richard P. Feynman*

THE

BATIDA

B

BATIDA

THE OTHER NATIONAL DRINK OF BRAZIL.

The *Batida* is the national drink of Brazil, alongside the *Caipirinha*. The name translates as 'shaken' or 'milkshake' in Portuguese and it's made with cachaça, fruit juice, condensed milk and sugar.

Sweetened condensed milk is essential in making this cocktail, you can't make an authentic *Batida* by removing or substituting it for anything else. The most popular flavour variations for this classic in Brazil are the coconut *(Batida de Coco)* and the passion fruit *(Batida de Maracujá)*.

Many of us have fond childhood memories of eating Nestlé Carnation condensed milk straight out of the can with a spoon... no? Hmm, ok. Just me then.

SPECS

DE MARACUJÁ

CACHAÇA
60ML (2 OZ)

SWEETENED CONDENSED MILK
30ML (1 OZ)

PASSION FRUIT PUREE
45ML (1 ½ OZ)

SUGAR SYRUP (2:1)
5ML (1 TSP)

DE COCO

CACHAÇA
60ML (2 OZ)

SWEETENED CONDENSED MILK
30ML (1 OZ)

COCONUT CREAM
60ML (2 OZ)

METHOD

1. Blend with crushed ice, and serve in a highball or hurricane glass.

2. Garnish with a passion fruit halved (de Maracujá) or a sprinkling of desiccated coconut (de Coco).

BEE'S KNEES

B

THE

BEE'S KNEES

FOREVER ASSOCIATED WITH THE LATE SASHA PETRASKE.

SPECS

GIN
60ML (2 OZ)

LEMON JUICE
20ML (¾ OZ)

HONEY WATER (1:1)
20ML (¾ OZ)

METHOD

1. Shake and strain into a cocktail glass.
2. No garnish.

BEE'S KNEES

Gin ....½ jigger Orange ....1 spoon
Lemon ....1 spoon Honey ....1 spoon

Shake well with ice, strain into chilled cocktail glass and serve.

BEES' KNEES

1/6 jus de citron
1/6 Miel
faire ce mélange avant
2/3 Gordon's dry Gin
Frapper le tout

Frank Meier, ***Bar du « Ritz ».***

World Drinks and How to Mix Them, *William Boothby, 1934*
Cocktails de Paris, *Georges Gabriel Thenon aka RIP, 1929*

Forever associated with the late Sasha Petraske, a true drinks pioneer who birthed the modern-day speakeasy. The *Bee's Knees* came about during Prohibition and is the most famous cocktail to feature honey as an ingredient.

'Bee's knees' was a common saying during the era and meant something extraordinary or great, similar to phrases such as 'the cat's meow', 'the cat's pyjamas' or 'the kipper's knickers'. It first appears in print in *Cocktails de Paris* by Georges Gabriel Thenon *(also known as 'RIP')* in 1929; he attributes it to Frank Meier of the Ritz Bar in Paris. When it appears in William Boothby's *World Drinks and How to Mix Them (1934)* orange juice appears as an addition.

THE

BELAFONTE

B

NON-CLASSIC
AUTHOR'S OWN

HEY INTERN, GET ME A CAMPARI.

Created in 2014 as an aperitif style drink, the ***Belafonte*** is a riff on the way white port is popularly served with tonic in Portugal. It is named after Steve *(Bill Murray)* Zizzou's boat in the classic film *The Life Aquatic.*

SPECS

CAMPARI
30ML (1 OZ)

WHITE PORT
30ML (1 OZ)

TOP WITH
TONIC

METHOD

1. Build over ice in a highball; top up with tonic.
2. Garnish with an orange twist.

THE BELLINI

THE FAMOUS DRINK FROM HARRY'S BAR IN VENICE, ENJOYED THE WORLD OVER.

The ***Bellini*** was invented by Giuseppe Cipriani at Harry's Bar in Venice in 1945 and named after the Renaissance painter Giovanni Bellini *(1430-1516)*. Bellini was a native of Venice, who over the course of a 65-year career in the city, established himself as one of the most influential painters of his period. Bellini was particularly known for his superlative rendering of natural light, and the use of vivid colours, such as the blush-pink hues which inspired the naming of the ***Bellini*** cocktail.

On the topic of naming things, Harry's Bar in Venice takes its name from Harry Pickering, a young American from Boston who whilst spending time in Venice met and befriended Giuseppe Cipriani, a bartender at Hotel Europa.

Pickering ended up borrowing 10,000 lire from Cipriani and left Venice shortly afterwards without settling the debt. Harry returned a couple of years later, sat down at the Europa bar, and gave Cipriani back the 10,000 lire he'd borrowed – as well as an additional 40,000 lire – to open and run his own bar for him. It opened in 1931, called Harry's. Harry's gained much fame and notoriety after illustrious writer/reprobate Ernest Hemingway started drinking there; they also frequently hosted everyone from F. Scott Fitzgerald to Orson Welles, Truman Capote and Dorothy Parker at the bar.

A heavy flow of tourist traffic demanding endless litres of ***Bellinis*** daily has continued for the intervening decades. The drink has become quite a draw for tourists in Venice from all over the world.

Pass me the shakers.

B BELLINI

SPECS

WHITE PEACH PUREE
50ML (1 ½ OZ)

PROSECCO
100ML (3 OZ)

METHOD

1. Add peach puree to a mixing glass or tin.

2. Pour prosecco in slowly at an angle; give it a gentle stir, then pour directly into a short thin tumbler or champagne flute.

3. No garnish.

NOTES

A true *Bellini* should only comprise of fruit and prosecco, without any additional liqueurs or spirits.

Bellinis are served at Harry's in a small thin tumbler as opposed to a flute. They're mixed carefully in a large metal shaker, and served by white-coated gentlemen who probably never want to see another *Bellini* again.

White peaches are abundant throughout Italy during the summer months *(June to September)* and peaches would be hand pitted, squeezed and strained in the kitchen at Harry's. Initially, due to the seasonal nature of the peaches, the *Bellini* was only available for those four months of every year. Now, one can drink them year-round, a feat made possible by the use of Boiron frozen peach puree.

There are several fruit variations of the *Bellini* such as the *Rossini (made with strawberry puree)* though none are as good as the original.

THE

BENTLEY

A TRIBUTE TO THE BENTLEY BOYS AND THEIR VICTORY IN THE 1927 LE MANS.

½ Calvados, or Apple Brandy.
½ Dubonnet.
Shake well and strain into cocktail glass.

BENTLEY COCKTAIL.

The Savoy Cocktail Book, *Harry Craddock, 1930*

In the 1920s and 30s, a group of pioneering adventurers, race car drivers, and playboys known as the *'Bentley Boys'* became famous the world over for their hedonistic, play-hard reputation.

Founder W.O. Bentley described the Boys thus: *"The public liked to imagine them living in expensive Mayfair flats, drinking Champagne in night clubs, playing the horses and the Stock Exchange, and beating furiously around the racing tracks at the weekend. Of several of them, this was not such an inaccurate picture."*

The Bentley Boys became virtual household names owing to their success in 24 hours of Le Mans, a famous prestige car race held annually in France since 1923. They won an astonishing five times in eight years.

The ***Bentley*** cocktail was said to have been created by Harry Craddock when the Boys celebrated their 1927 Le Mans victory at the Savoy where he worked. Craddock features the cocktail in *The Savoy Cocktail Book (1930)*.

B

BENTLEY

SPECS

CALVADOS
45ML (1 ½ OZ)

DUBONNET
45ML (1 ½ OZ)

METHOD

1. Stir and strain into a cocktail glass.

2. Garnish with an orange twist.

The Bentley Boys.
A Bentley in the Savoy.

As part of this raucous post-win celebration, they even managed to get the actual Bentley car into the Savoy dining room, where they proceeded to sit down to an elaborate eleven-course banquet.

BETWEEN THE SHEETS

B

THE

BETWEEN THE SHEETS

TO ALL THE LADIES IN THE PLACE WITH STYLE AND GRACE.

BETWEEN-THE-SHEETS COCKTAIL.	1 Dash Lemon Juice. 1/3 Brandy. 1/3 Cointreau. 1/3 Bacardi Rum. *Shake well and strain into cocktail glass.*

The Savoy Cocktail Book, *Harry Craddock, 1930*

Between the Sheets is a variant of the classic *Sidecar,* with the base split between cognac and white rum. The finger usually points to Harry MacElhone as having invented this drink at Harry's New York Bar in Paris in the 1920s; another story is that it was invented at the Berkeley Hotel, London in 1921, by a manager named Mr. Polly – however, both stories remain unsubstantiated.

Its first print appearance is in Harry Craddock's *The Savoy Cocktail Book (1930).*

The *Between the Sheets* is not as good as a *Sidecar* (or the Isley Brothers song, or the Big Poppa sample).

SPECS

WHITE RUM
30ML (1 OZ)

COGNAC
30ML (1 OZ)

COINTREAU
30ML (1 OZ)

LEMON JUICE
15ML (½ OZ)

METHOD

1. Shake and strain into a cocktail glass.

2. No garnish.

THE

BIJOU

EACH INGREDIENT A DIFFERENT JEWEL.

> **BIJOU COCKTAIL.**
> **(Use a large bar glass.)**
> ¾ glass filled with fine shaved ice;
> 1/3 wine glass chartreuse (green);
> 1/3 wine glass vermouth (Italian);
> 1/3 wine glass of Plymouth gin;
> 1 dash of orange bitters.
> Mix well with a spoon, strain into a cocktail glass; add a cherry or medium-size olive, squeeze a piece of lemon peel on top and serve.

Bartender's Manual, *Harry Johnson, 1900*

The name, ***Bijou,*** means *'Jewel'* in French; some say it derives from the three ingredients, each representing a different jewel: gin for a diamond, sweet vermouth for a ruby, and green Chartreuse for an emerald.

Note: The Bijou first appears in print in Harry Johnson's Bartender's Guide (1900) and was possibly his creation.

SPECS

PLYMOUTH GIN
30ML (1 OZ)

SWEET VERMOUTH
30ML (1 OZ)

GREEN CHARTREUSE
30ML (1 OZ)

ORANGE BITTERS
1 DASH

METHOD

1. Shake and strain into a cocktail glass.

2. Zest a lemon twist over the drink, but discard the peel. Drop a cherry into the drink.

THE

BLACK VELVET

EACH IS THE PERFECT COMPLEMENT OF THE OTHER.

Prince Albert, *1848*

B

BLACK VELVET

The Black Velvet is believed to have been invented at Brook's Club in London in 1861, to commemorate the death of Queen Victoria's husband, Prince Albert.

Albert, her Prince Consort, died prematurely from typhoid fever at the age of 42 on 14th December 1861 at Windsor Castle. The cocktail is a fitting tribute to the Prince – the celebratory connotation of champagne, shrouded by the moribund contrast of the black stout.

People often instinctively recoil at the thought of these two ingredients – champagne and stout beer – being mixed together!

Continued on next page...

SPECS

GUINNESS
1 PART

CHAMPAGNE
1 PART

METHOD

1. Build in a champagne flute; stir gently before serving.

2. No garnish.

Queen Victoria and Leopold of Albany

One camp wonders *'why you would ruin perfectly good champagne with stout?'* and the other, *'why you would sully a perfectly good stout with fizz?'* – but as David Embury says in *The Fine Art of Mixing Drinks (1948):*

"The combination of champagne and stout sounds terrifying – something like molasses and horseradish. Actually, it is excellent. The champagne cuts the heavy, syrupy consistency of the stout, and the stout takes the sharp, tart edge off the champagne. Each is the perfect complement of the other."

Queen Victoria famously wore black for the rest of her life, as a sign of her perpetual mourning. Until her death, in January 1901 she is said to have had the maids lay out Albert's clothes each night for the next day, as well as replacing the water in the basin in his room daily. Their tragic love story cut short captured the hearts and imaginations of many and has been portrayed in numerous books, TV series and films.

THE

BLINKER

IT'S NOT EVERY DAY THAT YOU MIX RYE AND GRAPEFRUIT.

First printed in Patrick Duffy's *The Official Mixer's Manual (1934)*, the *Blinker* was plucked from obscurity by drinks historian and writer, Ted Haigh – he included it in his work entitled *Vintage Spirits and Forgotten Cocktails (2004)*. Duffy's recipe calls for:

1 jigger Rye, 1 ½ jiggers Grapefruit juice, ½ jigger Grenadine.

The name ***'Blinker'*** most likely comes from the blinkers put on horses to keep their eyes on the road.

Haigh switched out the grenadine for raspberry syrup according to his personal preference, as well as adding a lemon twist garnish.

SPECS

RYE WHISKEY
45ML (1 ½ OZ)

GRAPEFRUIT JUICE
45ML (1 ½ OZ)

GRENADINE
15ML (½ OZ)

METHOD

1. Shake and strain into a cocktail glass.
2. No garnish.

THE

BLOOD AND SAND

A YOUNG BOY BORN INTO POVERTY GROWS UP TO BE THE GREATEST MATADOR IN SPAIN. HE RATS AROUND AND DIES. THE END.

BLOOD AND SAND COCKTAIL.

¼ Orange Juice.
¼ Scotch Whisky.
¼ Cherry Brandy.
¼ Italian Vermouth.
Shake well and strain into cocktail glass.

The Savoy Cocktail Book, *Harry Craddock, 1930*

This classic was brought to life in 1922 and named for the silent movie Blood and Sand, a film about bullfighting starring Rudolph Valentino (pictured). The plot of the movie was a reworking of Vicente Blasco Ibáñez's 1909 novel of the same name, and the subsequent play by Thomas Cushing. On his death bed in 1926 Valentino, the starring actor said he considered this his finest role.

It first appears in print in Harry Craddock's *The Savoy Cocktail Book (1930)*, although we're not completely sure who invented it.

The Blood and Sand is a delicious tipple, perfect for those who remain convinced they don't like scotch cocktails.

Not today, Satan. Not today.

People can be put off when you list the ingredients, but there are numerous unlikely pairings that are better than they sound: chocolate and sea salt; Metallica and a symphony orchestra; ramen and sliced cheese. It may surprise you.

B BLOOD AND SAND

SPECS

SCOTCH
25ML (1 OZ)

CHERRY HEERING
25ML (1 OZ)

SWEET VERMOUTH
25ML (1 OZ)

ORANGE JUICE
25ML (1 OZ)

METHOD

1. Shake and strain into a cocktail glass.

2. Garnish with an orange twist.

THE

BLOODHOUND

IF THE FRUIT MARTINI WERE A TRACKSUIT, THE BLOODHOUND WOULD BE A DINNER JACKET. THEY'RE BOTH FRUIT-BASED DRINKS AND SERVED IN THE SAME WAY, BUT THEY'RE NOT IN THE SAME LEAGUE OF REFINEMENT AND SOPHISTICATION.

BLOOD-HOUND COCKTAIL.

¼ French Vermouth.
¼ Italian Vermouth.
½ Dry Gin.
2 or 3 Crushed Strawberries.
Shake well and strain into cocktail glass.

The Savoy Cocktail Book, *Harry Craddock, 1930*

This cocktail first appears in its most rudimentary form in Tom Bullock's *The Ideal Bartender* in 1917:

one jigger of Old Tom gin, shaken with a half a dozen strawberries.

We take a step closer to the modern version in Robert Vermeire's *Cocktails and How to Mix Them (1922)* as the signature sweet and dry vermouth come into play.

To the vermouth and maraschino, Vermeire calls for raspberries, eschewing the traditional strawberries. His exact recipe is:

... equal parts (⅙ gill) Dry gin, French & Italian vermouth, with ½ tsp of Maraschino and six raspberries.

B

BLOODHOUND

SPECS

GIN
45ML (1 ½ OZ)

SWEET VERMOUTH
30ML (1 OZ)

DRY VERMOUTH
30ML (1 OZ)

STRAWBERRIES
2-3

METHOD

1. Crush strawberries in a shaker, then add the remaining ingredients.
2. Shake and strain into a cocktail glass.
3. No garnish.

The recipe had reached full maturity by the time it featured in Harry MacElhone's *Barflies and Cocktails (1927)* and Harry Craddock's *The Savoy Cocktail Book (1930)*, albeit with different ratios. MacElhone chooses equal parts; Craddock goes for a ratio of two parts gin to one part vermouth.

Note: Underneath his spec, MacElhone includes a little notation that the (9th) Duke of Manchester introduced this drink to London (where it was popular during the 1920s).

THE

BOBBY BURNS

PROBABLY NAMED AFTER A BRAND OF CIGAR, NOT RABBIE.

BOBBY BURNS COCKTAIL.*

½ Italian Vermouth.
½ Scotch Whisky.
3 Dashes Bénédictine.
Shake well and strain into cocktail glass. Squeeze lemcn peel on top.

*One of the very best Whisky Cocktails. A very fast mover on Saint Andrew's Day.

BOBBY BURNS COCKTAIL

½ Italian Vermouth
½ Scotch Whiskey
2 dashes Benedictine
Stir well in a mixing glass with cracked ice, strain and serve with a twist of Lemon Peel on top of glass.

The Savoy Cocktail Book, *Harry Craddock, 1930*
Recipes for Mixed Drinks, *Hugo R. Ensslin, 1917 (2nd Edition)*

The ***Bobby Burns*** is a Manhattan-esque cocktail that was first seen in print in Hugo R. Ensslin's *Recipes for Mixed Drinks (1917)*. It pops up again in Harry Craddock's *The Savoy Cocktail Book (1930)*.

A drink with slightly different ingredients *(no Benedictine; a dash of absinthe in its place)* appears in *Jacques Straub's Drinks (1914)* under the name ***Robert Burns Cocktail.***

B

BOBBY BURNS

Seventeen years later the same *Robert Burns* appears in Albert Stevens Crockett's *Old Waldorf Bar Days (1931)*, though in this incarnation we see the addition of orange bitters.

How did the drink get its name? – The *Bobby Burns* was thought to have been created to commemorate the famed Scottish poet Robert Burns (1759-1796) however, Crockett mentions under his 1931 recipe that it was probably named after the Robert Burns brand of cigar, rather than the Scottish Poet.

Adding to the farrago, Martin Doudoroff has found another cocktail called a *Baby Burns* with the same ingredients as a *Bobby Burns* - scotch, red vermouth and Benedictine; it appeared in a 1902 catalogue by The Bishop & Babcock Company.

SPECS

SCOTCH
50ML (2 OZ)

SWEET VERMOUTH
25ML (1 OZ)

BENEDICTINE
5ML (¼ OZ)

METHOD

1. Stir and strain into a cocktail glass.
2. Garnish with a lemon twist.

THE

BOULEVARDIER

A STRAIGHT-UP BOURBON NEGRONI, NAMED AFTER A LITERARY MAGAZINE.

Sometimes referred to as a ***Bourbon Negroni,*** the ***Boulevardier*** was created for Erskine Gwynne at Harry MacElhone's Harry's New York Bar in Paris, and features in his book *Barflies and Cocktails (1927).*

As you can see from what MacElhone says in his spec, it's implied that the recipe might have been Gwynne's invention:

"Now is the time for all good Barflies to come to the aid of the party, since Erskinne Gwynne crashed in with his Boulevardier Cocktail; 1/3 Campari, 1/3 Italian vermouth, 1/3 Bourbon whisky (sic)."

Erskine Gwynne was an American expat known to be a writer, socialite and nephew of the railroad tycoon Alfred Vanderbilt. He started a monthly literary magazine, which he edited, called The Boulevardier (a full-page advert was featured at the back of Barflies).

B

BOULEVARDIER

SPECS

BOURBON
30ML (1 OZ)

CAMPARI
30ML (1 OZ)

SWEET VERMOUTH
30ML (1 OZ)

METHOD

1. Stir and strain into a cocktail glass.

2. Garnish with an orange twist.

The drink is often made with extra bourbon – one and a half parts bourbon to one part Campari and vermouth. This is attributable to Ted Haigh, who made it as such in his book *Vintage Spirits and Forgotten Cocktails*. Haigh can take credit for rediscovering this forgotten drink, and bringing it back to our attention.

THE

BRAMBLE

PICKING BLACKBERRIES ON THE ISLE OF WIGHT.

The ***Bramble*** *is a true modern classic created by the late Dick Bradsell. As with his other liquid inventions, such as the* ***Treacle,*** *he had a knack for nailing the perfect name.*

Bradsell invented the ***Bramble*** whilst working at Fred's Club in Soho in the mid-1980s. Fred's was a members' club and celebrity hangout opened by Fred Taylor to rival some of the existing stuffy members' clubs in inner London. Taylor's venue was aimed at a younger crowd.

One day, an importer for liqueur brand *Cave de Bissey* brought a bottle of their Crème de Mûre to the club. Upon tasting it Bradsell described being immediately transported back to his childhood picking blackberries on the Isle of Wight.

As inspiration for the ***Bramble,*** Bradsell used as a template the *Singapore Sling* recipe from The Zanzibar Club, where he worked prior. He put it in a short glass, started with the same *Gin Sour* base (gin, lemon and sugar) and then laced it with this new Crème de Mûre. Originally he garnished it with a lemon and raspberry, but blackberries soon became the norm.

B

BRAMBLE

Dick once told me that the gin in his first iteration was Bombay Original, the precursor to Bombay Sapphire (with two fewer botanicals). However, he's also been quoted by Robert Simonson in *A Proper Drink* as saying it was Booth's Finest, so we can't be 100% sure.

The reason an exact measure for Crème de Mûre isn't stated in the recipe is a nod to how Bradsell made it. He would simply cover the air hole of the speed pourer in order to slow the pour, and deftly lace the mure with a few circular rotations around the inside rim of the glass.

SPECS

GIN
50ML

LEMON JUICE
25ML

SUGAR SYRUP (2:1)
10ML

CRÈME DE MÛRE
FLOAT

METHOD

1. Shake the gin, lemon and sugar; pour over crushed ice in a rocks glass; lace the Crème de Mûre in a circular motion around the inside rim of the glass, so it bleeds down through the crushed ice.

2. Garnish with a blackberry and a lemon wedge.

NOTE

Be careful not to be heavy-handed when lacing the Mûre, as the drink can become too sweet.

THE

BRANDY ALEXANDER

IF ANY OTHER ALEXANDERS WOULD LIKE TO LAY A CLAIM, PLEASE LEAVE YOUR NAME AT THE BAR.

ALEXANDER COCKTAIL

⅓ El Bart Gin
⅓ Crême de Cocoa
⅓ Sweet Cream

Shake well in a mixing glass with cracked ice, strain and serve.

Recipes for Mixed Drinks, *Hugo R. Ensslin, 1917 (2nd Edition)*

The *Brandy Alexander* is a variation on the gin-based *Alexander* cocktail made with equal parts gin, crème de cacao and cream. It made its cocktail book debut in Hugo Ensslin's *Recipes for Mixed Drinks (1917 edition).*

Historian Barry Popkin presents several possible origin stories for the original *Alexander,* the most likely of which is that it was created at the turn of the century by bartender Troy Alexander at Rectors, a famous pre-Prohibition eatery in New York.

The cocktail was conceived to celebrate the advent of the successful cartoon Phoebe Snow – a character used in advertising campaigns by the Delaware, Lackawanna & Western Railroad (DL&W) to promote the use of clean-burning anthracite, a revolutionary development in rail travel at the time. Snow was illustrated dressed in all white, to show passengers they could expect to arrive clean after their journey, as opposed to covered in black soot, which had been the norm.

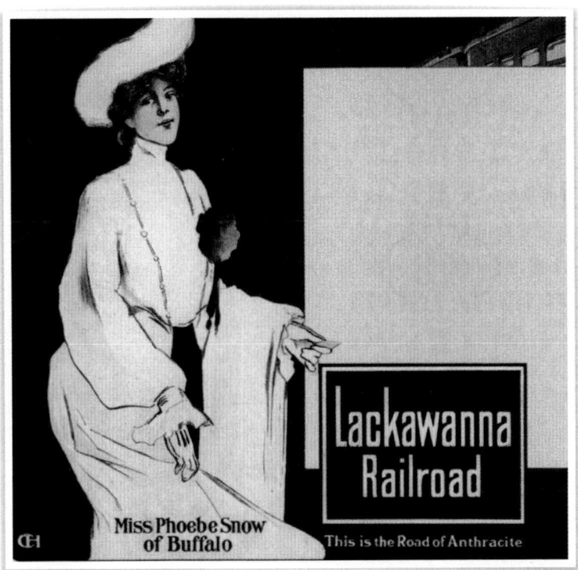

Lackawanna
Railroad
This is the Road of Anthracite
Miss Phoebe Snow
of Buffalo

Touch my dress and I'll cut you.

Interestingly, Popkin also mentions an article in the 1915 edition of the *Philadelphia Inquirer,* which claims the *Alexander* was invented in honour of Philadelphia pitcher Grover Cleveland Alexander just prior to the 1915 World Series against Boston, however, this is an unlikelier background story – no recipe is given, so we have no idea what this drink was like, or indeed if it has any relevance to the *Alexander* we are talking about here.

Several other Alexander's have also laid claim to this cocktail: Alexander Woollcott (of the Algonquin Round Table); Tsar Alexander II; and opera critic Alexander Dragon – all of these claims are as yet unsubstantiated.

Continued on next page...

B

BRANDY ALEXANDER

SPECS

COGNAC
50ML (2 OZ)

DARK CRÈME DE CACAO
25ML (1 OZ)

HEAVY CREAM
25ML (1 OZ)

METHOD

1. Shake and strain into a cocktail glass.

2. Garnish with grated nutmeg.

NOTES

Use 25ml (1 oz) gin for the original *Alexander* cocktail.

PRINCESS MARY COCKTAIL

There was also a cocktail invented in 1922 which is identical in all but name to the *Alexander* called the *Princess Mary.* It was created by Harry MacElhone (at Ciro's) to honour the marriage that year of Princess Mary and Viscount Lascelles, in London. Whether MacElhone rehashed Ensslin's *Alexander* cocktail or came up with the same combination independently, we'll never know. What we do know is that the *Princess Mary* appears in several notable cocktail books (usually in addition to the Alexander), including Robert Vermeire's *Cocktails - How to Mix Them (1922), Harry of Ciro's ABC of Mixing Cocktails* by Harry MacElhone (1923), and Harry Craddock's *The Savoy Cocktail Book (1930).*

THE SWITCH FROM GIN TO BRANDY

The brandy-based *Alexander* soon overtook its original incarnation in popularity, and never looked back. This change in spirit preference can be seen for the first time in the book *Harry of Ciro's ABC of Mixing Cocktails (1923)*: *Alexander Cocktail: ⅓ Crème de Cacao, ⅓ Brandy, ⅓ Fresh Cream.* In Harry Craddock's *The Savoy Cocktail Book (1930)* he covers all the bases, calling the gin version the *'no.1'* and the brandy *'no.2'*:

Alexander Cocktail (No.1):
½ Dry Gin, ½ Crème de Cacao,
¼ Sweet Cream.

Alexander Cocktail (No.2):
⅓ Brandy, ⅓ Crème de Cacao,
⅓ Fresh Cream.

Note: He also includes a 'Panama Cocktail' which is an exact duplicate of his Alexander (No.2).

By the time it appears in W.J. Tarling's Café Royal Cocktail Book (1937), it appears with the 2:1:1 ratio that is common today: Alexander: ½ Brandy, ¼ Crème de Cacao, ¼ Cream. As we see from these texts, it seems the spirit changed before the name did. The Brandy Alexander has so eclipsed its gin-based forefather that these days few are even aware of its original juniper-based incarnation.

"I've got to paint."

– *Charles Strickland*

THE

BRANDY CRUSTA

GO EASY ON THE MODIFIERS FOR THIS ONE.

116. Brandy Crusta.

(Use small bar glass.)

BRANDY CRUSTA.

Crusta is made the same as a fancy cocktail, with a little lemon juice and a small lump of ice added. First, mix the ingredients in a small tumbler, then take a fancy red wine-glass, rub a sliced lemon around the rim of the same, and dip it in pulverized white sugar, so that the sugar will adhere to the edge of the glass. Pare half a lemon the same as you would an apple (all in one piece) so that the paring will fit in the wine-glass, as shown in the cut, and strain the crusta from the tumbler into it. Then smile.

The Bon Vivant's Guide or How to Mix Drinks, *Jerry Thomas, 1862*

The *Brandy Crusta* is thought to have been invented by Joseph Santini around the 1850s in New Orleans, either at the City Exchange bar or the Jewel of the South bar on Gravier Street. It was purely a locals' drink until it scored a feature in Jerry Thomas' *The Bon Vivant's Guide or How to Mix Drinks (1862)* after Thomas visited New Orleans in the 1850s.

B BRANDY CRUSTA

The name *Crusta* refers to the crust of sugar around the rim of the elaborately garnished cocktail. The ***Brandy Crusta*** is the drink credited with introducing citrus as a popular cocktail ingredient.

The biggest mistake – too often made – is to put too much lemon juice (and everything else), making this more like a *Sour,* or a *Sidecar.* Although it was the precursor and grandaddy to such drinks, the *Crusta* was designed to have only small dashes of citrus and sweetener, subtly flavouring the brandy.

Maraschino is sometimes used instead of (or as well as) orange curaçao, as in Harry Craddock's Savoy recipe.

SPECS

COGNAC
60ML (2 OZ)

LEMON JUICE
5ML (1 TSP)

SUGAR SYRUP (2:1)
5ML (1 TSP)

PIERRE FERRAND ORANGE CURAÇAO
2.5ML (½ TSP)

BOKER'S BITTERS OR ANGOSTURA
2 DASHES

METHOD

1. Rim a small wine or sour glass with a lemon wedge and dip in sugar. Stir ingredients with ice and strain into the glass.

2. Cut a long peel using a whole lemon and balance it around the inside of the rim to garnish.

NOTES

Angostura bitters are often used as a substitute where Boker's bitters are not available.

THE

BRONX

THE MOST FAMOUS COCKTAIL TO HAVE ORANGE JUICE AS AN INGREDIENT.

BRONX COCKTAIL.

A LA BILLY MALLOY, PITTSBURG, PA.

One-third Plymouth gin, one-third French vermouth and one-third Italian vermouth, flavored with two dashes of Orange bitters, about a barspoonful of orange juice and a squeeze of orange peel. Serve very cold.

The World's Drinks and How to Mix Them, *William Boothby, 1908*

The *Bronx* cocktail was invented at the turn of the twentieth century. Shortly after it entered the drinking scene, it became immensely popular right through Prohibition. It made its cocktail book debut in 1908 in William Boothby's *The Worlds Drinks and How to Mix Them*, listed as equal parts gin, dry and sweet vermouth, two dashes of orange bitters and a bar spoon of orange juice. It also appears in other cocktail books that same year, but in a less recognisable state - without the crucial orange juice.

As with many classics, there are various accounts of its genesis; the following are the main culprits...

THE TWO JOHNS AT THE WALDORF

The first name thrown into the ring comes courtesy of the *Everythinginthebar* blog which catalogues a thorough timeline of the *Bronx's* print appearances. We learn from this detailed account that the first-ever mention of a *Bronx* cocktail was in the newspaper *The Virginia Enterprise* in 1901.

B BRONX

The Waldorf-Astoria, *New York City, 1901*

In a short blurb, it is announced that the invention committee of the Bartenders' Association had been tasked to invent three new cocktails, to mark the impending visit to Virginia of Carrie Nation of Kansas.

Before we go any further, it's important to mention that this endeavour was in no way to honour Mrs. Nation, but rather a tongue-in-cheek middle-finger of sorts. Nation was one of the most fervent members of the temperance movement and was regularly photographed holding a bible and a hatchet, which she would use to smash bottles in saloons (the hatchet that is). As such, she was an unpopular figure for many... but back to our story.

Continued on next page...

SPECS

GIN
40ML (2 OZ)

ORANGE JUICE
20ML (1 OZ)

DRY VERMOUTH
10ML (½ OZ)

SWEET VERMOUTH
10ML (½ OZ)

METHOD

1. Shake and strain into a cocktail glass.
2. No garnish.

NOTES

Adding two dashes of Angostura bitters will transform it into an *Income Tax Cocktail.*

Solon says he named it the Bronx after the Bronx Zoo, which he had visited a few days prior.

This invention committee was made up of three bartenders of repute:

> "Frank Curtis of the Gilsey house, inventor of 'Long Branch punch'; J.E. O'Connor of the Waldorf-Astoria, inventor of the 'Bronx cocktail' and William Gilbert of the Manhattan hotel, inventor of the 'Clover Club Mystery'."
> – *Virginia Enterprise (1901).*

Of these three, it's J. E. O'Connor we're interested in. John *'Curley'* O'Connor was a bartender who started at the Waldorf in 1893, worked his way up to chief bartender and stayed on until his retirement in 1939.

Until the discovery of *The Virginia Enterprise* article, no one had heard of O'Connor before. People assumed it was created at the Waldorf-Astoria, and by a bartender named John, however, this is not the John most people think of when discussing the *Bronx* cocktail... that John is yet another Waldorf alumnus: teetotaler Johnnie Solon. Solon would forever be associated with the *Bronx* after Albert Stevens Crockett tells the story of Solon's invention of the drink, in his influential books *Old Waldorf Bar Days (1931)* and *The Waldorf Astoria Bar Book (1935).* Crockett flatters him with a lengthy description, name-checking Solon as the creator; both titles include what he says is Solon's own account of its invention.

To paraphrase Crockett's account, Johnnie Solon was asked to invent an entirely new cocktail for a dinner guest – a challenge laid down by his colleague Traverson, head waiter in the Empire room (the Waldorf's main dining room). Solon happened to be making a *Duplex* cocktail at the time: equal parts dry and sweet vermouth, with orange zest and bitters. Solon put a clever twist on the cocktail he was presently making, using ⅔ Gordon's gin, ⅓ orange juice, and dashes of dry and sweet vermouth. He shook it up, and presented the drink to Traverson who gave it the thumbs up – and soon they were going through several cases of oranges a day.

Solon says he named it the *Bronx* after the Bronx Zoo, which he had visited a few days prior, which may seem arbitrary. But, assuming that Solon was the creator, he must have invented it sometime between 1899 (when he started at the Waldorf) and 1901 (when it's mentioned in *The Virginia Enterprise)*. In November 1899 (within that established time window) the Bronx Zoo opened. Brand spanking new, it caused quite the stir in New York City, which would lend some weight to the idea that Solon visited it, and then chose it as a name.

Whether it was O'Connor or Solon who originated the drink, we can't be 100% sure, but whoever it was, it does seem to have sprung into existence at the Waldorf.

CONTESTANT NUMBER THREE

Magnus Bredenbek in his book *What Shall We Drink? (1934)* puts forth another, albeit less plausible (and interesting), story. Bredenbek states that it was invented in Philadelphia, and only discovered in 1905 by Bronx restauranteur Joseph S. Sormani. This seems implausible, given that in 1901 the *Bronx* cocktail tied to the Waldorf had already been mentioned in *The Virginia Enterprise* newspaper.

THE

BROOKLYN

DRY OR SWEET VERMOUTH?

BROOKLYN COCKTAIL

1 dash Amer. Picon bitters
1 dash Maraschino
50% rye whiskey
50% Ballor Vermouth
Fill glass with ice.
Stir and strain. Serve.

Jack's Manual, *J.A.Grohusko, 1908*

The recipe for the *Brooklyn* cocktail I've given uses sweet vermouth, which is *not* how it's usually made these days.

It's now thought of as a dry vermouth drink, largely due to the success of the versions printed in Jacque Straub's two books, *Manual of Mixed Drinks (1913)* and *Drinks (1914)*, and later the far-reaching influence of Harry Craddock's *The Savoy Cocktail Book (1930)*.

Now, there's nothing wrong with a *Brooklyn* made with dry vermouth, that is until you've tried it the original way, as found in J. A. Grohusko's *Jack's Manual (1908)*. Grohusko (who was possibly the creator of the drink) specifies Ballor vermouth, a classic sweet variety from Torino.

B

BROOKLYN

BROOKLYN COCKTAIL
1 Dash Amer Picon.
1 Dash Maraschino.
½ Jigger French Vermouth.
½ Jigger good Rye Whiskey.
Stir.

Straub's Manual of Mixed Drinks, *Jacques Straub, 1913*

Made this way, with a quality sweet vermouth (Cocchi Torino would be my choice), the ***Brooklyn*** dumps on its ilk from a great height.

It's time for Clark Kent to take his glasses off and reveal his true self.

SPECS

RYE WHISKEY
45ML (1 ½ OZ)

SWEET VERMOUTH
45ML (1 ½ OZ)

AMER PICON
5ML (1 TSP)

MARASCHINO
5ML (1 TSP)

METHOD

1. Stir and strain into a cocktail glass.
2. No garnish.

THE

BUCK'S FIZZ & MIMOSA

HELLO, ROOM SERVICE?

The story of the ***Buck's Fizz*** begins in 1921 at Buck's Club, a members-only venue on Clifford Street in Mayfair, London. The first bartender there, Pat McGarry, apparently thought it up as a cunning ruse to allow the members to unashamedly drink before noon.

Four years later the ***Mimosa*** is invented at the Ritz Hotel in Paris, by Frank Meier. It takes its name from the exotic Australian flower *'Acacia dealbata'*, which is more commonly known as the ***mimosa***, and recognisable for its yellow colour. Oddly, Meier didn't claim to be the inventor of the cocktail when he included it in *The Artistry of Mixing Drinks (1936)*, as he did for his other creations throughout that title. Perhaps that's because of the overwhelming similarity with the ***Buck's Fizz*** which preceded it. Meier's recipe calls it a ***Mimosa*** or *Champagne Orange;* made with the juice of half an orange and a top-up of champagne, and served with a piece of ice in a wine glass.

The ***Buck's Fizz*** and the ***Mimosa*** are almost thought of interchangeably these days, but if we had to delineate them it would be in two ways: Firstly the ***Buck's Fizz*** usually has a 2:1 ratio of champagne to orange juice, whereas the ***Mimosa*** has equal parts. Secondly, the ***Mimosa*** was originally served in a wine glass with ice, whereas the ***Buck's Fizz*** came neatly in a flute. Having said that, you'll find that these days both drinks are usually served without ice, in a flute glass. Some also stipulate that the ***Buck's Fizz*** has the addition of dashes of gin and cherry liqueur, although that's very uncommon nowadays.

B

BUCK'S FIZZ & MIMOSA

SPECS

BUCK'S FIZZ

ORANGE JUICE
1 PART

CHAMPAGNE
2 PARTS

MIMOSA

ORANGE JUICE
1 PART

CHAMPAGNE
1 PART

METHOD

1. Build in a flute.
2. No garnish.

The ***Buck's Fizz*** is particularly popular at weddings, and the ***Mimosa*** is a brunch staple. However you make it, a hotel room service breakfast wouldn't be complete without one.

As with all drinks containing orange juice, use freshly squeezed. Made with carton juice from concentrate, it would be tastier to eat the glass.

CAIPIRINHA

TO

CULROSS

CAS OH

THE

CAIPIRINHA

THE NATIONAL DRINK OF BRAZIL.

There are conflicting accounts of the origin of the *Caipirinha,* but here are the main three.

The first has it stemming from a medicinal home remedy used during the Spanish Flu epidemic at the end of World War I. It was comprised of cachaça, lime, garlic and honey. In time the garlic fell to the wayside and honey was replaced with sugar; eventually, ice was added.

Similarly, the second account riffs on the same general theme: a medicinal drink that morphs into a mainstream tipple. This one asserts that the centuries-old mix of cane spirit, lime and citrus was brought over to Brazil by sailors, well versed in mixing up rum-based remedies for scurvy – they just switched out the rum for the more readily available local spirit.

The third account is that the rural folk of São Paolo were already drinking the combination of these three ingredients by the end of the 19th century, which if true blows up at least one of these other stories (as this was evidently prior to World War I).

While the drink's roots may be unclear, we do know that the word ***Caipirinha*** derives from the diminutive of *Caipira*, a term used to denote someone from the countryside, akin to a yokel. Knowing this, story number three might have some credibility – indicating that perhaps it was a drink traditionally popular with rural folk, rather than the well to do. Finding its way from rural Brazil to bright city lights, even the ***Caipirinha*** can't escape gentrification.

C CAIPIRINHA

SPECS

CACHAÇA
60ML (2 OZ)

CASTER SUGAR
10ML (2 TSP)

LIME
HALF

METHOD

1. Choose a nice plump lime, roll it, cut off the ends and slice it in half lengthwise.

2. Cut out the strip of white pith, then slice into four equal quarters.

3. Place these pieces with two teaspoons of caster sugar into a rocks glass and muddle.

4. Add the cachaça, stir, then fill the glass with cracked ice.

5. Finish it off with a quick stir in a gentle churning motion.

You'll often see this drink served with crushed ice, or shaken and the contents poured right into the glass without straining. Muddling in the glass itself, and then serving with cracked ice is more authentically Brazilian, but each to their own.

Note: This drink is probably the reason so many bartenders have an aversion to muddling. Anyone who has been in the game for long enough remembers the time when this was flying out of every bar (thank you Mr. John Gakuru) and can recall having tennis elbow to prove it.

CAMERON'S KICK

C

THE

CAMERON'S KICK

AN UNUSUAL COMBINATION OF SCOTCH AND IRISH WHISKEY THAT REALLY WORKS.

SPECS

SCOTCH
30ML (1 OZ)

IRISH WHISKEY (SINGLE POT STILL)
30ML (1 OZ)

LEMON JUICE
15ML (½ OZ)

ORGEAT
15ML (½ OZ)

METHOD

1. Shake and strain into a cocktail glass.

2. No garnish.

Who is Cameron? Why is he kicking? Nobody knows. What we do know is that in this cocktail, scotch and Irish whiskey get along as well as cheese and red wine.

The *Cameron's Kick* first appears in Harry's *ABC of Mixing Cocktails (1922)*. Author Harry MacElhone stipulates:

⅓ Scotch whisky

⅓ Irish whiskey

⅙ Lemon juice

⅙ Orgeat syrup

THE

CASINO

WE CALL HIM 'DOUBLE DOWN'.

CASINO COCKTAIL
2 dashes Maraschino
2 dashes Orange Bitters
2 dashes Lemon Juice
1 drink of Tom Gin
Stir well in a mixing glass with cracked ice, strain and serve with a cherry.

CASINO COCKTAIL.
2 Dashes Maraschino.
2 Dashes Orange Bitters.
2 Dashes Lemon Juice.
1 Glass Old Tom Gin.
Stir well and add cherry.

Recipes for Mixed Drinks, *Hugo R. Ensslin, 1917 (2nd Edition)*
The Savoy Cocktail Book, *Harry Craddock, 1930*

The *Casino* cocktail first appears in Hugo Ensslin's *Recipes for Mixed Drinks (1917)* and then later in Harry Craddock's *The Savoy Cocktail Book (1930).*

Modern-day casinos are, more often than not, havens of sadness, interrogation lighting, and the perfunctory feeding of slot machines – as futile as trying to fill an impact crater with crackers. The *Casino* cocktail, in contrast, harks back to a time when they had a decidedly more glamorous evocation: classy, opulent venues filled with tuxedo and ball gown adorned guests. As such the *Casino* is a sophisticated drink – gin-heavy in the martini-style, with dashes of lemon juice and maraschino providing nuance. These additions are designed to be subtle, so it's important not to add too much of either, lest the drink veer into *Aviation* territory.

SPECS

OLD TOM GIN
60ML (2 OZ)

LEMON JUICE
5ML (1 TSP)

MARASCHINO
5ML (1 TSP)

ORANGE BITTERS
2 DASHES

METHOD

1. Shake and strain into a cocktail glass.
2. Garnish with a cherry.

THE

CHAMPAGNE COCKTAIL

THE QUINTESSENTIAL CHAMPAGNE COCKTAIL.

110. Champagne Cocktail.

(One bottle of wine to every six large glasses.)

(Per glass.)

¼ teaspoonful of sugar.
1 or 2 dashes of bitters.
1 piece of lemon peel.
Fill tumbler one-third full of broken ice, and fill balance with wine. Shake well and serve.

The Bon Vivant's Guide or How to Mix Drinks,
Jerry Thomas, 1862

The *Champagne Cocktail* is mentioned in print for the first time in Robert Tomes' book *Panama in 1855: An Account of the Panama Rail-road, of the cities of Panama and Aspinwall with sketches of life and characters on the Isthmus (1855)*. (Catchy title). Tomes describes in detail his friend making him the *Champagne Cocktail*, and how delightful he found it to be. We learn from his description that this early iteration of the cocktail was served in a tumbler, over cracked ice.

C CHAMPAGNE COCKTAIL

Seven years later, it makes its first cocktail book appearance in Jerry Thomas' *The Bon Vivant's Guide or How to Mix Drinks (1862)*. As with Tomes, this recipe is also served in a tumbler over cracked ice, although Thomas says to shake the drink – we'll give him the benefit of the doubt that it's a typo, and that he didn't actually intend for you to shake champagne.

According to drinks historian David Wondrich, the champagne used at this time would have been sweeter – a sec or a demi-sec – with brut only coming onto the scene at the end of the century.

The addition of cognac (which is commonplace nowadays) was first recorded in 1898 by a bartender from Delaware named Joseph Haywood, although the recent trend for its inclusion is most likely attributable to its addition in W.J. Tarling's *Café Royal Cocktail book* in 1937. His recipe is copied straight out of Harry Craddock's *The Savoy Cocktail Book (1930)*, except for the note at the end, adding *"A dash of Brandy as required."*

SPECS

SUGAR CUBE
1

ANGOSTURA BITTERS
DASHES

CHAMPAGNE
TOP WITH

COGNAC (OPTIONAL)
20ML (¾ OZ)

METHOD

1. Lay a bar napkin on top of a champagne flute.

2. Placing a sugar cube in the centre, soak with Angostura bitters (the napkin will catch any excess), then drop the sugar cube into the flute.

3. Add cognac if desired; top up with champagne.

4. Garnish with a lemon twist.

"...the nights were
mainly made
for saying things
that you can't say
tomorrow day."

– *Alex Turner*

THE

CHAMPS ELYSÉES

AS BEAUTIFUL AS ITS NAMESAKE.

CHAMPS ELYSÉES COCKTAIL. (6 people)

3 Glasses Cognac.
1 Glass Chartreuse.
1½ Glasses Sweetened Lemon Juice.
1 Dash Angostura Bitters.
Shake well and strain into cocktail glasses.

The Savoy Cocktail Book, *Harry Craddock, 1930*

First appearing in Nina Tote and A.H. Adair's *Drinks - Long & Short (1925)*, the same recipe is then reprinted in Harry Craddock's *The Savoy Cocktail Book (1930)*.

"Three glasses of brandy, one glass of Chartreuse and one and a half glasses of sweetened lemon juice, put in the shaker with a dash of Angostura Bitters."

The *Champs Élysées* cocktail is named after the famous Parisian boulevard. Champs Élysées translates as *'Elysian Fields'*, which was the heavenly realm imagined in Greek mythology.

C CHAMPS ELYSÉES

Champs Élysées, *1900*

The *Champs Élysées* is certainly one of the best cognac cocktails in existence unless of course, you hate Chartreuse… in which case… well, why do you hate Chartreuse?

SPECS

COGNAC
50ML (2 OZ)

LEMON JUICE
20ML (¾ OZ)

GREEN CHARTREUSE
15ML (½ OZ)

SUGAR SYRUP (2:1)
5ML (1 TSP)

ANGOSTURA BITTERS
1 DASH

METHOD

1. Shake and strain into a cocktail glass.

NOTES

Which type of Chartreuse to use is not specified in the original recipe, but the green works better than the yellow in this drink.

CHARLIE CHAPLIN

C

THE

CHARLIE CHAPLIN

A COCKTAIL NAMED AFTER THE LEGENDARY SILENT FILM STAR.

SPECS

APRICOT BRANDY
30ML (1 OZ)

SLOE GIN
30ML (1 OZ)

LIME JUICE
30ML (1 OZ)

METHOD

1. Shake and strain into a cocktail glass.

The *Charlie Chaplin* was thought to have been created and served at New York's Old Waldorf Astoria as early as pre-1920 but was first published in 1931 in *Old Waldorf Bar Days* by Albert Stevens Crockett. In this print appearance, it is listed as a simple one-third ratio for each of the three ingredients.

This drink is named for Charles Spencer (Charlie) Chaplin – the English silent movie actor, comedian and filmmaker – who remains one of the most important figures in the history of film. Chaplin would have been at the height of his fame when this cocktail was invented.

A perfectly balanced tripartite of ingredients – a cocktail deserving of wider prominence.

THE CHATHAM ARTILLERY PUNCH

AS A VANQUISHER OF MEN, ITS EQUAL HAS NEVER BEEN FOUND.

Two early champions of punch, who played a significant role in the modern-day resurgence we're presently enjoying, are Nick Strangeway and David Wondrich.

Strangeway was in charge of the bar at the original Hawksmoor in Spitalfields, London, back in its infancy... before it became the multi-headed giant it is today. He served up an array of forgotten punches in an Aladdin's-cave worth of unique vintage bowls, cups and glassware that he sourced himself; during that time he was no doubt known in every antique shop in London, and smoke could be seen flying from his eBay account. Such items are ubiquitous in cocktail bars nowadays, but Strangeway was an early pioneer who kicked off this trend, as well as opening our eyes to the virtues of this, most English of cocktails.

Continued on next page...

SPECS

COGNAC
30ML (1 OZ)

BOURBON
30ML (1 OZ)

JAMAICAN RUM
30ML (1 OZ)

LEMON SHERBET
30ML (1 OZ) SEE RECIPE

CHAMPAGNE
90ML (3 OZ)

METHOD

1. Pour ingredients except for champagne into a double rocks glass with some cracked ice.

2. Give it a gentle stir then add the champagne.

3. Grate nutmeg over the top of the drink to garnish.

The second modern champion of the punch is polymath David Wondrich, who with his books *Imbibe! (2007)*, and *Punch (2010)* educated a new generation about the history and wonders of this long-neglected cocktail category.

In Wondrich's seminal book *Punch (2010)*, he includes the earliest account of the ***Chatham Artillery Punch***, from *The Augusta Chronicle: "The concoction was thus made: One of the horse buckets of ordinary size was filled with finely crushed ice; a quart of good brandy, whisky and rum each was poured into the ice, and sugar and lemon added. The bucket was filled to the brim with Champagne, and the whole stirred into delirious deliciousness. Rumor hath it every solitary man of the Blues was put under the table by this deceiving, diabolical and most delightful compound."* - *The Augusta Chronicle, quoted in the San Antonio Light (1885)*

The actual birthdate of the drink was in the 1850s: the Chatham Artillery Regiment of Savannah, Georgia held a welcome home banquet in Macon for another local regiment — an all-volunteer group stationed in Fort Jackson called the Republican Blues.

The man responsible for the concoction was a local patriot by the name of A.H.Luce, who *"proposed to brew a new punch in honour of the Blues."*

With time the recipes became varied (and weaker) with ingredients such as sweet wine, pineapple, tea, Benedictine, orange and maraschino being added. None of these later versions are as good as the devastating original — certainly the most enjoyable way to take heavy fire.

The *Augusta Chronicle* says of the Chatham: *"As a vanquisher of men, its equal has never been found".*

If you don't have time to make a proper lemon sherbet, balance with lemon juice and sugar, and then zest in the oils from several lemons. To make the full-size punch version, use:

1 bottle lemon sherbet
1 bottle cognac
1 bottle dark Jamaican rum
1 bottle bourbon
3 bottles champagne

Add to a punch bowl with a big piece of block ice and serve in small cups or glasses.

THE

CHICAGO FIZZ

HE DIDN'T PUSH OFF BYRON RUSSELL.

CHICAGO FIZZ
Juice of one-half a Lemon.
1 Barspoonful of Sugar.
½ Jigger Jamaica Rum.
½ Jigger Port Wine.
1 White of Egg.
Shake, strain.
Fill glass with Siphon.

The Savoy Cocktail Book, *Harry Craddock, 1930*

The *Chicago Fizz* was invented by Michael Jordan, after hitting the game-winning jumper to claim his 6th NBA Championship... okay, maybe that's not true. Maybe the real story (which is less fun) is that it was a pre-Prohibition drink from Chicago, said to have been made famous at The Old Waldorf Astoria in New York.

It appears in Albert Stevens Crockett's *Old Waldorf Bar Days (1931)*, but its first appearance in a cocktail book is in Jacque Straub's *Manual of Mixed Drinks (1913)*. So, nothing very interesting in terms of its backstory, but nevertheless it's an attractive looking drink with a mauve colour, rich flavour and great texture.

SPECS

JAMAICAN RUM
30ML (1 OZ)

RUBY PORT
30ML (1 OZ)

LEMON JUICE
15ML (½ OZ)

CASTER SUGAR
5ML (1 TSP)

EGG WHITE
1

SODA
TOP WITH SODA

METHOD

1. Dry shake, then shake with ice.

2. Strain into a highball glass without ice and top up with soda.

3. No garnish.

THE

CLOVER CLUB

FRUITY AND FLUFFY.

*The **Clover Club** was an exclusive society of 35 members, established in 1882 and lasting until the 1920s. The Club's regular meetings were held at the Bellevue Stratford Hotel in Philadelphia, and the **Clover Club** cocktail was said to have been invented at the hotel bar during this period.*

According to the Club's charter, members would meet once a month for *"social enjoyments, the cultivation of literary tastes, and the encouragement of hospitable intercourse"*. Thanks to drinks writer David Wondrich we know that the first recorded recipe is in Paul E. Lowe's *Drinks - How to Mix and Serve (1909)*.

Lowe's original recipe includes the use of dry vermouth which adds complexity, and dramatically improves the drink.

He does miss out the lemon juice, but the general consensus is that this was likely a mistake. *Drinks - How to Mix and Serve, Paul E. Lowe, 1909:*

Fill large bar glass ½ full fine ice
½ pony raspberry syrup,
½ jigger dry gin
½ jigger French Vermouth
White of 1 egg
Shake well; strain into cocktail glass and serve.

C

CLOVER CLUB

There are two other noteworthy appearances that fiddle with the citrus element: In *Cocktails - How to Mix Them (1922)* by Robert Vermeire lime juice is used; lemon juice is specified in the later title *Old Waldorf Bar Days (1931)* by Albert Stevens Crockett. These days lemon juice is more commonly used.

A preference for the use of fresh raspberries (instead of syrup) is first seen in a 1911 recipe from the Hotel Belvedere in Baltimore, Maryland. In addition to the use of fresh raspberries, the recipe uses both dry and sweet vermouth – which is a change that hasn't been as readily adopted.

Note: The Clover Club will sink or swim based on the quality of the syrup you use; it's worth the effort to make a homemade syrup (made with fresh raspberries). However, if you don't have the time, I'd suggest going the Hotel Belvedere route instead, using fresh fruit and sugar.

SPECS

GIN
50ML (2 OZ)

LEMON JUICE
25ML (3/4 OZ)

DRY VERMOUTH
25ML (3/4 OZ)

RASPBERRY SYRUP
15ML (1/2 OZ)

EGG WHITE
1

METHOD

1. Dry shake, then shake with ice.

2. Strain into a cocktail glass.

3. No garnish.

NOTES

If you were to float a mint leaf on top of this drink it would become a *Clover Leaf.*

CLUBLAND

C

THE

CLUBLAND

I GENERALLY LIKE MY VODKA FROZEN AND NEAT, BUT THIS IS A PLEASANT ALTERNATIVE.

SPECS

VODKA
45ML (1 ½ OZ)

WHITE PORT
45ML (1 ½ OZ)

ANGOSTURA BITTERS
1 DASH

METHOD

1. Stir and strain into a cocktail glass.

Clubland advert: Courtesy of Grace's Guide to British Industrial History.

The brand of white port after which the *Clubland* was named sadly no longer exists, so now when it's made, a generic white port appears in its place. Its first print appearance is in W.J. Tarling's *Café Royal Cocktail Book (1937)*, and the recipe calls for equal parts of Clubland White Port and Wolfschmidt vodka, with a dash of Angostura bitters. A note appears under the recipe giving inventor credit to an A. Mackintosh, though no more than this is known about the supposed inventor.

THE

COCKTAIL À LA LOUISIANE

A ROSE BY ANY OTHER NAME.

This short and sweet cocktail, invented in New Orleans, is a relation of the *Vieux Carré* and the *Sazerac*. It's known by a few names: the *A la Louisiane, La Louisiane,* or *De la Louisiane.*

Note: Many modern interpretations of this drink increase the ratio of rye to other ingredients.

SPECS

RYE WHISKEY
30ML (1 OZ)

SWEET VERMOUTH
30ML (1 OZ)

BENEDICTINE
30ML (1 OZ)

ABSINTHE
3 DASHES

PEYCHAUD'S BITTERS
3 DASHES

METHOD

1. Stir and strain into a cocktail glass.

2. Garnish with a maraschino cherry.

“Put that coffee down, coffee’s for closers only.”

– Blake

THE

COFFEE COCKTAIL

THE COFFEE COCKTAIL WITH NO COFFEE.

SPECS

RUBY PORT
60ML (2 OZ)

COGNAC
30ML (1 OZ)

SUGAR SYRUP (2:1)
5ML (1 TSP)

WHOLE EGG
1

METHOD

1. Shake and strain into a wine glass or goblet.
2. Grate nutmeg over the top of the drink.

NOTE

If you further reduce the amount of cognac (relative to the port), you have a *Porto Flip*.

This drink is rather unusually named, being that it doesn't actually contain any coffee, but like its namesake it's just as pleasant after dinner (and might actually help rather than hinder a good night's sleep).

The *Coffee Cocktail* was first published in 1887 in Jerry Thomas' *Bar-Tender's Guide*; it's widely believed to have come from New Orleans, though given the lack of documentation of this drink's history it's hard to state anything definitively.

Coffee Cocktail.

(Use a large bar-glass.)

Take 1 tea-spoonful powdered white sugar.
1 fresh egg.
1 large wine-glass of port wine.
1 pony of brandy.
2 or 3 lumps of ice.

Break the egg into the glass, put in the sugar, and lastly the port wine, brandy and ice.

Shake up very thoroughly. and strain into a medium bar goblet. Grate a little nutmeg on top before serving.

The name of this drink is a misnomer, as coffee and bitters are not to be found among its ingredients, but it looks like coffee when it has been properly concocted, and hence probably its name.

Bar-Tender's Guide, *Jerry Thomas, 1887*

THE

COMMODORE

OBVIOUSLY, THE TWO COMMODORES COMMAND TWO DIFFERENT FLEETS.

The *Commodore,* which first appeared in the early 1920s, has taken a number of different forms. The recipe I've chosen is based on the *Commodore No.2* which is one of two versions that appeared in Albert Stevens Crockett's book *Old Waldorf Bar Days (1931).* Crockett's version is printed as: *⅓ Bourbon, ⅓ Lemon juice, ⅓ Crème de cacao, Dash Grenadine. Frappé in a Champagne glass.*

Crockett's *Commodore* is a separate beast entirely consisting of rum, lemon, grenadine, raspberry and egg white. However, it's the *Commodore No.2* (with a bourbon base) that is the more commonly known these days. There is another, more obscure *Commodore Cocktail,* found in Harry MacElhone's *Harry's ABC of Mixing Cocktails (1922),* as well as in *Barflies and Cocktails (1927).* This is a drink made of rye whiskey, lime juice, sugar and orange bitters.

Drinks writer David Embury reprints Crockett's 1931 *Commodore* recipe in *The Fine Art of Mixing Drinks (1948),* however, he does also mention MacElhone's version, jokingly stating; *"Obviously, the two Commodores command two different fleets."*

SPECS

BOURBON
45ML (1 ½ OZ)

DARK CRÈME DE CACAO
15ML (½ OZ)

LEMON JUICE
15ML (½ OZ)

GRENADINE
5ML (1 TSP)

METHOD

1. Shake and strain into a cocktail glass.

2. No garnish.

CORPSE REVIVER No.1

THE CORPSE REVIVER No.1

CONSUMED LIKE 'THE HAIR OF THE DOG' TO REVIVE ONESELF.

¼ Italian Vermouth.
¼ Apple Brandy or Calvados.
½ Brandy.
Shake well and strain into cocktail glass.

CORPSE REVIVER. (No. 1.)

To be taken before 11 a.m., or whenever steam and energy are needed.

The Savoy Cocktail Book, *Harry Craddock, 1930*

SPECS

COGNAC
40ML (1 ½ OZ)

APPLE BRANDY OR CALVADOS
20ML (¾ OZ)

SWEET VERMOUTH
20ML (¾ OZ)

METHOD

1. Stir and strain into a cocktail glass.

2. No garnish.

NOTE

Compared to its sibling, the *Corpse Reviver No.1* is Danny DeVito in Twins.

Corpse Revivers are a category of drink, rather than a single recipe – they fall into the family of 'pick me ups' akin to 'the hair of the dog' type drinks; designed to bring you back from the dead after a heavy night.

The first recipe for a *Corpse Reviver* was in E. Ricket and C. Thomas' *The Gentleman's Table Guide (1871)* and appears as: *"Half wineglass of brandy, half glass of Maraschino, and two dashes of Boker's bitters."*

The *Corpse Reviver No.1* is lesser known than the *Corpse Reviver No. 2,* though both versions appear in Harry Craddock's *The Savoy Cocktail Book (1930).* Although Craddock advises shaking this drink, stirring is preferable.

THE

CORPSE REVIVER No.2

A WORD OF WARNING ABOUT OVERINDULGING IN THIS 'HANGOVER CURE'.

CORPSE REVIVER (No. 2.)

¼ Wine Glass Lemon Juice.
¼ Wine Glass Kina Lillet.
¼ Wine Glass Cointreau.
¼ Wine Glass Dry Gin.
1 Dash Absinthe.
Shake well and strain into cocktail glass.

Four of these taken in swift succession will unrevive the corpse again.

No. 92.—CORPSE REVIVER.

USE a wineglass. Half wineglass of brandy, half glass of Maraschino, and two dashes of Boker's bitters.

The Savoy Cocktail Book, *Harry Craddock, 1930*
The Gentleman's Table Guide, *E.Ricket and C.Thomas, 1871*

The *Corpse Reviver No.2* is the most popular and well known of the revivers today, a wonderfully complex cocktail and very well balanced. It was first printed, along with the *Corpse Reviver No.1* in Harry Craddock's *The Savoy Cocktail Book (1930)*, where he comments: *"Four of these taken in swift succession will unrevive the corpse again."* A *Corpse Reviver No.3* is featured in *1700 Cocktails For The Man Behind The Bar* by R. de Fleury in 1934. Consisting of brandy, maraschino and curaçao, it's meant to be layered in the pousse-café style. W.J. Tarling also includes three different *Corpse Reviver* recipes in his 1937 tome the *Café Royal Cocktail Book.*

SPECS

GIN
25ML (¾ OZ)

COCCHI AMERICANO
25ML (¾ OZ)

COINTREAU
25ML (¾ OZ)

LEMON JUICE
25ML (¾ OZ)

ABSINTHE
1 DASH

METHOD

1. Shake and strain into a cocktail glass.

2. No garnish. You're hungover, you don't have time for that.

THE COSMOPOLITAN

"OH SO PRETTY IN PINK".

EARLY REFERENCES

The first mention of a ***Cosmopolitan*** cocktail was in *Pioneers of Mixing at Elite Bars in 1934*. It may not resemble a modern-day ***Cosmo***, but isn't actually too dissimilar in flavour profile: *Jigger of Gordons' gin, 2 dashes Cointreau, juice of one lemon, a teaspoon of raspberry juice.*

A more familiar recipe turns up three decades later when Ocean Spray (which had started to promote their new cranberry juice in the 1960s), printed a cocktail on their packaging labels in 1968 called a ***Harpoon***.

This consisted of cranberry juice, vodka and a squeeze of lime – three essential building blocks of the modern ***Cosmopolitan***.

COSMOPOLITAN

EAST COAST TO WEST COAST, THEN BACK AGAIN

Toby Cecchini is the man responsible for the *Cosmopolitan* as we know it, but prior to that, the person who started it all off is said to be Cheryl Cook, a bartender working in South Beach, Miami.

In the 1980s, when test-marketing began for the newly released Absolut Citron, she put a spin on the *Kamikaze* (vodka, triple sec and Rose's lime cordial) by combining: *"Absolut Citron, a splash of triple sec, a drop of Rose's lime, and just enough cranberry to make it oh so pretty in pink, and topped with a curled lemon twist."*

The *Cosmopolitan* quickly spread across the country and was a big hit in the gay scene in San Francisco, eventually making its way onto the menu at the city's famous Fog City Diner.

Continued on next page...

SPECS

CITRUS VODKA
45ML (1 ½ OZ)

COINTREAU
15ML (½ OZ)

LIME JUICE
15ML (½ OZ)

CRANBERRY JUICE
30ML (1 OZ)

METHOD

1. Shake and strain into a cocktail glass.
2. Garnish with a flamed orange zest.

Back on the East Coast, it was brought to The Odeon in TriBeCa, New York by bartender Melissa Huffsmith, who'd been working in San Francisco. Shortly afterwards, in 1988, her colleague, Toby Cecchini reformulated the recipe she'd brought over (which was vodka, Rose's lime cordial and grenadine) and changed it to Absolut Citron, Cointreau, lime and cranberry.

"I'd like a cheeseburger, large fries and a *Cosmopolitan*."

Although Toby Cecchini may be responsible for inventing the modern-day *Cosmopolitan*, it's Dale Degroff who put rocket boosters on its popularity when he tweaked the recipe – complete with a flamed orange zest – while working at the iconic Rainbow Room in New York. It was a hit and quickly became the fashionable tipple amongst the glitterati, especially after Madonna was photographed sipping on one at a Grammys after-party.

When Sex and the City aired in the late 90s, the *Cosmopolitan* made regular appearances on the show and by the end of its run, the drink would be synonymous in people's minds.

THE

CULROSS

NAMED AFTER THE VILLAGE IN FIFE? – PERHAPS, PERHAPS NOT.

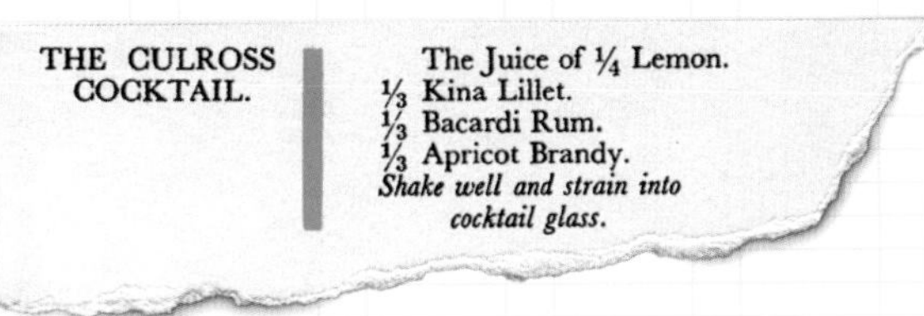

THE CULROSS COCKTAIL.

The Juice of ¼ Lemon.
⅓ Kina Lillet.
⅓ Bacardi Rum.
⅓ Apricot Brandy.
Shake well and strain into cocktail glass.

The Savoy Cocktail Book, *Harry Craddock, 1930*

The *Culross* is one of the lesser-known cocktails from *The Savoy Cocktail Book (1930)* and one whose name is a mystery.

Culross is a coastal village in Fife, Scotland, and perhaps it was named after a guest from the area visiting The Savoy; this is mere speculation, mind you.

SPECS

WHITE RUM
30ML (1 OZ)

APRICOT BRANDY
30ML (1 OZ)

COCCHI AMERICANO
30ML (1 OZ)

LEMON JUICE
15ML (½ OZ)

METHOD

1. Shake and strain into a cocktail glass.

2. No garnish.

DAIQUIRI

TO

DELMONICO

CO-SPECS

CAS OH

THE

DAIQUIRI

THE KING OF RUM COCKTAILS.

"Daiquiri" {Original Mr. Cox's.
for 6 persons—
The juice of 6 lemons
8 teaspoons full of Sugar
6 Bacardi cups—"Carta Blanca"
2 small cups of Mineral Water
Plenty Crushed ice—
Put all ingredients in a cocktail shaker—and shake well—
Do not strain as the glass may be served with some ice—

Cox's original hand written recipe, recorded in his diary.

Pronounced Dye-Ker-Ree, the *Daiquiri* is believed to be the creation of American engineer Jennings Cox. Cox managed the iron ore mining interests of the 'Spanish-American Iron Ore Company' in the Sierra Mountains, Cuba, by the coastal town of Daiquiri.

According to his granddaughter, he's said to have created the *Daiquiri* one afternoon in 1896 – he was hosting some surprise American guests and ran out of gin. Wary of giving them straight rum, he mixed it with lime and sugar and served it with shaved ice. His guests loved the drink, and so the *Daiquiri* was born.

Jennings Cox note: Courtesy of University of Miami Special Collections

DAIGUIRI COCKTAIL
$\frac{2}{3}$ Jigger Lime Juice.
$\frac{1}{3}$ Jigger Rum.
1 Barspon Powdered Sugar.
Shake well in fine ice and strain into
Cocktail glass.

Straub's Manual of Mixed Drinks, *Jacques Straub, 1913*

For many years the drink didn't have a name, and there are two stories about how it was christened.

The popular tale is the one told by Basil Woon in his 1928 book *When It's Cocktail Time in Cuba*. One morning, Cox and some of his workers were drinking them at their local bar the Hotel Venus (as was their morning ritual), when Cox exclaimed: "Boys, we've been drinking this delicious little drink for some time, but we've never named it... I'll tell you what, lads - we all work at Daiquiri and we all drank this drink first there. Let's call it a *Daiquiri*!"

The second is from chemist Josh Linthicum, who worked with Cox – he says it was named by a bartender serving Cox at the San Carlos Club. Lucius Johnson, a US Admiral who had fought in the ten-week Spanish-American War of 1898, took the drink stateside and introduced it to the Army and Navy Club in Washington DC, where a plaque still stands.

Continued on next page...

OUR RECIPE

WHITE RUM
60ML

LIME JUICE
25ML

CASTER SUGAR
10ML (2 TSP)

METHOD

1. Add sugar and lime juice to a shaker tin without ice and stir to dissolve the granules. Add rum, shake and strain into a cocktail glass.

2. Garnish with a lime wedge.

It might be most accurate to say that Cox was the first to pen the recipe, as the simple combination of rum, lime and sugar is centuries old. Case in point is the *El Draque* – associated with the legendary Sir Francis Drake in the late 1500s – it was a precursor to the *Mojito,* consisting of aguardiente, lime, sugar, mint and tree bark. This combination can also be seen in the form of the *Grog,* from 1740, when Admiral Edward Vernon issued an order that the sailors daily rum rations be diluted with water, adding that members of the crew could *"purchase sugar and limes to make it more palatable to them."*

Jennings Cox *(possibly the inspiration for Toad of Toad Hall).*

A similar combination is seen again, in the *Ti Punch* from Martinique in the second half of the 19th century, and even on home soil in Cuba there was a drink called a *Canchanchara* – popular with Cuban independence fighters in the late 19th century, this consisted of aguardiente, lime and molasses (or honey) and was drunk without ice.

Cox's original handwritten recipe for the drink can be seen on the previous pages. When he says lemons, he almost certainly means limes as lemons were virtually unheard of in Cuba, whereas limes were ubiquitous. Interestingly, Cox initially used brown sugar, but the wrong recipe (made with white sugar) was unknowingly spread by publicist Gerry Swinehart, who had been employed in the early 1930s by the Cuban government to promote American tourism.

He did such a great job in spreading the drink throughout bars in Havana and Manhattan that the white sugar version is the one that stuck. Jeff Berry, in his excellent book *Potions of the Caribbean (2013),* says it was either Emilio *'El Maragato'* Gonzalez of Hotel Plaza, or Eddie Woelke, who changed the drink to serve it straight up.

The first cocktail book that features the *Daiquiri* is *Jacque Straub's Manual of Mixed Drinks (1913)*, although it's spelt Daiguiri, and his recipe is a little confused, with double the lime to rum. Hugo Ensslin prints a more familiar recipe in *Recipes for Mixed Drinks (1917);* he lists two identical cocktails called *Bacardi Cocktail* and *Cuban Cocktail,* both with a measure of rum, juice of ½ a lime, and two dashes of gum syrup.

The first mention in a novel is in F. Scott Fitzgerald's *This Side of Paradise (1920).*

The man who mastered the *Daiquiri* was Catalan born Constantino Ribalaigua Vert, bartender and part-owner of the famous La Floridita bar in Havana. His venue would later become known as the 'Cradle of the Daiquiri.' It was here that he numbered his different *Daiquiris* 1 to 4, each with a different twist on the original three ingredients. It was at Floridita that Constante's *Daiquiris* were consumed by the man who would become synonymous with the drink (and the venue), the writer Ernest Hemingway.

Continued on next page...

COX'S RECIPE

JUICE
6 LEMONS (LIMES)

SUGAR
6 TSP

BACARDI CARTA BLANCA
6 CUPS

MINERAL WATER
2 SMALL CUPS

CRUSHED ICE

METHOD

1. Put all ingredients in a cocktail shaker and shake well - do not strain as the glass may be served with some ice.

NOTE

David Embury, in *The Fine Art of Mixing Drinks (1948),* lists the *Daiquiri* as one of his 'Six Basic Drinks', his preferred ratio being 8:2:1.

Hemingway at the La Floridita bar with friends, including Spencer Tracy.

The Floridita bar was the place to enjoy a ***Daiquiri*** *during the 30s and 40s, earning Constante the nickname of 'El Rey de Los Coteleros' or 'King of Cocktails'.*

By his death in 1952, after 50 years behind the bar, he's said to have made several million *Daiquiris.*

To make an authentic *Daiquiri* you'll need to use white rum. In terms of the sugar, there are different schools of thought, with some advocating caster or fine sugar and others, sugar syrup.

Hemingway at Floridita - Courtesy of Ernest Hemingway Collection. John F. Kennedy Presidential Library and Museum, Boston.

DAIQUIRI NUM. 1

2 Ounces Bacardí Rum.
1 Teaspoonful Sugar.
juice of half a lemon.
Cracked ice.
Shake well and strain into cocktail glass.

DAIQUIRI NUM. 2

2 Ounces Bacardí Rum.
Several Dashes Curacao.
1 Teaspoonful Orange Juice.
1 Teaspoonful Sugar.
Juice of Half a Lemon.
Cracked ice.
Shake well and strain into cocktail glass.

DAIQUIRI NUM. 3
(Maidique Style)

2 Ounces Bacardí Rum.
1 Spoonful Sugar.
1 Teaspoonful Grape Fruit Juice.
1 Teaspoonful Marraschino.
Juice of half a lemon.
Shake well and strain into cocktail glass. Serve frappe.

DAIQUIRI NUM. 4
(Florida Style)

2 Ounces Bacardí Rum.
1 Teaspoonful Sugar.
1 Teaspoonful Marraschino.
Juice of half a lemon.
Shake in an electric shaker with crushed ice.
Serve frappe.

Bar La Florida, *Constante Ribalaigua Vert, 1934*

DAIQUIRI #1	*DAIQUIRI #2*	*DAIQUIRI #3*	*DAIQUIRI #4*
WHITE RUM 60ML (2 OZ)	WHITE RUM 60ML (2 OZ)	WHITE RUM 60ML (2 OZ)	WHITE RUM 60ML (2 OZ)
LIME JUICE 15ML (½ OZ)	LIME JUICE 15ML (½ OZ)	LIME JUICE 15ML (½ OZ)	LIME JUICE 15ML (½ OZ)
CASTER SUGAR 5ML (1 TSP)	ORANGE CURAÇAO 5ML (1 TSP)	MARASCHINO 5ML (1 TSP)	MARASCHINO 5ML (1 TSP)
SHAKEN	ORANGE JUICE 5ML (1 TSP)	GRAPEFRUIT JUICE 5ML (1 TSP)	CASTER SUGAR 5ML (1 TSP)
	CASTER SUGAR 5ML (1 TSP)	CASTER SUGAR 15ML (1 TBSP)	BLENDED
	SHAKEN	BLENDED	

Note: See also Hemingway Daiquiri for more recipes.

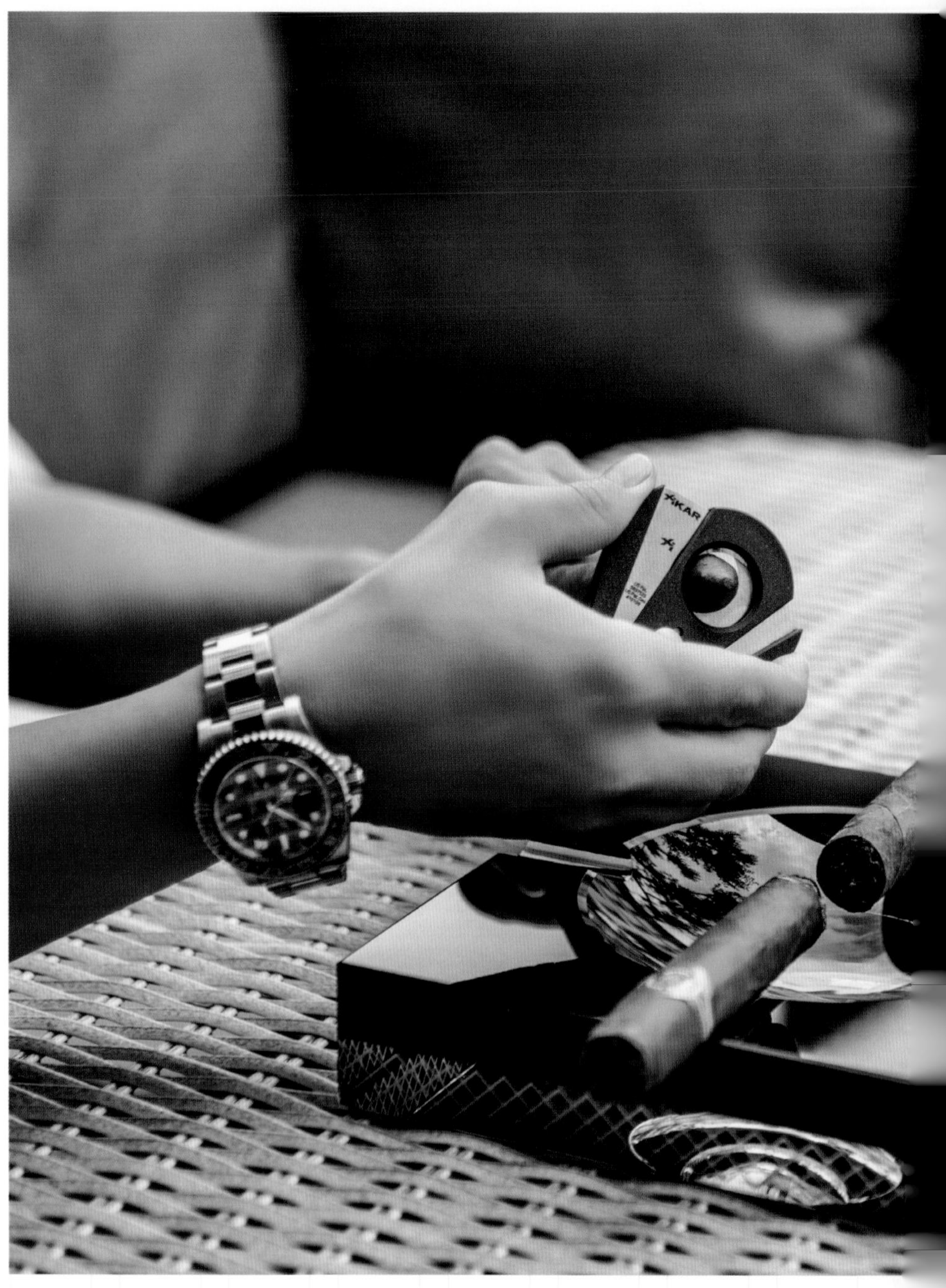

THE

DARK 'N' STORMY

THE COLOUR OF A CLOUD ONLY A FOOL OR DEAD MAN WOULD SAIL UNDER.

The *Dark 'n' Stormy* is the national drink of Bermuda (alongside the *Bermuda Rum Swizzle)*. The history of this cocktail begins with the British Royal Navy, which in 1809 acquired a dockyard site on Ireland Island in Bermuda.

At the turn of the 20th century, they added a ginger beer plant to the site, and in no time, this soft drink was being combined with the popular local rum Gosling's Black Seal.

Legend has it that the name was bestowed by a sailor, who on observing the visual effect of rum poured over iced ginger beer remarked it was: *"the colour of a cloud only a fool or dead man would sail under"*.

D

DARK 'N' STORMY

BLACK SEAL

Gosling's Rum established themselves in Bermuda in 1806, and in 1857 they began blending rums. Three years later, in 1860, they released 'Old Rum' which today is known as 'Black Seal'.

The 'Black Seal' name has, in fact, nothing to do with the cartoon seal on the label balancing a barrel on its snout. Rather, it hails from the fact that rum was initially only distributed in barrels, with people bringing their own bottles to fill up. The most common receptacle at the time were leftover champagne bottles from the British Naval officer's mess, which once filled with rum were then sealed with black wax.

People started asking for the 'black seal' rum, eventually leading to an official name change. As a nod to this tradition, Gosling's Rum makes a 'Family Reserve Old Rum' (same blend as black seal but aged longer) which is sold in a wax-sealed champagne bottle.

Note: Gosling's Rum has actually trademarked the Dark 'n' Stormy so it's technically illegal to make it with any other rum.

SPECS

GOSLING'S BLACK SEAL RUM
50ML (2 OZ)

GINGER BEER
TO TOP

METHOD

1. Pour ginger beer over ice in a highball, then add the rum.

2. Garnish with a lime wedge, optional but native Bermudians usually swear by it.

THE

DEATH IN THE AFTERNOON

AFTER SIX OF THESE COCKTAILS THE SUN ALSO RISES.

So Red the Nose, or Breath in the Afternoon, 1935:

Pour 1 jigger of absinthe into a champagne glass. Add iced champagne until it attains the proper opalescent milkiness. Drink 3 to 5 of these slowly.

The ***Death in the Afternoon*** was actually invented by Ernest Hemingway himself and named after his 1932 novel of the same name. It was his contribution to a 1935 collection of celebrity cocktail recipes titled ***So Red the Nose, or Breath in the Afternoon.***

On how it was created, Hemingway writes: *"This was arrived at by the author and three officers of H.M.S Danae after having spent seven hours overboard trying to get Capt. Bra Saunders' fishing boat off a bank where she had gone with us in a N.W. gale."*

Jeez – almost makes you feel lazy for coming up with that signature cocktail drinking wine in your pants at home.

D

DEATH IN THE AFTERNOON

SPECS

ABSINTHE
45ML (1 ½ OZ)

CHAMPAGNE
TO TOP

METHOD

1. Pour absinthe into a flute and top up slowly with champagne, allowing it to louche.

2. No garnish.

Hemingway, a man known for his tungsten constitution, notes that one should "... drink three to five of these slowly".

The editor also adds a note at the bottom saying: *"After six of these cocktails The Sun Also Rises."* (I assume he means in hospital). If you like absinthe (check) and you like champagne (check), meet your new best friend.

THE

DELICIOUS SOUR

I STAY MODEST 'BOUT IT, AY, SHE ELABORATE IT, AY.

4. The Delicious Sour.

A goblet with the juice of a lime,
a squirt of seltzer,
a spoonful of sugar,
½ of apple-jack,
½ of peach brandy,
the white of an egg.
Fill your glass with ice, shake well, strain, and serve.

The Flowing Bowl, *A. William Schmidt, 1892*

The *Delicious Sour* was invented by A. William Schmidt, or as he modestly called himself: *"The Only William"*.

Schmidt was one of the most celebrated bartenders of his time; nowadays he's been referred to as the 'godfather of modern mixology' for the creativity of his inventions – some working better than others – as evidenced by his book *The Flowing Bowl (1891)*.

Delicious indeed, but not the most humble naming of a cocktail on record. Schmidt's editor probably had to talk him out of calling it the *'William is Handsome Sour'*.

D

William Schmidt

There are rumoured to be lips under that moustache.

SPECS

LAIRD'S STRAIGHT APPLE BRANDY
50ML (2 OZ)

CRÈME DE PÊCHE
10ML (2 TSP)

LIME JUICE
25ML (¾ OZ)

SUGAR SYRUP (2:1)
10ML (2 TSP)

EGG WHITE
1

SODA
SPLASH OF

METHOD

1. Dry shake, then shake with ice and strain into a cocktail glass. Add a splash of soda at the end.

2. No garnish.

THE

DELMONICO

EGGS BENEDICT, BAKED ALASKA, LOBSTER NEWBERG, DELMONICO STEAK AND CHICKEN À LA KING.

Sometimes this drink is known as a *Delmonico Special* or a *Delmonico No.1.* The *Delmonico* cocktail was invented at what some consider America's first 'real' restaurant.

In the 1820s a pair of Swiss brothers – Giovanni (John) and Pietro (Peter) Del-Monico – opened a pastry shop on South William Street, New York. A few years later, in 1831, they opened their first official restaurant with the help of their nephew Lorenzo. This legendary restaurant changed the dining landscape, introducing the 'à la carte' menu concept to the USA, and while other eating establishments offered simple fixed menus or sandwiches, *Delmonico's* menu was over 100 pages long, with over 300 menu items and a massive wine cellar to boot.

At the time, eating out was not yet considered a leisure activity in its own right, but something to be done quickly; food merely as fuel. *Delmonico's* pioneered dining as an occasion, and a place where the wealthy could see and be seen. Dishes such as Eggs Benedict, Baked Alaska, Lobster Newberg, Delmonico Steak and Chicken à la King were all invented there.

Over the years it closed, re-opened and moved location several times. The photo shown is the restaurant on Fifth Avenue and 26th Street, which was open from 11th September 1876 through to 18th April 1899. The last New York City restaurant owned by the *Delmonico* family was on 44th Street and Fifth, and closed in 1923.

D

DELMONICO

DELMONICO'S : FIFTH AVENUE, BROADWAY AND 26TH STREET.

It's uncertain which of the many iterations of the restaurant spawned the *Delmonico* cocktail, but David Wondrich's guess is that it probably came about in 1876, originating at Delmonico's Madison Square outfit.

*Note: A lot of the **Delmonico** recipes out there are just a 'perfect' Cognac Manhattan; the additional gin is essential to differentiate this drink.*

SPECS

GIN
30ML (1 OZ)

COGNAC
15ML (½ OZ)

DRY VERMOUTH
15ML (½ OZ)

SWEET VERMOUTH
15ML (½ OZ)

ANGOSTURA BITTERS
2 DASHES

METHOD

1. Stir and strain into a cocktail glass.

2. Garnish with an orange twist.

EAST INDIA COCKTAIL

TO

ESPRESSO MARTINI

E

CAS OH

THE

EAST INDIA COCKTAIL

A GREAT FAVOURITE WITH THE ENGLISH LIVING IN THE DIFFERENT PARTS OF EAST INDIA.

175. EAST INDIA COCKTAIL.

(Use a large bar glass.)

Fill the glass with shaved ice;
1 tea-spoon of raspberry syrup;
1 tea-spoon of Curacao (red);
2 or 3 dashes of bitters (Angostura);
2 dashes of Maraschino;
1 wine glass of brandy;
stir up with a spoon, strain into a cocktail glass, and twist a piece of lemon peel on top, and serve.

EAST INDIA COCKTAIL.

(Use a large bar glass.)

Fill the glass with shaved ice;
1 teaspoonful of curaçoa (red)
1 teaspoonful of pineapple syrup;
2 or 3 dashes of bitters (Boker's genuine only);
2 dashes of maraschino;
1 wine glass full of brandy (Martell).
Stir up with a spoon, strain into a cocktail glass, putting in a cherry or medium-sized olive, twist a piece of lemon peel on top, and serve.

This drink is a great favorite with the English living in the different parts of East India.

Bartender's Manual, *Harry Johnson, 1882*
Bartender's Manual, *Harry Johnson, 1900*

E

EAST INDIA COCKTAIL

Fort William, the headquarters of the British East India Company in Kolkata, India.

The *East India Cocktail* was first printed in Harry Johnson's *Bartender's Manual* in 1882. His recipe specified raspberry syrup – which was changed to pineapple syrup by the time the 1888 and 1900 editions of his book came out. In these later editions, he adds a note saying: *"This drink is a great favourite with the English living in the different parts of East India."* East India was the term used to describe the lands of South and Southeast Asia that were under British and Dutch colonial rule. These included India, Singapore, Burma, Pakistan, Malaysia, Indonesia and several others.

David Wondrich rightly points out that it's essentially a slightly fancy *Brandy Cocktail* (brandy, curaçao, aromatic bitters and gum syrup). There is another identical cocktail called the *Bengal,* featured in a later book, R. De Fleury's *1700 Cocktails For The Man Behind The Bar (1934).*

SPECS

COGNAC
60ML (2 OZ)

PIERRE FERRAND ORANGE CURAÇAO
5ML (1 TSP)

PINEAPPLE SYRUP
5ML (1 TSP)

MARASCHINO
2.5ML (½ TSP)

BOKER'S (OR ANGOSTURA) BITTERS
3 DASHES

METHOD

1. Stir and strain into a cocktail glass.
2. Garnish with lemon twist and cherry.

NOTES

The red curaçao mentioned in Johnson's recipe is just curaçao with added red food colouring (Bols still make a version of it). In light of this, just use normal orange curaçao instead.

EGGNOG

E

SPECS

SERVES 4-5
LARGE WHOLE EGGS 4

ICING SUGAR
6 TBSP

WHOLE MILK
360ML (12 OZ)

HEAVY DOUBLE CREAM
180ML (6 OZ)

COGNAC
120ML (4 OZ)

DARK RUM
60ML (2 OZ)

GRATED NUTMEG
1 TSP

METHOD

1. Separate egg yolks and whites into bowls. Whisk yolks with icing sugar until smooth. In the other bowl, whisk whites until you get stiff peaks. Optionally add ½ tsp of cream of tartar to stop it separating.

2. Add all other ingredients to the mixture and whisk. Fold in egg whites with a spoon and stir. Serve, or bottle and refrigerate.

THE

EGGNOG

A WINTERTIME FAVOURITE.

Eggnog is traditionally made like a classic creme anglaise: raw eggs are beaten in a bowl with a combination of milk, sugar, spirits, and optional cream and spices. The recipe here is for 4-5 servings and is the unheated variety, though some prefer to make it on a stove, gently heating and thickening the mixture into a smooth custard.

It is thought to have originated in East Anglia but made its way across to the United States during the 18th century. It is now a highly popular drink, served throughout the wintertime in Canada and North America.

The origins of the name are up for debate... Some believe it comes from the combination of 'egg' and 'noggin' (a wooden mug used in English taverns of the time). Others think it is a contraction of 'egg-and-grog' (grog being North American slang for alcohol).

Eggnog remains a popular holiday drink across the Western world. It is often made by the batch and served at holiday parties from Thanksgiving through to New Year.

Trivia: George Washington, America's first president, was quite the fan of Eggnog, and devised his own booze-heavy recipe containing rum, rye and sherry.

THE

EL DIABLO

HELL IS EMPTY, AND ALL THE DEVILS ARE HERE!

Where are my pants?

El Diablo translates to 'the devil' in Spanish. Alongside the *Paloma* it's the best known long tequila cocktail, in a category that's rather sparse. The first cited mention of it is in a Ronrico rum pamphlet from the late 1930s found by drinks writer Greg Boehm. Trader Vic includes a *Mexican El Diablo* in his 1946 *Book of Food and Drink,* with 1 oz tequila, juice of ½ lime and ½ oz cassis, built over ice and topped with ginger ale.

Illustration: Satan, as drawn by Gustave Doré, from John Milton's Paradise Lost, 1866.

SPECS

TEQUILA BLANCO
45ML (1 ½ OZ)

LIME JUICE
15ML (½ OZ)

CREME DE CASSIS
15ML (½ OZ)

GINGER ALE
TO TOP

METHOD

1. Build over ice in a highball.
2. Garnish with a lime wedge.

THE

EL PRESIDENTE

SOMETIMES DESCRIBED AS A RUM MANHATTAN.

*The **El Presidente** is very likely a creation of Constantino Ribalaigua (of 'El Floridita' fame), but this would have been created prior to his **Daiquiri** days at the iconic bar.*

According to David Wondrich, it was probably invented in the mid-1910s, when Ribalaigua was working at a cafe off the Parque Central in Havana.

The earliest known recipe comes from John B. Escalante's *Manual del Cantinero* in 1915 (as shown). It uses two parts Chambery vermouth to one part Bacardi, with curaçao and grenadine (or simple syrup), as well as the unusual addition of Angostura bitters.

Manual del Cantinero, *John B. Escalante, 1915:*

- *Curacao, a few drops*
- *Angostura bitters, a few drops*
- *Grenadine or simple syrup, ½ barspoon*
- *Orange, 1 twist*
- *Chambery vermouth, 2 parts*
- *Bacardi rum, 1 part*

Mix with a spoon, stir and strain into cocktail glass, garnish with a cherry.

Manual del Cantinero, *Leon Pujol & Oscar Muniz, 1924:*

- *½ Bacardi rum*
- *½ Chambery*
- *a little grenadine, or better, curaçao.*

Serve with carbonated water, orange peel & a cherry.

EL PRESIDENTE

PRESIDENTE COCKTAIL

½ Vermouth Chambery.	½ Chambery Bermouth
½ Bacardí Oro.	½ Bacardí Gold.
½ Cucharadita de Curacao.	½ Teaspoonful of Curacao.
Hielo menudo.	Crushed ice.
Enfríese perfectamente y cuélese.	Cold well and strain.
Sírvase con guindas y una corteza de naranja.	Serve with cherris and a peel of orange.

Bar La Florida, *Constante Ribalaigua Vert, 1934*

In the *Manual del Cantinero (1924)* by Leon Pujol and Oscar Muniz (also shown), the proportions are altered to equal parts rum and vermouth, with either grenadine or curaçao. This version is closer to Ribalaigua's formula, as it appears in *Bar La Florida (1934)*, where he also omits grenadine in favour of curaçao. All three of these recipes call for 'Chambery', a type of French vermouth made in the Alps by Dolin. After investigation, Wondrich found that the Chambery that would have been ubiquitous at the time (and for which this French town was historically known), would likely not have been the dry version but the Blanc, which is a semi-dry. Made this way, the drink is far richer and more complex than the rum and dry vermouth combo often used today.

In 1919 *The New York Evening Telegram* described it as a mix of *"Bacardi, granatin (sic) and French vermouth"* and noted it was a *"favourite of the Cubans."* The name is said to have been a tribute to the President of the time, Mario Garcia Menocal, who was the leader of Cuba from 1913 to 1921. The 1:1 original ratio is too much like a glass of vermouth - the 2:1 ratio provides a better balance of flavours.

SPECS

WHITE RUM
50ML (2 OZ)

DOLIN BLANC
25ML (1 OZ)

PIERRE FERRAND ORANGE CURAÇAO
2.5ML (½ TSP)

GRENADINE
2.5ML (½ TSP)

METHOD

1. Stir and strain into a cocktail glass.
2. Garnish with an orange twist.

NOTES

When made with Dolin Blanc, full-flavoured white rum, Pierre Ferrand curaçao and real pomegranate grenadine, this drink sings.

ESPRESSO MARTINI

E

THE

ESPRESSO MARTINI

DICK BRADSELL'S MODERN CLASSIC.

SPECS

VODKA
50ML (1 ½ OZ)

COFFEE LIQUEUR
25ML (¾ OZ)

ESPRESSO
1 DOUBLE

SUGAR SYRUP (2:1)
10ML (2 TSP)

METHOD

1. Shake and strain into a cocktail glass.
2. Lay three coffee beans on top of the drink in a star pattern to garnish.

Invented by the inimitable Dick Bradsell in the early 1980s, he came up with it whilst working at the Soho Brasserie in London. He created it for a famous model (who shall remain nameless and blameless) who asked him for something that would be sure to "wake her up, and fuck her up." Originally called a *Vodka Espresso,* it transitioned to the now common *Espresso Martini.* For a brief spell, while he worked at Notting Hill's 'The Pharmacy' it was called *The Pharmaceutical Stimulant* – a very apt name indeed. Is there another modern classic that has so entrenched itself globally? I think not.

I do miss Mr Dick Bradsell, may he rest in peace – he really was one of a kind. Decades ago, when I was still an ignorant woofy-haired cartoon, knowing nothing but pretending I did (that part hasn't changed), he fielded all my basic questions with patience and tact and was the first one to show me how deep the cocktail rabbit hole could go. In the various bars in which he held fort, I can't count how many times he's seen me completely cabbaged, acting a fool and looking like a smashed crab – and through it all, he remained a friend. I raise my glass to you, sir.

THE

FALCONI

FALCONI

NON-CLASSIC
AUTHOR'S OWN

DON'T BE THAT GUY.

Created in 2007, the ***Falconi*** is named for my friend Sasha Ash; prolific inventor of words and phrases that would quickly be taken up and become part of the lexicon of those he mingled with. ***'Falconi'*** was a term he used to describe a 'sleazy rat-bastard'... so, basically, him.

Note: Noilly Ambre is produced in the same way as the dry or rouge versions of the vermouth, with the inclusion of orange, cinnamon, vanilla, and some additional herbs and spices.

SPECS

RYE WHISKEY
50ML (2 OZ)

NOILLY PRAT AMBRE
25ML (¾ OZ)

TAWNY PORT
15ML (½ OZ)

ORANGE BITTERS
2 DASHES

METHOD

1. Stir and strain into a cocktail glass.
2. Garnish with an orange twist.

"They lose the day
in expectation of the
night, and the night
in fear of the dawn."

– *Seneca*

THE

FANCY GIN OR BRANDY COCKTAIL

THAT'S A FANCY GLASS YOU HAVE THERE.

107. Brandy Cocktail.

(Use small bar glass.)

3 or 4 dashes of gum syrup.
2 do. bitters (Bogart's).
1 wine-glass of brandy.
1 or 2 dashes of Curaçoa.
Squeeze lemon peel; fill one-third full of ice, and stir with a spoon.

108. Fancy Brandy Cocktail.

(Use small bar glass.)

This drink is made the same as the brandy cocktail, except that it is strained in a fancy wine-glass, and a piece of lemon peel thrown on top, and the edge of the glass moistened with lemon.

The Bon Vivant's Guide or How to Mix Drinks,
Jerry Thomas, 1862

David Wondrich points out that in 1862 there wasn't yet a dedicated cocktail glass, so these would have been served in small wine glasses. The only difference between the standard *Gin or Brandy Cocktail* and the *'Fancy'* version is that it would have been served in a fancier wine glass, and with a lemon-juiced rim and a twist dropped in as garnish.

In Jerry Thomas' *The Bon Vivant's Guide or How to Mix Drinks (1862)* – as with the related category of 'Improved Cocktails' in later editions – it says to shake the cocktail. Having said that, I prefer to stir these particular drinks.

FANCY GIN OR BRANDY COCKTIAL

F

111. Gin Cocktail.

(Use small bar glass.)

3 or 4 dashes of gum syrup.
2 do. bitters (Bogart's).
1 wine-glass of gin.
1 or 2 dashes of Curaçoa.
1 small piece lemon peel; fill one-third full of fine ice shake well, and strain in a glass.

112. Fancy Gin Cocktail.

(Use small bar glass.)

This drink is made the same as the gin cocktail, except that it is strained in a fancy wine-glass and a piece of lemon peel thrown on top, and the edge of the glass moistened with lemon.

The Bon Vivant's Guide or How to Mix Drinks,
Jerry Thomas, 1862

FANCY GIN COCKTAIL

SPECS

GENEVER
60ML (2 OZ)

SUGAR SYRUP (2:1)
2.5ML (½ TSP)

PIERRE FERRAND ORANGE CURAÇAO
2.5ML (½ TSP)

BOKER'S BITTERS (OR ANGOSTURA)
2 DASHES

METHOD

1. Stir and strain into a cocktail glass; rub a lemon wedge around the rim to wet it.

2. Lemon twist.

FANCY BRANDY COCKTAIL

SPECS

COGNAC
60ML (2 OZ)

SUGAR SYRUP (2:1)
2.5ML (½ TSP)

PIERRE FERRAND ORANGE CURAÇAO
5ML (1 TSP)

BOKER'S BITTERS (OR ANGOSTURA)
2 DASHES

METHOD

1. Stir and strain into a cocktail glass; rub a lemon wedge around the rim to wet it.

2. Lemon twist.

THE

FISH HOUSE PUNCH

...AN EXPERIENCE FOLLOWED BY THREE BLANK PAGES IN HIS OTHERWISE FASTIDIOUSLY KEPT DIARY.

*The history of the **Fish House Punch** (sometimes referred to as the **Philadelphia Fish House Punch**) begins in the state of Pennsylvania – one of America's thirteen founding states. There, in 1732, America's oldest social club formed, under the name the 'Schuylkill Fishing Company of Pennsylvania' (pronounced school-kul). This punch was their 'house drink'.*

The first mention of the ***Fish House Punch*** was likely in 1744; the secretary of an embassy of Virginia Commissioners, William Black, was greeted by members of the club on the banks of Schuylkill River, who "very kindly welcomed [him] into their Province, with a Bowl of fine Lemon Punch big enough to [have] half a dozen young swimming geese. From *The Philadelphia Telegraph, 1880: To 1 pint of lemon or lime juice add 3 pints of mixture given below; 10 pints of water, 4 pounds of best loaf sugar. When ice is put in use less water. The Mixture; 1/2 pint Jamaica rum, 1/4 pint Cognac brandy. 1/4 pint best peach brandy.* The receipt is dated 1795.

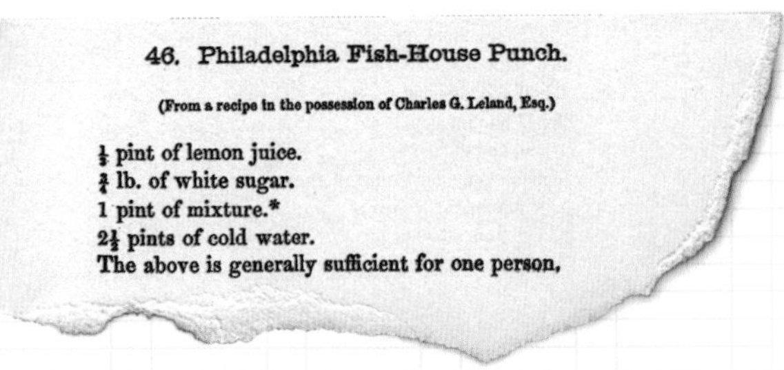

46. Philadelphia Fish-House Punch.

(From a recipe in the possession of Charles G. Leland, Esq.)

¼ pint of lemon juice.
¾ lb. of white sugar.
1 pint of mixture.*
2½ pints of cold water.
The above is generally sufficient for one person.

The Bon Vivant's Guide or How to Mix Drinks,
Jerry Thomas, 1862

F

FISH HOUSE PUNCH

In *The Joy of Mixology (2003),* Gary Regan tells the amusing tale of George Washington's brief visit; he once stayed at the club and sampled their *Fish House Punch* – an experience followed by three blank pages in his otherwise fastidiously kept diary. Quite a testament to its potency!

The first cocktail book it appears in is Jerry Thomas' *The Bon Vivant's Guide or How to Mix Drinks (1862)*, where he notes that the recipe had come from Charles Godfrey Leland, a lawyer and early member of the club. However, the earliest printed recipe, found by David Wondrich, is a cutting from 1795 reprinted in *The Philadelphia Telegraph* in 1880 – it was found as a clipping inside the pages of a book detailing the history of the club.

One challenge with accurately recreating this drink is that peach brandy is no longer available; créme de pêche is the most common substitute. Another alternative, suggested by David Wondrich, is to use three parts bonded applejack, to one part créme de pêche. This is the perfect punch to welcome guests at a dinner party – a crowd-pleaser, and so easy to drink. Ice will be broken in short order... sometimes a bit too much.

SPECS

SMITH & CROSS JAMAICAN RUM
20ML (1 OZ)

APPLETON 12 YEAR
20ML (1 OZ)

COGNAC
20ML (1 OZ)

CRÈME DE PÊCHE
10ML (½ OZ)

LEMON JUICE
20ML (1 OZ)

SUGAR SYRUP (2:1)
10ML (½ OZ)

WATER
25ML (1 OZ)

METHOD

1. Stir and strain into a rocks glass over ice.

2. Garnish with a lemon wedge.

THE

FLORADORA

THAT ONE FRIEND WHO JUST HAS TO BE 'EXTRA'.

FLORADORA—IMPERIAL STYLE
Juice ½ a Lime.
1 Jigger Brandy.
1 Pint Ginger Ale.

FLORADORA COOLER
Juice of ½ a Lime.
¼ Jigger Raspberry.
¼ Jigger Dry Gin.
1 Lump cube ice.
1 Pint Schweppes Ginger Ale.

Straub's Manual of Mixed Drinks,
Jacques Straub, 1913

David Wondrich sheds light on the *Floradora's* background, saying it's probably the first time the infamous orange-cherry-flag garnish was used.

Floradora was a successful comedy musical which debuted in London and then moved across the Atlantic in 1900 to open at New York's 'Casino Theatre'. The title of the drink is also the name of the fictitious Philippine Island on which the play unfolds.

F FLORADORA

The show's main attraction was the six beautiful girls that featured in it, known as the ***'Floradora Girls.'*** They were quite a sensation at the time, especially with New York's elite – in fact, all six of them went on to marry millionaires.

According to the *New York Evening World* newspaper, the drink was invented in 1901: a crowd, including one of the *Floradora* girls, Susie Drake (not one of the original sextette) visited a Colombus Avenue restaurant... To the annoyance of her companions she refused to drink, saying she'd only have one *"if you'll get me something brand new"* (so extra) to which Jimmy O'Brien, the fella in charge of the bar, obliged her by whipping up a new creation; from showgirl petulance the *Floradora* was born.

The first time it appears in print is Jacques Straub's *Manual of Mixed Drinks (1913)*. He also lists a variation, the *Floradora 'Imperial Style'*, made with brandy instead of gin, and without raspberry.

SPECS

PLYMOUTH GIN
50ML (2 OZ)

LIME JUICE
15ML (½ OZ)

RASPBERRY SYRUP
10ML (2 TSP)

GINGER ALE
TO TOP

METHOD

1. Build in a highball glass, add ice and stir.

2. Top with ginger ale, and stir again gently to combine.

3. Garnish with an orange slice and a cherry.

THE

FOG CUTTER

"FOG CUTTER, HELL. AFTER TWO OF THESE, YOU WON'T EVEN SEE THE STUFF."

SPECS

ORIGINAL FOG CUTTER

WHITE RUM
60ML (2 OZ)

COGNAC
30ML (1 OZ)

GIN
15ML (½ OZ)

LEMON JUICE
45ML (1 ½ OZ)

ORANGE JUICE
30ML (1 OZ)

ORGEAT
15ML (½ OZ)

PEDRO XIMENEZ SWEET SHERRY
15ML (½ OZ)

METHOD

1. Shake all ingredients except the sherry and pour over ice in a tall Tiki mug. Float the sherry; serve with a straw and no garnish.

The *Fog Cutter* is an original drink invented by Victor Bergeron, more widely known by his moniker *'Trader Vic'*. ***The Mai Tai, Scorpion*** and ***Fog Cutter*** are a few of his most famous creations.

The *Fog Cutter*, listed in his 1947 book Trader Vic's Bartender's Guide, is a shaken drink, served over cracked ice in a 14 oz glass. His recipe is:

2 oz Puerto Rican rum,

1 oz brandy,

½ oz gin,

2 oz lemon juice,

1 oz orange juice,

½ oz orgeat, with a sherry float.

FOG CUTTER

By the 1950s Vic had created a weaker variation called the Samoan *Fog Cutter,* which was featured in the 1972 edition of his *Bartender's Guide.* This iteration reduced the gin and brandy, was blended instead of shaken, and then garnished with fresh mint.

The recipe he gives is:

1½ oz light Puerto Rican rum,
½ oz gin & brandy,
2 oz lemon juice,
1 oz orange juice,
½ oz orgeat, and
¼ sweet sherry floated on top.

In the 1972 edition of his book, Trader Vic jokes of his creation: *"Fog Cutter, hell. After two of these, you won't even see the stuff."*

Note: I've reduced the lemon juice in both from 60ml to 45ml for better balance.

SPECS

SAMOAN FOG CUTTER

WHITE RUM
45ML (1½ OZ)

COGNAC
15ML (½ OZ)

GIN
15ML (½ OZ)

LEMON JUICE
45ML (1 ½ OZ)

ORANGE JUICE
30ML (1 OZ)

ORGEAT
15ML (½ OZ)

PEDRO XIMENEZ SWEET SHERRY
15ML (½ OZ)

METHOD

1. Blend all ingredients except the sherry with one scoop of crushed ice. Pour into a tall Tiki mug, then top up with cubed ice and float sherry to finish.

2. Garnish with a mint sprig.

THE

FORD COCKTAIL

AN OLD TOM MARTINI WITH A HERBAL FLOURISH.

CAPRICE

Gin	⅔ jigger	Benedictine	1 spoon
Fr. Vermouth	1 spoon	Orange Bitters	2 dashes

Shake well with ice, strain into chilled cocktail glass, add ripe olive and serve.

World Drinks and How to Mix Them, *William Boothby, 1934*

Despite presumptions to the contrary, the *Ford Cocktail* is not named after industrial titan Henry Ford – it predates his rise and the launch of his automobile. It might possibly be named for the famous 'all-around athlete' of the time, Malcolm Webster Ford, who was also the great-grandson of Noah Webster, the renowned poet and creator of Webster's dictionary.

F

FORD COCKTAIL

Ford Cocktail.

Three dashes benedictine, three dashes orange bitters, half a jigger Tom gin, half a jigger French vermouth. Mix in a mixing-glass half-full fine ice. Strain into a cocktail-glass. Add a piece twisted orange-peel.

Modern American Drinks, *George J. Kappeler, 1895*

The print debut of the *Ford Cocktail* is in George J. Kappeler's *Modern American Drinks (1895)*. There are several other drinks with similar or even identical ingredients, most notably the *Caprice,* although that came into view 39 years later in William Boothby's *World Drinks and How To Mix Them (1934).*

Note: The amount of Benedictine to use is contentious. As with all recipes involving the ambiguous measuring of 'dashes'; it's vital to achieve balance with the Old Tom and the vermouth, so taste-testing may be required to finesse this.

SPECS

OLD TOM GIN
30ML (1 OZ)

DRY VERMOUTH
30ML (1 OZ)

BENEDICTINE
5ML (1 TSP)

ORANGE BITTERS
3 DASHES

METHOD

1. Stir and strain into a cocktail glass.
2. Garnish with an orange twist.

THE

FRENCH 75

ONE OF THE BEST KNOWN CHAMPAGNE COCKTAILS, NAMED AFTER A WWI CANNON.

The *French 75* is named after the 75mm field gun used by the French army during WWI. It began its life as a completely different cocktail to the version we know today.

"There has been brought back to Broadway from the front by War Correspondent E. Alexander Powell the Soixante Quinze cocktail - the French Seventy-five. It is one-third gin, one-third grenadine, one-third applejack and a dash of lemon juice. Frank Leon Smith, the story writer, says he drank one and immediately paid his rent." – Washington Herald, December 2nd 1915.

It first appeared in print as the ***Soixante Quinze (Seventy Five) Cocktail*** in an issue of the *Washington Herald* published 2nd December 1915. There it's listed as: one third gin, one third applejack, one third grenadine and a dash of lemon juice.

The first cocktail book appearance is in 1922, as the ***'75' Cocktail*** in Robert Vermeire's *Cocktails and How to Mix Them*. His recipe looks like this: *one third gill Dry Gin, one sixth gill Calvados, 2 dashes of Grenadine, 1 tsp of Lemon juice.* Harry MacElhone also includes the ***'75' Cocktail*** in his *ABC of Mixing Cocktails*, published the same year – 1922. MacElhone also uses a base of gin, calvados and grenadine, but eschews the lemon for absinthe and Anis Del Oso instead.

F FRENCH 75

Faculty officers of the Yale R.O.T.C. firing the famous French 75's in Artillery Hall, *Connecticut, 1917.*

It's in 1927, in Judge Jr's *Here's How* that it first appears as *The French "75"* with the recipe taking the recognisable modern form: *2 jiggers Gordon water; 1 part lemon juice; a spoonful of powdered sugar; cracked ice. Fill up the rest of a tall glass with Champagne!* Above the recipe, Judge Jr. states: *"This drink is really what won the War for the Allies"*, and underneath, *'If you use club soda instead of champagne, you have a Tom Collins.'* It was this version that Harry Craddock later replicated in *The Savoy Cocktail Book,* and it's this name and set of ingredients that have endured.

Robert Vermeire believes it was invented by Henry Tépé, of Henry's bar in Paris, while others say it was created at Harry's New York Bar, also in Paris.

Note: In New Orleans, the French 75 is commonly made with cognac instead of gin.

SPECS

GIN
30ML (1 OZ)

LEMON JUICE
20ML (3/4 OZ)

SUGAR SYRUP (2:1)
10ML (1/2 OZ)

CHAMPAGNE
TO TOP

METHOD

1. Shake the first three ingredients and strain into a flute; top with champagne.

2. Garnish with a lemon twist.

GIBSON
TO
GRASSHOPPER

CO-SPECS

G

T H E

GIBSON

YOU CAN NEVER HAVE ENOUGH ONIONS.

Gibson Cocktail
½ jigger French vermouth.
½ jigger dry gin.
Stir, strain and serve.

Drinks, *Jacques Straub, 1914*

Often recognised simply as a ***Dry Martini*** *with a pickled onion garnish, this is a misnomer. In fact, the evolution of the* ***Gibson*** *involves more than just a switch of garnish – it's emergence is significant because it's the first time we see a prototype for a* ***Dry Martini*** *without any bitters.*

In fact, the earliest recipes for the *Gibson* have no onion garnish to speak of. An olive is specified in William Boothby's *The World's Drinks and How to Mix Them (1908)* – which seems to be the first appearance in a cocktail book – but many of the early recipes don't feature any garnish at all. When bitters started to fall by the wayside from the *Dry Martini*, the onion might have been added as a means of differentiating between two otherwise identical drinks.

GIBSON

ORIGIN STORIES

There are several accounts of how the *Gibson* came about; the two most prevalent being:

• It was invented at the Players Club in New York, by a bartender named Charlie Connolly. He named it after the famous illustrator Charles Dana Gibson (late 19th to early 20th century), who was a member of the club, and challenged Connolly to make him a *Martini* – but an improved version. Gibson was the creator of the iconic 'Gibson Girl' drawings, which represented the glamorous ideal of an American woman. Connolly added two onions as a garnish, to represent the breasts of the Gibson Girls.

• The competing story is that it was invented in the late 1890s, at the Bohemian Club in San Francisco. There, financier Walter D.K. Gibson would order his *Martinis* without bitters, and soon the version of his drink took on his name. Eric Felton of the *Wall Street Journal* found a printed mention of the cocktail by fellow Bohemian Club member Ward Thompson, from way back in 1898.

The problem is that as we know, the *Gibson* existed for years before the onion garnish was added. The Charles Dana Gibson story is certainly the more colourful of the two, but the Walter D.K. Gibson story also has legs; we can't say for sure either way.

Continued on next page…

SPECS

GIN
60ML (2 OZ)

DRY VERMOUTH
15ML (½ OZ)

METHOD

1. Stir and strain into a cocktail glass.
2. Garnish with two pickled onions on a skewer.

NOTABLE COCKTAIL BOOK APPEARANCES

• In William Boothby's *The World's Drinks and How to Mix Them (1908)* the *Gibson* is listed as equal parts dry gin and French vermouth, no onion to speak of. And, importantly, a note states *"No bitters should ever be used in making this drink"* (which falls into line with the Walter D.K. Gibson version of its origin).

• In *Drinks,* by Jacques Straub (1914), it's comprised of equal parts dry gin and French vermouth, stirred with no garnish.

An onion makes an appearance in George R. Washburne and Stanley Bronner's *Beverages de Luxe (1914)* in the *Onion Cocktail:*

ONION COCKTAIL

Fill mixing glass up with fine ice
Two or three dashes of Orange Bitters
One-third French Vermouth
Two-thirds Dry Gin
Three of four dashes of Onion Juice

Stir well and serve in fancy cocktail glass with small pearl onion in place of olive.

• It appears again as an *Onion Cocktail* in Tom Bullock's *The Ideal Bartender* in 1917. Bullock's recipe calls for sweet vermouth to be added to Old Tom and the very specific instruction that no bitters are to be used. In the same book, Bullock also lists another cocktail garnished with pickled onions, called an *L.P.W.*; that drink adds both sweet and dry vermouth to Old Tom gin.

• In his 1948 book *The Fine Art of Mixing Drinks,* David Embury says *"The distinction between a Martini and the Gibson is simple. The Martini is served with an olive, the Gibson with a small pickled onion."* For the ratio of gin to vermouth, Embury says 5:1 is pleasing to most, though he personally likes it 7:1 – as with the *Martini,* apply your preferred ratio.

Robert Vermeire's Cocktails and How to Mix Them (1922) finally put ***Martini*** *and onion together under the* ***Gibson*** *name. He also makes a slightly arbitrary observation: that the cocktail is well known in Japan, principally in Yokohama.*

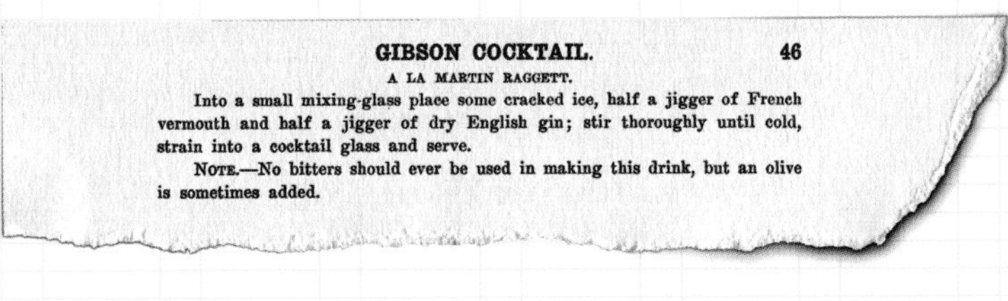

GIBSON COCKTAIL. **46**

A LA MARTIN RAGGETT.

Into a small mixing-glass place some cracked ice, half a jigger of French vermouth and half a jigger of dry English gin; stir thoroughly until cold, strain into a cocktail glass and serve.

NOTE.—No bitters should ever be used in making this drink, but an olive is sometimes added.

The World's Drinks and How to Mix Them,
William Boothby, 1908

Personally, I can never have enough onions in my *Gibson,* so I usually ask for extra in a small glass on the side.

Note: You'll sometimes (although very rarely) find a Gibson garnished with a pickled hazelnut. This stems from a reference plucked from obscurity by David Wondrich, found in Ernest P. Rawling's Rawling's Book of Mixed Drinks (1914).

THE

GIMLET

A COCKTAIL ORIGINATING FROM THE BRITISH ROYAL NAVY.

*The **Gimlet** is a drink that originated in the British Royal Navy, either at the end of the 19th century or beginning of the 20th. Since the 18th century, the juices of limes and other citrus fruits had been consumed by sailors in order to combat the scourge of scurvy, a disease arising from a lack of vitamin C.*

Sailors had begun by drinking Grog, a crude mix of rum and lime. They would preserve the lime juice on board by fortifying it with alcohol (usually adding circa 15% rum).

The threat of scurvy was serious enough that in 1867 the 'Merchant Shipping Act' was passed into law, making it mandatory for British ships to carry lime juice on board.

That same year, in Leith, Scotland, a savvy businessman named Lauchlan Rose invented a way to preserve lime juice without alcohol, using sugar and sulphur dioxide instead – Rose's lime juice cordial was released in short order. His aim was to tap into a broader market, which he achieved, but in addition to this, his new lime cordial became the defacto choice for the Royal Navy.

SPECS

PLYMOUTH NAVY STRENGTH OR FORD'S OFFICER'S RESERVE GIN
60ML (2 OZ)

LIME CORDIAL
15ML (½ OZ)

METHOD

1. Stir and strain into a cocktail glass.
2. No garnish.

In terms of who put two and two together to make the *Gimlet* cocktail, the credit usually goes to Sir Thomas Desmond Gimlette, Surgeon General of the British Royal Navy from 1879 to 1913, for whom the drink could be named after. He is said to have mixed gin and lime cordial in order to encourage consumption of the citrus fruit. Another story asserts that the name derives from a small corkscrew-like tool called a 'gimlet' used to bore a hole in a spirit barrel.

These days it's common for cocktail bars to eschew lime cordial for fresh lime juice and sugar instead. But, much as fresh lime juice is always preferable in cocktails, a ***Gimlet*** with just gin, lime juice and sugar doesn't feel like a ***Gimlet***, but more like a ***Gin Sour.***

Continued on next page...

NOTES ON THE USE OF CORDIAL

Rose's lime cordial undoubtedly has an artificial taste and doesn't work in most cocktails, but for some reason, it does work in the *Gimlet.* Some add both lime cordial and fresh lime juice, and for those who just can't stomach lime cordial at all you could substitute it for one of the many homemade lime cordial recipes out there – just ensure it also includes the zest of a lime.

The *Gimlet's* first cocktail book appearance is in the 1922 edition of *Harry's ABC of Mixing Cocktails.* His ratio is equal parts Plymouth gin to Rose's lime cordial. When you consider that on the ships it would have been mixed without any ice, this makes sense as the gin was 57% ABV. MacElhone's notes under the recipe state: *"Stir and serve in same glass. Can be iced if desired. A very popular beverage in the Navy."*

Note: British sailors consumed so many limes, they adopted the nickname 'Limeys'.

THE

GIN & IT

GIN INNIT?

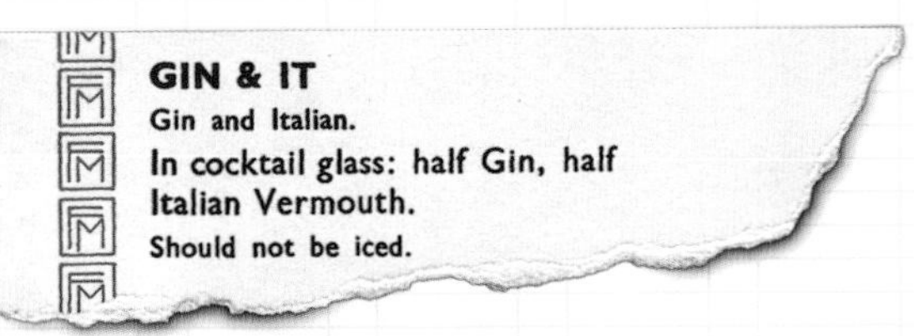

GIN & IT
Gin and Italian.
In cocktail glass: half Gin, half Italian Vermouth.
Should not be iced.

The Artistry of Mixing Drinks, *Frank Meier, 1936*

There is scant information to be found on the history of this drink however, we do know that *Gin & It* stands for gin and Italian vermouth (in other words, sweet vermouth).

Popular around the end of the 19th century, it was originally called the *Sweet Martini* or *Sweet Vermouth Martini.* Later this changed to the *Gin & Italian,* and eventually to the much catchier *Gin & It.*

SPECS

GIN
45ML (1½ OZ)

SWEET VERMOUTH
45ML (1½ OZ)

METHOD

1. Shake and strain into a cocktail glass.
2. No garnish.

NIKKA WHISKY
TAKETSURU
PURE MALT
ウイスキー

THE

GIN DAISY

IT'S A DAISY AGE.

SPECS

OLD SCHOOL JERRY THOMAS

GENEVER
60ML (2 OZ)

ORANGE CURAÇAO PIERRE FERRAND
10ML (2 TSP)

LEMON JUICE
20ML (¾ OZ)

SUGAR SYRUP (2:1)
5ML (1 TSP)

SODA WATER
A SPLASH

METHOD

1. Shake and strain into short 5-8 oz tumbler (or small coupe). Splash soda on top.

2. No garnish.

The *Gin Daisy* was originally a whiskey-based cocktail, but soon became a category of drink to encompass different base spirits including brandy, rum and gin. In time, the *Gin Daisy* separated itself from the pack and became the most ubiquitous of the group.

The story of the ***Daisy's*** invention is featured in David Wondrich's revised and updated book *Imbibe! (2015)*.

Paraphrasing, the short version is that: *On July 7th, 1873, Billy Taylor walked into Fred Eberlin's basement bar, around the corner from the New York Stock Exchange. Taylor dictated the ingredients for the Daisy to resident bartender Frank who mixed it for him. Upon trying it, Taylor exclaimed: "By George, that's a Daisy!"*

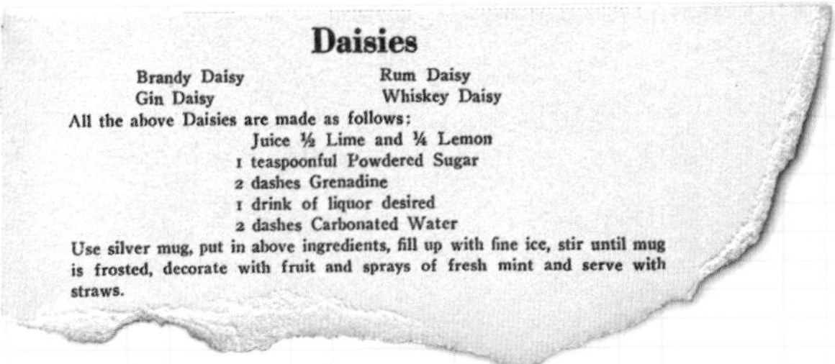

Daisies

Brandy Daisy — Rum Daisy
Gin Daisy — Whiskey Daisy

All the above Daisies are made as follows:

Juice ½ Lime and ¼ Lemon
1 teaspoonful Powdered Sugar
2 dashes Grenadine
1 drink of liquor desired
2 dashes Carbonated Water

Use silver mug, put in above ingredients, fill up with fine ice, stir until mug is frosted, decorate with fruit and sprays of fresh mint and serve with straws.

Recipes for Mixed Drinks, *Hugo R. Ensslin, 1917*

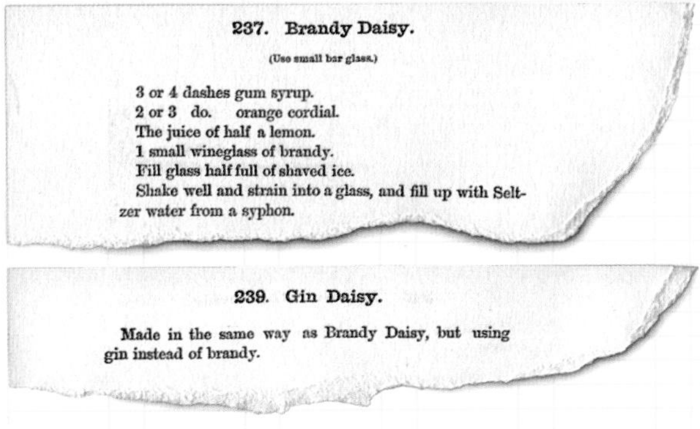

237. Brandy Daisy.

(Use small bar glass.)

3 or 4 dashes gum syrup.
2 or 3 do. orange cordial.
The juice of half a lemon.
1 small wineglass of brandy.
Fill glass half full of shaved ice.
Shake well and strain into a glass, and fill up with Seltzer water from a syphon.

239. Gin Daisy.

Made in the same way as Brandy Daisy, but using gin instead of brandy.

Bar-Tender's Guide, *Jerry Thomas, 1876*

The *Daisy* cocktail has taken many forms over the years, spawning numerous divergent interpretations. In order to differentiate them, Wondrich makes two clear category distinctions: 'old school' as seen in the 1876 edition of Jerry Thomas' *Bar-Tender's Guide* (the *Daisy's* first cocktail book appearance), or 'new school', which became popular in the early 1900s, as found in Hugo R. Ensslin's *Recipes for Mixed Drinks (1916).*

Continued on next page...

G GIN DAISY

SPECS

NEW SCHOOL HUGO ENSSLIN

GIN
60ML (2 OZ)

LEMON JUICE
10ML (2 TSP)

LIME JUICE
10ML (2 TSP)

CASTER SUGAR
5ML (1 TSP)

GRENADINE
5ML (1 TSP)

SODA WATER
SPLASH OF

METHOD

1. Add ingredients to a silver mug or small highball, add crushed ice and churn with a spoon to mix.

2. Garnish with a mint sprig, raspberry and orange slice (or any other fruits in season).

SPECS

MODERN VARIATION DAVID EMBURY

GIN
60ML (2 OZ)

LEMON JUICE
20ML (¾ OZ)

GRENADINE
10ML (2 TSP)

YELLOW CHARTREUSE
5ML (1 TSP)

METHOD

1. Pour ingredients into a goblet or silver mug, add crushed ice and churn with a spoon to mix.
2. Garnish with seasonal fruit - dealers choice.

I've included recipes for both, as well as a third 'modern' recipe from David Embury which includes Chartreuse. Harry Johnson was actually the first to add yellow Chartreuse to a *Daisy* in his *Bartender's Manual (1888)*, but Embury improved upon Johnson's recipe by reducing the amount and adding grenadine.

ON DAISIES & FIXES

Both the *Daisy* and the *Fix* are derivations of the *Sour;* the difference between a *Daisy* and a *Fix* – which are very similar drinks – is that the *Daisy* uses orange cordial (originally) or raspberry syrup/grenadine, whereas the *Fix* uses pineapple syrup.

NOTES ON GLASSWARE

The type of glass used has also changed over the years; from a small tumbler-style bar glass, as used by Thomas (where the drink was served straight up) to the silver mugs, goblets or highballs of later recipes, which were filled with crushed ice. These days a *Gin Daisy* is most likely to be served over crushed ice, in a highball or tumbler.

"What matters most is how well you walk through the fire."

– *Charles Bukowski*

THE

GIN FIZZ

I'LL DRINK THIS STANDING.

244. Whiskey Fiz.

(Use small bar glass.)

4 or 5 dashes of gum syrup.
Juice of ½ a lemon.
1 small wineglass of whiskey.
Fill the glass half full of shaved ice, shake up well and strain into a glass.
Fill up the glass with Seltzer water from a syphon and drink without hesitation.

246. Gin Fiz.

The same as Whiskey Fiz, substituting gin for whiskey.

Bar-Tender's Guide, *Jerry Thomas, 1876*

The *Gin Fizz*, and its cousin the *Tom Collins* are thought of interchangeably – both have the same ingredients and are essentially just lemonades spiked with gin. However, although they may be indistinguishable if ordered nowadays, that wasn't always the case...

When both drinks make their first cocktail book appearance in the 1876 edition of Jerry Thomas' *Bar-Tender's Guide*, we see the delineation: the key differences are the presentation and the way they were intended to be consumed.

G GIN FIZZ

Gin Fiz.

(Use medium bar-glass.)

Take 1 tea-spoonful of powdered white sugar.
3 dashes of lemon juice.
1 wine-glass of Holland gin.
1 small piece of ice.

Fill up the glass with Apollinaris or Seltzer water, stir thoroughly and serve.

Bar-Tender's Guide, *Jerry Thomas, 1887*

The Fizz was meant to be a short drink, served in a small 6 to 8 oz highball-style glass, without ice, designed to be quaffed quickly. One can imagine a *Fizz* being drunk by a busy 19th century industrialist who had moves to make – the 'time is money; I'll drink this standing' type.

The Collins, on the other hand, was served in a much larger glass, with ice, and with its roots as a classic *'Punch'* it was a drink for those in less of a rush; more suited to a patron of languid disposition.

RECIPE VARIATIONS

SILVER FIZZ
Add egg white.

ROYAL FIZZ
Add 1 whole egg.

GOLDEN FIZZ
Add one egg yolk.

DIAMOND FIZZ
Use champagne instead of soda.

SPECS

GIN
50ML (2 OZ)

LEMON JUICE
20ML (¾ OZ)

SUGAR SYRUP (2:1)
10ML (½ OZ)

SODA
TO TOP

METHOD

1. Shake and strain into a small highball (6-8 oz) without ice and top up with chilled soda.

2. No garnish or straw.

T H E

GIN RICKEY

NO SUGAR!

GIN RICKEY.

(Use a medium size fizz glass.)

1 or 2 pieces of ice;
Squeeze the juice of 1 good-sized lime or 2 small ones;
1 wine glass of Tom or Holland gin if required;
Fill up the glass with club soda, carbonic or selters if required, and serve with a spoon.

Bartender's Manual, *Harry Johnson, 1900*

The history of the *Rickey* is covered in great detail in David Wondrich's seminal book *Imbibe!*

Wondrich tells us that, of the several venues mentioned as contenders for the potential birthplace of the *Gin Rickey*, the one cited most often is Shoomaker's in Washington DC. It was here in 1883 that Colonel Joe Rickey, a Democratic lobbyist from Missouri, is said to have invented the drink – asking bartender George Williamson to squeeze half a lime into his bourbon and top it up with soda. *Rickey* had just won a large sum of money betting on underdog John G.Carlisle to be elected as the new speaker of the House, and he celebrated his win with an epic dining and drinking binge, ending up at Shoomaker's the next day (which he owned at the time).

As mentioned in Imbibe!, the *Rickey* was originally a whiskey drink, but the preferred spirit soon changed to gin (much to Colonel Joe's annoyance).

G GIN RICKEY

SPECS

GIN (OR OLD TOM)
50ML (2 OZ)

LIME JUICE
OR HALF A LIME
15ML (½ OZ)

SODA
TO TOP

METHOD

1. Build over cubed ice in a highball.
2. Garnish with a lime wedge.

Pretty soon the drink was a sensation that had spread across the country, as well as internationally. The *Rickey* is now a category of drinks, although the gin version remains the most popular. The *Gin Rickey's* first cocktail book appearance is in the 1900 edition of *Harry Johnson's Bartender's Manual.*

It is absolutely crucial that no sugar is added to this drink; the lack of a sweetener is the essence of a *Rickey.* Adding sugar to a *Gin Rickey* is like asking a native from the beautiful city of Napoli if they would like pineapple on their pizza – punishable by death!

In the Brooklyn Eagle, 1892, Colonel Rickey is quoted as saying: *"Any drink with sugar in it... heats the blood, while the Rickey, with its blood cooling lime juice, is highly beneficial."*

Indeed, the refreshingly light and tart combination of gin, soda and lime juice makes this the most perfect summer drink, though it works just as well in other seasons.

“Keep searching for that sound you hear in your head until it becomes a reality.”

– *Bill Evans*

GODFATHER

G

THE

GODFATHER

THE SUGAR COATING TO THE CYANIDE PILL.

SPECS

SCOTCH
50ML (2 OZ)

AMARETTO
25ML (1 OZ)

METHOD

1. Build over cubed ice in a rocks glass.
2. No garnish.

Not that one.

Not much is known about this cocktail, but it's believed to have come about in the 1970s.

Disaronno claim that the *Godfather* was a favourite of Marlon Brando, hence the name, however, this seems awfully convenient for the marketing department.

I can't really imagine Vito or Michael Corleone sipping one of these. Perhaps Fredo?

For die-hard I'd-rather-French-kiss-my-dad-than-drink-amaretto types, this could be the sugar coating to the cyanide pill.

VARIATIONS

GODMOTHER
Vodka instead of whisky.

GODSON
Add cream.

THE

GOLDEN CADILLAC

TOP UP AS NEEDED.

The *Golden Cadillac* was invented in 1952 at Poor Red's Bar-B-Q restaurant in El Dorado, California. A newly engaged couple came to celebrate and asked bartender Frank Klein to create their very own cocktail, matching it to their freshly purchased pride and joy – a golden Cadillac. Many attempts and recipes later, they landed on the recipe we know today.

It was originally made with Bols white cacao and blended, and is still made this way at Poor Red's today. They also serve the extra in a highball glass on the side, for you to top up your drink as needed, which seems like good old American hospitality.

TRIVIA

Poor Red's is the biggest consumer of Galliano in the world, and for their purchasing loyalty the Galliano group even gave them an actual golden Cadillac to display outside the bar.

SPECS

GALLIANO
30ML (1 OZ)

WHITE CRÈME DE CACAO
30ML (1 OZ)

HEAVY CREAM
30ML (1 OZ)

METHOD

1. Shake and strain into a cocktail glass.
2. No garnish.

GOLDEN DAWN

G

THE

GOLDEN DAWN

A SWEET COCKTAIL THAT'S MEANT TO RESEMBLE A SUNSET.

SPECS

CALVADOS
20ML (3/4 OZ)

GIN
20ML (3/4 OZ)

APRICOT BRANDY
20ML (3/4 OZ)

ORANGE JUICE
20ML (3/4 OZ)

GRENADINE
2.5ML (1/2 TSP)

METHOD

1. Shake first four ingredients and strain into a cocktail glass.

2. Add grenadine with a spoon into the middle of the drink so it sinks to the bottom.

*The **Golden Dawn** comes from W.J. Tarling's Café Royal Cocktail Book (1937) and was created in September 1930 by one Tom Buttery, at the Berkeley Hotel in London.*

Some claim it was named after the 1927 Rogers and Hammerstein operetta (or the movie spin-off three years later). However, it's more likely the name came from the appearance of the drink: layered with grenadine at the bottom, it looks convincingly like a red-orange summer sunrise.

*Note: You'll find many different recipes for the **Golden Dawn** out there, some with Cointreau, others omitting calvados.*

THE

GRASSHOPPER

G

GRASSHOPPER

DO YOU LIKE AFTER EIGHTS?

The *Grasshopper* was invented at Tujague's, the second oldest restaurant in New Orleans – it opened in 1856, and is still going. In 1910 the owners Guillaume and Marie Tujague sold the business to the family of Philibert Guichet, who invented the drink for a cocktail competition in New York in 1919 (in which he claimed second place). Some assert that this competition took place in 1928; this would mean it was held during Prohibition (which ran from 1920-1933), so that seems highly unlikely, especially in New York.

Adding weight behind the original story, in a 2014 article by Erin DeJesus, she writes that Poppy Tooker (a New Orleans food historian) has found *Grasshopper* references in newspapers dated 1919, and makes the excellent point that if the competition had taken place during Prohibition, there wouldn't have been a written record.

The *Grasshopper* was very popular during the 50s and 60s, especially in the American South. It is sometimes served as a blended drink, with ice cream replacing the cream.

SPECS

GREEN CRÈME DE MENTHE
30ML (1 OZ)

WHITE CRÈME DE CACAO
30ML (1 OZ)

HEAVY DOUBLE CREAM
30ML (1 OZ)

METHOD

1. Shake and strain into a cocktail glass.
2. No garnish.

HAMMER OF GOD

TO

HURRICANE

CO-SPECS

H

THE

HAMMER OF GOD

NON-CLASSIC / AUTHOR'S OWN

I DON'T SEE THE DIFFERENCE BETWEEN THE TWO QUESTIONS...?

A fortified beer cocktail invented in 2012 which pairs Innis & Gunn Original beer (aged in whisky barrels, with vanilla and toffee notes) with blended scotch; balanced with lemon and cinnamon syrup.

The late great Christopher Hitchens was once asked two questions: what was his favourite thing to travel with, and also his favourite whisky, to which he replied: *"I don't see the difference between the two questions?..."* Elaborating on his answer he quipped: *"Johnnie Walker Black, the breakfast of champions, accept no substitute."* Indeed, as in life, so for the Hammer – only *'Mr. Walker's amber restorative will do'*.

One ill-advised patron had fifteen of these in an evening and woke up the next day looking like he'd been chasing parked cars.

The ***Hammer of God*** should be served in a handled beer glass, such as a trigger mug. It's designed to be consumed swiftly, while it's cold and frothy.

SPECS

JOHNNIE WALKER BLACK
50ML (2 OZ)

LEMON JUICE
20ML (2/3 OZ)

MONIN CINNAMON SYRUP
15ML (1/2 OZ)

INNIS & GUNN ORIGINAL BARREL AGED SCOTCH ALE
TO TOP

METHOD

1. Pour Innis & Gunn about halfway in a chilled beer glass with a handle.

2. Shake the whisky, lemon and cinnamon syrup and pour straight into a mug (don't fine strain) to create a frothy head.

THE

HANKY PANKY

THE SIGNATURE COCKTAIL OF LEGENDARY SAVOY BARTENDER ADA COLEMAN.

HANKY PANKY COCKTAIL.

2 Dashes Fernet Branca.
½ Italian Vermouth.
½ Dry Gin.
Shake well and strain into cocktail glass. Squeeze orange peel on top.

The Savoy Cocktail Book, *Harry Craddock, 1930*

The excellently named ***Hanky Panky*** *was created by legendary Ada Coleman – head bartender of The American Bar at The Savoy Hotel, London.*

The American Bar opened in 1898, the same year as the newly rebuilt Claridges. Coleman's late father had been a steward at one of Rupert D'Oyly Carte's golf clubs, and he gave the 24-year-old Ada *'Coley'* a job at the bar in Claridges, one of his hotels, in 1899.

When Rupert later became the Chairman of The Savoy (in 1903), she was given a position at the hotel's American Bar, where she would become head bartender and stay until she retired in December 1924.

Ada Coleman, master of the no-look pour.

H

HANKY PANKY

SPECS

GIN
45ML (1 ½ OZ)

SWEET VERMOUTH
45ML (1 ½ OZ)

FERNET-BRANCA
5ML (1 TSP)

METHOD

1. Stir and strain into a cocktail glass.

2. Garnish with an orange twist.

During her tenure, she made drinks for some of the most famous people of her time.

Luminaries such as Mark Twain, The Prince of Wales, Prince Wilhelm of Sweden, and the person for whom the *Hanky Panky* was invented, Charles Hawtrey – leading comedy actor of his generation, and mentor to Noel Coward (not to be confused with the Charles Hawtrey of the Carry On movies).

Continued on next page...

"The late Charles Hawtrey... was one of the best judges of cocktails that I knew. Some years ago, when he was overworking, he used to come into the bar and say, 'Coley, I am tired. Give me something with a bit of punch in it.'

It was for him that I spent hours experimenting until I had invented a new cocktail. The next time he came in, I told him I had a new drink for him.

He sipped it, and, draining the glass, he said, 'By Jove! That is the real hanky-panky!' and ***Hanky-Panky*** *it has been called ever since."*

Coleman describing the story behind the creation of the drink to *The People* newspaper in 1925.

THE

HARVARD

HOW DO YOU LIKE THEM APPLES?

> **Harvard Cocktail.**
>
> **One dash gum-syrup, three dashes Angostura bitters, half-jigger Italian vermouth, half-jigger brandy in half a mixing-glass of fine ice. Mix, strain into cocktail-glass, fill up with seltzer.**

Modern American Drinks, *George J. Kappeler, 1895*

The *Harvard* first appears in George J. Kappeler's *Modern American Drinks (1895)*, and unsurprisingly it's named after the Ivy League university in Cambridge, Massachusetts; indeed, the drink is crimson, the official colour of the college.

Kappeler designed it to be a small drink, using an equal parts ratio – half a jigger each of cognac and sweet vermouth. By contrast, it's usually made 2:1 nowadays.

The *Harvard* is often thought of as a ***Cognac Manhattan.***

SPECS

COGNAC
50ML (2 OZ)

SWEET VERMOUTH
25ML (1 OZ)

ANGOSTURA BITTERS
3 DASHES

SODA
A SPLASH

METHOD

1. Stir and strain into a cocktail glass.
2. Top with a splash of soda.
3. No garnish.

T H E

HEMINGWAY DAIQUIRI

15 PAPA DOBLES IN ONE SESSION BETWEEN 10:30AM AND 7PM.

DAIQUIRI NUM. 3
(Maidique Style)

2 Ounces Bacardí Rum.
1 Spoonful Sugar.
1 Teaspoonful Grape Fruit Juice.
1 Teaspoonful Marraschino.
Juice of half a lemon.
Shake well and strain into cocktail glass. Serve frappe.

DAIQUIRI NUM. 4
(Florida Style)

2 Ounces Bacardí Rum.
1 Teaspoonful Sugar.
1 Teaspoonful Marraschino.
Juice of half a lemon.
Shake in an electric shaker with crushed ice.
Serve frappe.

Bar La Florida, *Constante Ribalaigua Vert, 1934*

Constantino Ribalaigua Vert, the famous head bartender of La Floridita, numbered his Daiquiris 1 to 4, depending on the ingredients and the type of ice he used. Jeff Berry wrote a fantastic piece about Ernest Hemingway in his book *Potions of the Caribbean (2013)*, and according to him, Hemingway asked for the Daiquiri #4 without the sugar, and with double the rum.

He also asked the same for the Daiquiri #3, but with twice the lime and thrice the grapefruit. This version became known as the *Papa Doble* or the *E. Hemingway Special.* La Floridita became a destination bar, and the fame for the *Papa Doble* spread, with Hemingway fans coming in droves to see him and drink the cocktail.

Trivia: Hemingway had a hereditary disease called haemochromatosis, which can lead to diabetes, so he preferred to eschew sugar. He is known to have once consumed 15 Papa Dobles in one session between 10:30am to 7pm.

HEMINGWAY DAIQUIRI

"E. HENMIWAY" SPECIAL

2 Onzas Bacardí.	2 Ounces Bacardí.
1 Cucharadita Jugo de Toronja.	1 Teaspoonful Grape Fruit Juice.
1 Cucharadita Marrasquino.	1 Teaspoonful Marraschino.
Jugo ½ limón verde.	The juice of ½ lemon.
Hielo frappe.	Frappe ice.
Batido y sírvase frappe.	Shake well and serve frappe.

Bar La Florida, *Constante Ribalaigua Vert, 1939*

SPECS

ORIGINAL

WHITE RUM
120ML (4 OZ)

JUICE OF 1/2 LIME
15ML (½ OZ)

MARASCHINO
5ML (1 TSP)

SPECS

PAPA DOBLE

WHITE RUM
120ML (4 OZ)

JUICE OF 1 LIME
30ML (1 OZ)

GRAPEFRUIT JUICE
15ML (½ OZ)

MARASCHINO
5ML (1 TSP)

Journalist, A.E. Hotchner, wrote a biography of Hemingway titled ***Papa Hemingway*** after he visited the bar in 1948 to meet him. He said the real specs of the ***Papa Doble***, what Constante actually used to make the drink for Hemingway and customers, was (different to the version he printed in the 1939 reprint of Bar La Florida): *"two and a half jiggers (approx 150ml/5oz) of Bacardi White Label Rum, the juice of two limes, half a grapefruit, and six drops of maraschino."* Blended and served.

SPECS

HEMINGWAY MODERN

WHITE RUM
60ML (2 OZ)

GRAPEFRUIT JUICE
30ML (1 OZ)

JUICE OF 1/2 LIME
15ML (½ OZ)

MARASCHINO
5ML (1 TSP)

SUGAR SYRUP (2:1)
5ML (1 TSP)

METHOD

1. Shake and strain into a cocktail glass.

2. Garnish with a lime wedge.

HORSE'S NECK

H

THE HORSE'S NECK

THANK YOU FOR THE DINNER AND A VERY PLEASANT EVENING.

Horse's Neck.

Cut the peel from a lemon in one long piece, place in a thin punch-glass, add a bottle of cold imported ginger ale.

HORSE'S NECK.
(Use a large size fizz glass.)

Peel a lemon in one long string, place in glass, so that one end hangs over the head of glass;
2 or 3 dashes of bitters (Boker's genuine only);
1 wine glass whiskey, rye, Scotch, or Irish, as requested;
3 or 4 lumps of broken ice;
Fill up with syphon vichy, or ginger ale, if required.

Modern American Drinks, *George J. Kappeler, 1895*
Bartender's Manual, *Harry Johnson, 1900*

SPECS

BOURBON
50ML (2 OZ)

GINGER ALE
TO TOP

ANGOSTURA BITTERS
2 DASHES (OPTIONAL)

METHOD

1. Build over cubed ice in a highball.
2. Garnish with a long spiral of lemon peel with one end hanging off the glass.

NOTES

Can also be made with cognac or rye.

The *Horse's Neck* has been around since the late 1890s, beginning its life as a non-alcoholic drink: a simple ginger ale over ice with a long twist of lemon, as seen in George J. Kappeler's *Modern American Drinks (1895).*

By the early 1900s people had begun adding whiskey to it, and a little later, brandy (this is sometimes known as a *Horse's Collar*). Any version of the drink made with alcohol could be referred to as a *Horse's Neck With A Kick.* The addition of bitters is optional – it's the garnish that is the trademark of this drink, with one long spiral of lemon peel placed in the drink, and half of it hanging off the edge of the glass, i.e. the *'Horse's Neck'.*

THE

HOT BUTTERED RUM

...ONE HELLUVA DRUG.

Although butter has been added to hot drinks since the time of Henry VIII, the *Hot Buttered Rum* most likely originated in New England, USA around the 18th century. New England was then a big-time producer and consumer of rum, and the *Hot Toddy* (another classic hot drink) was already popular in the region. There are numerous recipes for *Hot Buttered Rum;* the one listed above is technically a spiced version.

A perfect drink for those cold winter days and evenings, *Hot Buttered Rum* is one helluva drug.

METHOD

1. Make the batter by heating in a saucepan until the ingredients are melted.

2. It can then be used straight away or put in a tub in the fridge or freezer.

3. For each drink, in a pre-heated mug, add two tablespoons of batter, then the rum, and top up with boiling water. Stir the mixture before serving.

4. Garnish with a cinnamon stick and grated nutmeg.

SPECS

BATTER (ROUGHLY 20 PORTIONS)

UNSALTED BUTTER
250 G

BROWN SUGAR
350 G

GOLDEN SYRUP
3 TSP

GROUND CINNAMON
3 TSP

GRATED NUTMEG
1½ TSP

VANILLA PASTE
2 TSP

TO ADD AFTER

DARK RUM
50 ML (1 ½ OZ)

HOT WATER
TO TOP

THE

HOT TODDY

A COMMONLY USED (AND VALID) EXCUSE TO DRINK ALCOHOL WHEN YOU'RE SICK.

132. Apple Toddy.

(Use small bar glass.)

1 table-spoonful of fine white sugar.
1 wine-glass of cider brandy.
½ of a baked apple.
Fill the glass two-thirds full of boiling water, and grate a little nutmeg on top.

133. Brandy Toddy.

(Use small bar glass.)

1 teaspoonful of sugar.
½ wine-glass of water.
1 do. brandy.
1 small lump of ice.
Stir with a spoon.
For hot brandy toddy omit the ice, and use boiling water.

134. Whiskey Toddy.

(Use small bar glass.)

1 teaspoonful of sugar.
½ wine-glass of water.
1 do. whiskey.
1 small lump of ice.
Stir with a spoon.

3*

135. Gin Toddy.

(Use small bar glass.)

1 teaspoonful of sugar.
½ wine-glass of water.
1 do. gin.
1 small lump of ice.
Stir with a spoon.

The Bon Vivant's Guide or How to Mix Drinks, *Jerry Thomas, 1862*

H

HOT TODDY

It's important to note right off the bat that the recipe given here is not a traditional *Toddy,* but the modern iteration you're likely to find in the wild. The original would have been sugar, hot water and spirit only (also a fine drink). Ingredients-wise the *Toddys* and *Slings* (as featured in Jerry Thomas' *The Bon Vivant's Guide, or How to Mix Drinks (1862)* are essentially the same – just an addition of some nutmeg differentiates the *Sling.* Both could be served hot or cold. The way David Wondrich delineates them is to think of: *"Toddys as hot drinks, that can be made cold. Slings as cold drinks, that can be made hot."*

The etymology of the name possibly comes from the *Toddy* drink from India, which is an alcoholic drink made from fermented palm tree sap.

One of the earliest mentions of the *Toddy* is from the early 1750's: a young painter asks a Scottish doctor what is the best drink for health? – The doctor responds: *"Toddy, man. The Spirit must have something to act on, and therefore acts on the sugar and does nae injury to the Stomach."* ... Oh for the days when one could enjoy their booze 'medicinally'! Originally, a variety of pot still spirits were used in the *Toddy,* from rum, brandy, applejack, Holland gin and whisk(e)y. However, after the grape disease phylloxera destroyed France's vineyards in the late 1870s, scotch whisky soon became the standard choice (and still is today).

SPECS

SCOTCH
30ML (1 OZ)

LEMON JUICE
10ML (2 TSP)

HONEY
15ML (½ OZ)

CLOVES
4

CINNAMON STICK
1

HOT WATER
TO TOP

METHOD

1. In a preheated glass mug, stir honey with a little boiling water to dissolve.

2. Add lemon juice, whisky, a lemon slice speared with cloves and a cinnamon stick.

3. Top with more boiling water, stir and serve.

THE

HOTEL NACIONAL SPECIAL

A COCKTAIL HAILING FROM THE MOST FAMOUS HOTEL IN CUBA.

NATIONAL COCKTAIL

¼ Apricot Brandy.	¼ Apricot Brandy.
¼ Jugo piña.	¼ Pine-apple Juice.
½ Ron Bacardí.	½ Bacardí Rum.
Hielo menudo.	Cracked Ice.
Batido y colado.	Shake well and strain in cocktail glass.
Adórnese con lascas de piña y guindas.	Decorate glass with slices of pine-apple and cherries.

Bar La Florida, *Constante Ribalaigua Vert, 1934*

Occasionally this drink is also known as the *Nacional* or *Nacional Daiquiri* and was invented sometime between 1931 and 1933 by Wil P. Taylor, manager of the Hotel Nacional de Cuba.

According to drinks writer Jeff Berry, during this period two other chaps also worked in the bars at the Nacional, and both are sometimes credited with the creation of this drink. Fred Kaufman (of *Mary Pickford* fame), and Eddie Woelke – though Eddie worked at the Casino Nacional, not the hotel.

H

HOTEL NACIONAL

Although we don't know for sure if one of these two might have an inventor claim, when it appears in print in Charles H. Baker's *Gentleman's Companion (1939)*, it's printed as Taylor's recipe: *"1 jigger Bacardi gold, 1 jigger pineapple juice, Juice of ½ lime, 1 tsp dry apricot brandy, Shaken and served in a cocktail glass."* This drink also appears in the *Bar La Florida Guide* from 1934 but is listed without lime juice.

In its day, the Hotel Nacional de Cuba was one of the most resplendent hotels in the world, host to all the visiting A-listers from abroad. Famous visitors included Winston Churchill, Ernest Hemingway, Errol Flynn, Marlon Brando, John Wayne, Marlene Dietrich, Frank Sinatra and Rocky Marciano.

The hotel is also famed for being the host venue of the infamous 'Havana Conference' held in 1946. The meeting of the heads of the American and Italian crime families, organised by the infamous mobsters Meyer Lansky and Lucky Luciano. It was attended by the crème de la crème of the underworld, including Santo Trafficante Jr, Frank Costello, Vito Genovese, and Gaetano Lucchese, among others. This meeting was recreated in The Godfather Part II.

SPECS

GOLD RUM
45ML (1½ OZ)

PINEAPPLE JUICE
30ML (1 OZ)

LIME JUICE
15ML (½ OZ)

APRICOT BRANDY
15ML (½ OZ)

METHOD

1. Shake and strain into a cocktail glass.
2. Garnish with a lime wedge.

NOTES

Some modern interpretations switch the pineapple juice for pineapple syrup.

T H E

HURRICANE

A COCKTAIL WHOSE GLASS IS MORE FAMOUS THAN THE DRINK ITSELF.

The name comes from the hurricane glass in which it was first served, which in turn is named after the hurricane lamp (the shape of the glass mirrors and the shape of the classic lamp style).

In his book *Beachbum Remixed (2010)*, drinks writer Jeff Berry notes that the ***Hurricane*** was invented at Pat O'Brien's restaurant in New Orleans, around the 1940s. Scotch was in short supply after WWII whereas rum was plentiful, so head bartender Louis Culligan invented the ***Hurricane*** as a way of utilising this rum surplus.

There are numerous recipes for the ***Hurricane***, the three most common are as follows:

- Pat O'Brien's original recipe, listed in *Jeff Berry's Grog Log (1998)*. Berry says:

*"Although Pat O'Brien's is not a Polynesian restaurant, it's **Hurricane** was widely copied by tiki bars from coast to coast. Pat had the last laugh because his place is still here today."*

- Chuck Taggart's variation – featured on his website – has become increasingly popular, with Gary Regan featuring it in *The Joy of Mixology (2003)*. The recipe above tweaks the volumes a bit.

- Dale Degroff also prints a popular version with Galliano and pineapple juice in *The Essential Cocktail (2008)*.

H

HURRICANE

SPECS

DEGROFF

LIGHT RUM
1 OZ

MYER'S DARK RUM
1 OZ

GALLIANO
½ OZ

ORANGE JUICE
2 OZ

PINEAPPLE JUICE
2 OZ

PASSION FRUIT NECTAR OR SYRUP
1 OZ

LIME JUICE
¾ OZ

SIMPLE SYRUP (1:1)
1 OZ

ANGOSTURA BITTERS
DASH

METHOD

1. Shake and strain over ice into a hurricane glass.

2. Garnish with tropical fruit (pineapple, passion fruit, etc.)

SPECS

ORIGINAL

DARK JAMAICAN RUM
120ML (4 OZ)

LEMON JUICE
60ML (2 OZ)

PASSION FRUIT SYRUP
60ML (2 OZ)

METHOD

1. Shake and strain over ice into a hurricane glass.

SPECS

TAGGART

LIGHT RUM
25ML (1 OZ)

DARK RUM
25ML (1 OZ)

LIME JUICE
25ML (1 OZ)

ORANGE JUICE
50ML (2 OZ)

PASSION FRUIT SYRUP
20ML (¾ OZ)

GRENADINE
5ML (1 TSP)

METHOD

1. Shake and strain over ice into a hurricane glass.

2. Garnish with an orange wheel and a cherry.

IMPROVED COCKTAIL

TO

IRISH COFFEE

CO-SPECS

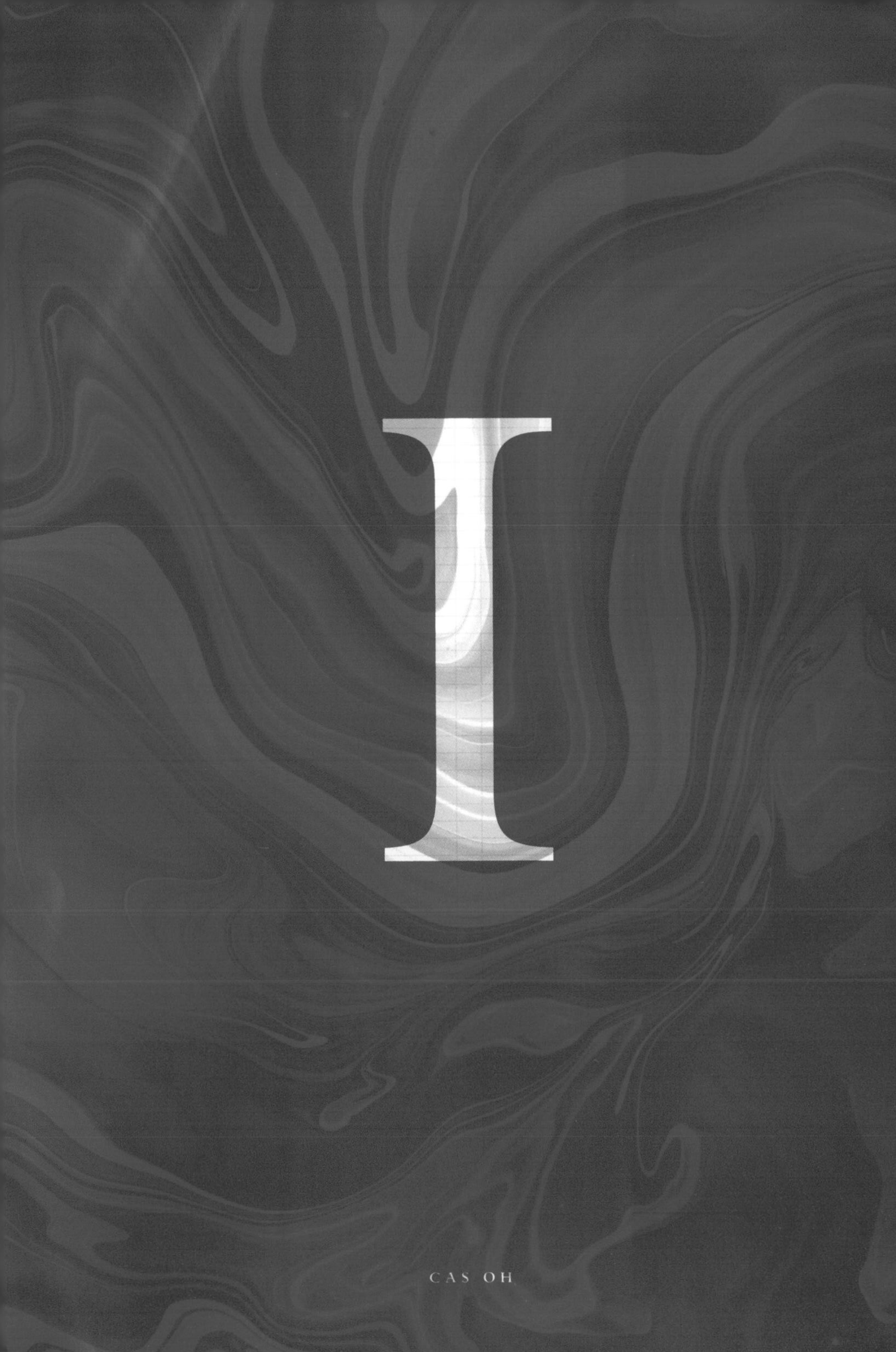
I
CAS OH

THE

IMPROVED COCKTAIL

GIN, WHISKEY & BRANDY

NEW YORK'S ANSWER TO THE SAZERAC.

Gin Cocktail.

(Use small bar-glass.)

Take 3 or 4 dashes of gum syrup.
2 dashes of bitters (Boker's).
1 wine-glass of Holland gin.
1 or 2 dashes of Curaçoa.

Fill the glass one-third full of shaved ice, and strain into a cocktail glass. Twist a small piece of lemon peel, place it in the glass, and serve.

Improved Gin Cocktail.

Made the same way as the Improved Brandy Cocktail substituting Holland or Old Tom gin for the brandy.

Bar-Tender's Guide, *Jerry Thomas, 1887*

*The **Improved** Holland Gin, Whiskey and Brandy Cocktails, which appear in Jerry Thomas' 1887 Bar-Tenders Guide are all variations of the classic Gin, Whiskey and Brandy Cocktails as featured in his original 1862 publication. The term 'Improved' is in reference to the addition of absinthe.*

THE ITERATIONS ARE:

IMPROVED HOLLAND GIN COCKTAIL	IMPROVED WHISKEY COCKTAIL	IMPROVED BRANDY COCKTAIL
Addition of absinthe and curaçao is replaced with maraschino.	Addition of absinthe and maraschino.	Addition of absinthe and curaçao is replaced with maraschino.

David Wondrich says that most of the gin recipes in Jerry Thomas' original book would have been made with genever as that was the predominant style exported to America at the time. He also notes that curaçao in the *Gin Cocktail* was a fanciful Jerry Thomas addition, and was not commonplace or necessary.

When the *Improved Gin Cocktail* is made with Hollands gin, Wondrich calls it *"New York's answer to the Sazerac."* In terms of the *Whiskey Cocktail,* he says the whiskey used would likely have been rye at this time, and that in 1862 there wasn't yet a dedicated cocktail glass so these would have been served in a small wine glass.

By the time the *'Improved'* versions were printed the coupe glass had been introduced. Note the similarity between the original *Whiskey Cocktail* and what we now know as the *Old Fashioned.*

Jerry Thomas' recipe calls for shaking these drinks, but stirring is actually preferable. Recipes in Harry Johnson's *Bartender's Manual (1882)* and O. H. Byron's *Modern Bartenders Guide (1884)* also recommend stirring.

Continued on next page...

THE IMPROVED COCKTAIL

Whiskey Cocktail.

(Use small bar-glass.)

Take 3 or 4 dashes of gum syrup.
2 dashes of bitters (Boker's).
1 wine-glass of whiskey.

Fill one-third full of fine ice ; shake and strain in a fancy red wine-glass. Put in a piece of twisted lemon peel in the glass and serve.

Improved Whiskey Cocktail.

Prepared in the same manner as the Improved Brandy Cocktail, by substituting Bourbon or rye whiskey for the brandy.

Bar-Tender's Guide, *Jerry Thomas, 1887*

GIN COCKTAIL

GENEVER
60ML (2 OZ)

PIERRE FERRAND ORANGE CURAÇAO
2.5ML (½ TSP)

SUGAR SYRUP (2:1)
2.5ML (½ TSP)

BOKER'S BITTERS (OR ANGOSTURA)
2 DASHES

METHOD

1. Stir and strain into a cocktail glass.

2. Garnish with lemon twist.

IMPROVED HOLLAND GIN COCKTAIL

GENEVER
60ML (2 OZ)

MARASCHINO
2.5ML (½ TSP)

SUGAR SYRUP (2:1)
2.5ML (½ TSP)

ABSINTHE
1 DASH

BOKER'S BITTERS OR ANGOSTURA
2 DASHES

METHOD

1. Stir and strain into a cocktail glass.

2. Garnish with a lemon twist.

WHISKEY COCKTAIL

RYE WHISKEY
60ML (2 OZ)

SUGAR SYRUP (2:1)
5ML (2 OZ)

BOKER'S BITTERS OR ANGOSTURA
2 DASHES

METHOD

1. Stir and strain into a cocktail glass.

2. Garnish with a lemon twist.

THE IMPROVED COCKTAIL

Improved Brandy Cocktail.

(Use ordinary bar-glass.)

Take 2 dashes Boker's (or Angostura) Bitters.
3 dashes gum syrup.
2 dashes Maraschino.
1 dash Absinthe.
1 small piece of the yellow rind of a lemon, twisted to express the oil.
1 small wine-glass of brandy.

Fill glass one-third full of shaved ice, shake well, and strain into a fancy cocktail glass, put the lemon peel in the glass and serve.

The flavor is improved by moistening the edge of the cocktail glass with a piece of lemon.

Bar-Tender's Guide, *Jerry Thomas, 1887*

IMPROVED WHISKEY COCKTAIL

RYE WHISKEY
60ML (2 OZ)

MARASCHINO
2.5ML (½ TSP)

SUGAR SYRUP (2:1)
2.5ML (½ TSP)

ABSINTHE
1 DASH

BOKER'S BITTERS OR ANGOSTURA
2 DASHES

METHOD

1. Stir and strain into a cocktail glass.

2. Garnish with a lemon twist.

BRANDY COCKTAIL

COGNAC
60ML (2 OZ)

SUGAR SYRUP (2:1)
2.5ML (½ TSP)

PIERRE FERRAND ORANGE CURAÇAO
2.5ML (½ TSP)

BOKER'S BITTERS OR ANGOSTURA
2 DASHES

LEMON PEEL

METHOD

1. Add ingredients into a mixing glass, zest lemon peel over the top.

2. Stir and strain into a cocktail glass.

IMPROVED BRANDY COCKTAIL

COGNAC
60ML (2 OZ)

MARASCHINO
2.5ML (½ TSP)

SUGAR SYRUP (2:1)
2.5ML (½ TSP)

ABSINTHE
1 DASH

BOKER'S BITTERS OR ANGOSTURA
2 DASHES

METHOD

1. Stir and strain into a cocktail glass.

2. Garnish with a lemon twist.

111. Gin Cocktail.

(Use small bar glass.)

3 or 4 dashes of gum syrup.
2 do. bitters (Bogart's).
1 wine-glass of gin.
1 or 2 dashes of Curaçoa.
1 small piece lemon peel; fill one-third full of fine ice shake well, and strain in a glass.

109. Whiskey Cocktail.

(Use small bar glass.)

3 or 4 dashes of gum syrup.
2 do. bitters (Bogart's).
1 wine-glass of whiskey, and a piece of lemon peel.
Fill one-third full of fine ice; shake and strain in a fancy red wine-glass.

107. Brandy Cocktail.

(Use small bar glass.)

3 or 4 dashes of gum syrup.
2 do. bitters (Bogart's).
1 wine-glass of brandy.
1 or 2 dashes of Curaçoa.
Squeeze lemon peel; fill one-third full of ice, and stir with a spoon.

The Bon Vivant's Guide or How to Mix Drinks,
Jerry Thomas, 1862

"Everything that needs to be said has already been said. But since no one was listening, everything must be said again."

– André Gide

THE

IRISH COFFEE

HEAD OVER TO THE DEAD RABBIT TO GET YOUR FIX.

The story goes that the ***Irish Coffee*** was invented in the 1940s at the Shannon Airport in County Clare, Ireland – the work of a local Head Chef by the name of Joe Sheridan.

A Pan Am flight bound for New York was cancelled due to a storm, and to warm the cold and tired passengers Sheridan added Irish whiskey, brown sugar and a float of whipped cream to hot coffee, and served it to them. One of the passengers remarked "Is this Brazilian coffee?" to which Joe replied, "No, that's ***Irish Coffee.***"

Stanton Delaplane, a travel writer for the *San Francisco Chronicle*, tried the drink at Shannon Airport and promptly brought it over to the States, where he worked with Jack Koeppler (owner of the Buena Vista cafe in San Francisco) to recreate it. They had some initial troubles getting the cream to float, and enlisted the help of the Mayor at the time, local dairy-owner George Christopher. He suggested they use cream aged for at least 48 hours, and his tip worked a treat.

I
IRISH COFFEE

The Buena Vista began serving *Irish Coffee* on 10th November 1952 and to date they have served more than 30 million of them, averaging 1,800 a day. Consequently, Buena Vista is the biggest consumer of Irish whiskey in America.

The Buena Vista recipe is two cubes of C&H brand white cane sugar, Peerless coffee and Tullamore Dew Irish whiskey (they used to use their own private brand made by the Cooley distillery, but switched some years ago).

Other than the Buena Vista (which is the original), without a doubt the best *Irish Coffee* served today can be found at The Dead Rabbit in New York.

SPECS

IRISH WHISKEY (SINGLE POT STILL)
45ML (1½ OZ)

DEMERARA SUGAR
2 TSP

FILTER COFFEE

FULL FAT CREAM

METHOD

1. Heat a 6 oz Irish coffee glass with boiling water.
2. Discard the water, then add the sugar and coffee, stir to dissolve.
3. Add whiskey, and float the cream (shake without ice to whip).

"Because I'd like to be the sort of person who can enjoy things at the time instead of having to go back in my head and enjoy them then."

– *David Foster Wallace*

JACK ROSE

TO

JUNGLE BIRD

CO-SPECS

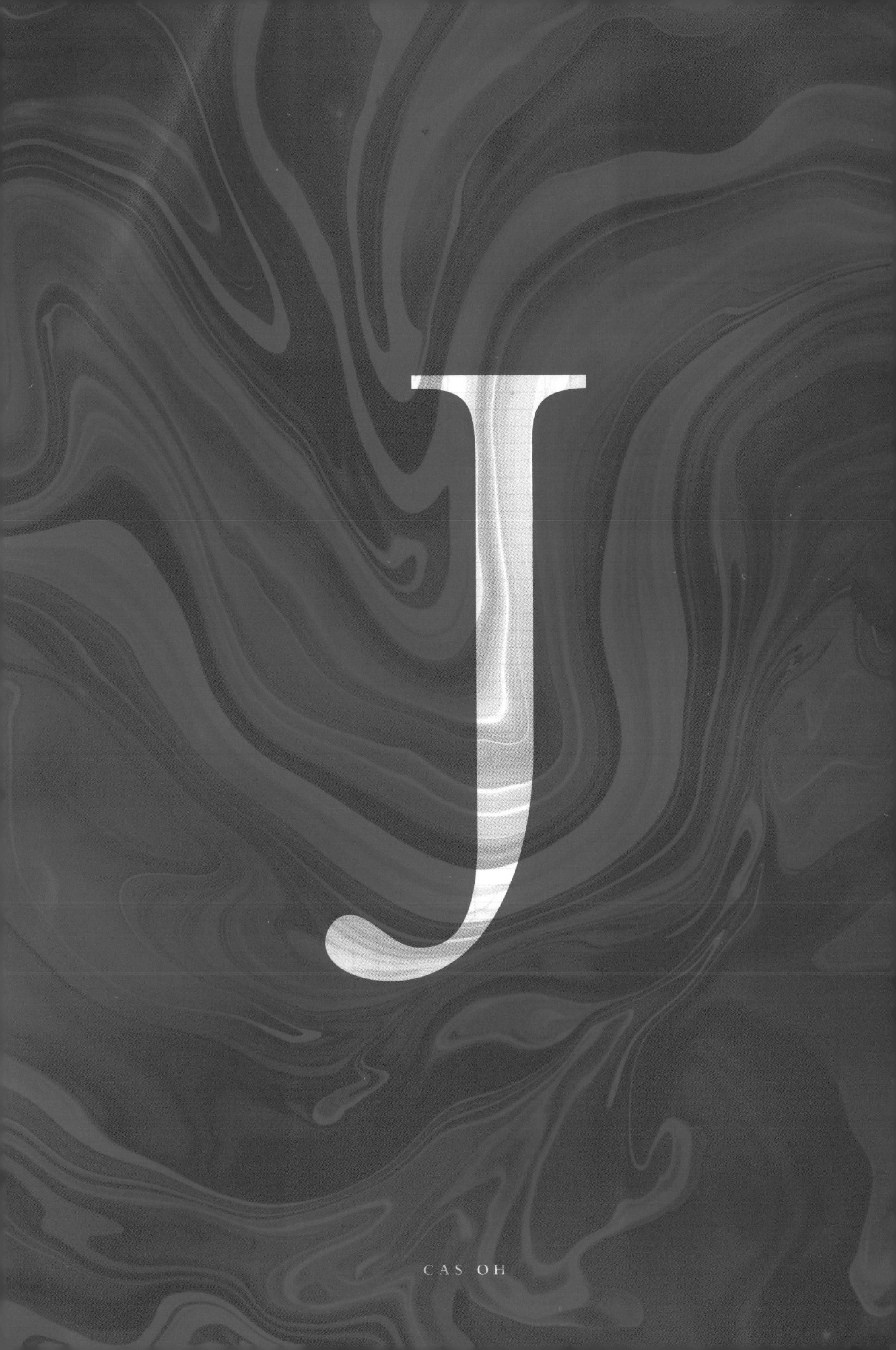
J
CAS OH

THE

JACK ROSE

ONE OF DAVID EMBURY'S 'SIX BASIC COCKTAILS'.

JACK ROSE COCKTAIL
1 Jigger Apple Jack.
½ Lime.
¼ Jigger Grenadine Syrup.
Shake well.

Straub's Manual of Mixed Drinks, *Jacques Straub, 1913*

There are numerous stories about where the ***Jack Rose*** was invented, and how it got its name. The most likely version we know from the very first printed ***Jack Rose*** reference, in 1905; the 22nd April edition of the *National Police Gazette* read:

"Frank J. May, better known as Jack Rose, is the inventor of a very popular cocktail by that name, which has made him famous as a mixologist. He is at present looking after the managerial affairs of Gene Sullivan's Cafe, at 187 Pavonia Avenue, Jersey City, N. J., one of the most popular resorts in that city."

This makes sense – Applejack is the state spirit of New Jersey, and Laird's has been made there since 1780.

Albert S. Crockett, in his 1935 *Old Waldorf-Astoria Bar Book*, claims it's named after the Jacqueminot rose (a flower with a blush pink hue), which in turn takes its name from French general, Jean-François Jacqueminot who served under Napoleon. Others say the 'Jack' comes from base spirit Applejack, and 'Rose' from the drink's colour, which is highly plausible.

J JACK ROSE

JACK ROSE
1 teaspoonful sugar
10 dashes Raspberry syrup
10 dashes lemon juice
5 dashes orange juice
Juice ½ lime
75% cider brandy.

Fill glass with cracked ice, shake and strain, fill with fizz water and serve.

Jack's Manual, *J.A.Grohusko, 1908*

The most famous story goes that it was named for (or possibly even invented by) the infamous New York gambler 'Bald Jack Rose' who turned informant in the notorious 1912 Becker-Rosenthal murder case.

A newspaper article at the end of 1912 says the *Jack Rose* fell out of favour because of the trial, so some bartenders took to calling it a *Royal Smile* instead. This certainly means it was already an established drink by that time.

Venerable drinks author David Embury included the *Jack Rose* as one of his 'Six Basic Cocktails'. As with many of his drinks, his preferred ratio is 8:2:1.

SPECS

LAIRD'S STRAIGHT APPLE BRANDY (BOTTLED IN BOND)
50ML (2 OZ)

LEMON JUICE
25ML (¾ OZ)

GRENADINE
15ML (½ OZ)

METHOD

1. Shake and strain into a cocktail glass.
2. No garnish.

JAPANESE

J

T H E

JAPANESE

CREATED IN HONOUR OF A STATE VISIT TO NEW YORK BY THE FIRST JAPANESE DELEGATION IN 1860.

SPECS

COGNAC
60ML (2 OZ)

ORGEAT
5ML (1 TSP)

BOKER'S BITTERS OR ANGOSTURA
3 DASHES

METHOD

1. Stir and strain into a cocktail glass.
2. Garnish with a lemon twist.

113. Japanese Cocktail.

(Use small bar glass.)

1 table-spoonful of orgeat syrup.
½ teaspoonful of Bogart's bitters.
1 wine-glass of brandy.
1 or 2 pieces of lemon peel.
Fill the tumbler one-third with ice, and stir well with a spoon.

The Bon Vivant's Guide or How to Mix Drinks,
Jerry Thomas, 1862

According to David Wondrich, the *Japanese Cocktail* is one of the only drinks in Jerry Thomas' 1862 book *The Bon Vivant's Guide or How to Mix Drinks* that we know for certain was invented by Thomas himself. It was created in honour of a state visit to New York by the first Japanese delegation, in June 1860. They stayed at the Metropole hotel, just a block from Thomas' bar, and would likely have visited his popular venue.

Note: Bogart's is simply a misspelling of Boker's bitters. Founded in 1828 by John G. Boker, it was a highly popular bitters during the 'golden age' of mixed drinks – the mid to late 19th century. However, sadly it was defunct by Prohibition. The original formula has been recreated and is now available for sale once again.

THE JOURNALIST

NOTHING.

JOURNALIST COCKTAIL.

2 Dashes Lemon Juice.
2 Dashes Curaçao.
1 Dash Angostura Bitters.
$\frac{1}{6}$ French Vermouth.
$\frac{1}{6}$ Italian Vermouth.
$\frac{2}{3}$ Gordon's Dry Gin.
Shake well and strain into cocktail glass.

The Savoy Cocktail Book, *Harry Craddock, 1930*

*The **Journalist** first appears in Harry Craddock's The Savoy Cocktail Book (1930).*

More is known about Jimmy Hoffa's burial whereabouts than about this cocktail.

SPECS

GIN
60ML (2 OZ)

DRY VERMOUTH
15ML (½ OZ)

SWEET VERMOUTH
15ML (½ OZ)

PIERRE FERRAND ORANGE CURAÇAO
2.5ML (½ TSP)

LEMON JUICE
2.5ML (½ TSP)

ANGOSTURA BITTERS
1 DASH

METHOD

1. Shake and strain into a cocktail glass.

2. No garnish.

JUNGLE BIRD

J

THE

JUNGLE BIRD

GREAT COMBINATION OF INGREDIENTS IN THIS TIKI CLASSIC.

SPECS

DARK JAMAICAN RUM
45ML (1½ OZ)

PINEAPPLE JUICE
45ML (1½ OZ)

CAMPARI
20ML (¾ OZ)

LIME JUICE
15ML (½ OZ)

SUGAR SYRUP (2:1)
10ML (2 TSP)

METHOD

1. Shake and strain over cubed ice (block) in a rocks glass.

2. Garnish with a pineapple leaf or dehydrated pineapple slice (optional).

The ***Jungle Bird*** *is a genuinely delicious drink that demonstrates the versatility of Campari. It was brought to our attention in the noughties, after featuring in Jeff 'Beachbum' Berry's Intoxica (2003); Berry says it was invented at the Aviary Bar in Kuala Lumpur, Malaysia in 1978.*

Note: The original garnish called for in the recipe is fairly elaborate: an orchid and a maraschino cherry, speared to lemon and orange wheels.

THE

KIR AND KIR ROYALE

PINK NOT PURPLE.

Simon Difford enlightens us about the genesis of the *Kir* on his website *diffordsguide.com.* The *Kir* dates back to 1904, when a waiter named Faivre mixed creme de cassis with locally produced Bourgogne Aligote wine, at the Café George on Rue de Montchapet, Paris (where Café Le Montchapet now stands). Originally called the *Cassis Blanc* it was popularised and made famous by the Mayor of Dijon, Canon Felix Kir (who was a former French Catholic priest, and who formed part of the French Resistance against the Nazi occupation in World War II). As Mayor, Kir was keen to promote local products, and would serve the drink at functions; his success in doing so led to the recipe eventually being named after him.

Bourgogne Aligoté (primarily made with Aligoté grapes, although 15% Chardonnay is allowed) is a dry, acidic white wine, lesser-known than the grape variety Burgundy is most famous for – Chardonnay. The proportions of cassis to wine vary, with some sources recommending a ratio of 1:3, and others 1:5 (which is very sweet). 1:10, or 1:12 is more suited to a modern palate. It should appear slightly pink, not the colour of grape drink.

SPECS

KIR

CREME DE CASSIS
10ML (¼ OZ)

BOURGOGNE ALIGOTÉ OR WHITE WINE
GLASS OF

METHOD

1. Pour a glass of wine, add creme de cassis and gently stir before serving.

SPECS

KIR ROYALE

CREME DE CASSIS
10ML (¼ OZ)

CHAMPAGNE
GLASS OF

METHOD

1. Pour a glass of champagne, add creme de cassis and gently stir before serving.

"Life is short, eat dessert first."

– Jacques Torres

THE

KNICKERBOCKER À LA MONSIEUR

THE GRANDDADDY OF ALL TIKI DRINKS.

184. Knickerbocker.

(Use small bar glass.)

½ a lime, or lemon, squeeze out the juice, and put rind and juice in the glass.

2 teaspoonfuls of raspberry syrup.

1 wine-glass Santa Cruz rum.

½ teaspoonful of Curaçoa.

Cool with shaved ice; shake up well, and ornament with berries in season. If this is not sweet enough, put in a little more raspberry syrup.

The Bon Vivant's Guide or How to Mix Drinks, *Jerry Thomas, 1862*

First appearing in Boston around the 1850s, and then in print in Jerry Thomas' *The Bon Vivant's Guide or How to Mix Drinks (1862)*, this drink has been referred to as the granddaddy of all Tiki drinks.

The cocktail has a male and female version – 'à la Monsieur' and 'à la Madame' – both of which feature in William Terrington's *Cooling Cups and Dainty Drinks (1869)*.

The term 'Knickerbockers' traces back to the 1600s, when Dutch settlers arrived in the New World (modern-day New York) – it was a reference to the style of knee pants they wore *(pictured right)*, and later was shortened to the more well-known term 'knickers'. This could well be what the cocktail's name is derived from. The recipe calls for Santa Cruz rum or rum from St. Croix in the Virgin Islands. Cruzan would be a contemporary option, though any gold rum would be fine.

K

KNICKERBOCKER À LA MONSIEUR

Knickerbocker à la Monsieur.—To the strained juice of 1 lemon, or orange, add 2 tablespoonfuls of raspberry syrup, 1 wine-glass of Jamaica rum, table-spoonful of Curaçoa; mix in soda-water glass; add balance with shaven ice.

Knickerbocker à la Madame.—½ pint lemon-water ice, ½ pint sherry or Madeira, 1 bottle seltzer water, ¼ pint shaven ice.

Cooling Cups and Dainty Drinks,
William Terrington, 1869

There are several other related cocktails with knickerbocker in the name:

- *Knickerbocker à la Madame:* Sherry or madeira, lemon water and seltzer.

- *Knickerbocker (Martini):* Gin, French vermouth, a dash of Italian vermouth.

- *Knickerbocker Special:* Rum, lemon and orange juice, curaçao, raspberry syrup and muddled pineapple chunk, served straight up.

- *White Lion:* Pretty much identical to a ***Knickerbocker à la Monsieur,*** with the exception that it's sometimes made with lime juice instead of lemon, sometimes has sugar added, and uses grenadine instead of raspberry in some recipes.

SPECS

GOLD RUM
40ML (2 OZ)

LEMON JUICE
20ML (1 OZ)

PIERRE FERRAND ORANGE CURAÇAO
10ML (½ OZ)

RASPBERRY SYRUP
10ML (½ OZ)

METHOD

1. Shake and strain over crushed ice into a rocks glass.
2. Garnish with a raspberry and orange slice (or berries in season).

THE

KNICKERBOCKER SPECIAL

THE OTHER KIND OF KNICKERBOCKER WITH PINEAPPLE AND ORANGE JUICE.

57. KNICKERBOCKER.

(Use a large bar glass.)

2 table-spoonsful of raspberry syrup;
2 dashes of lemon juice;
1 slice of pineapple;
1 slice of orange;
1 wine glass full of St. Croix rum;
One-half glass of Curacao;
then fill the glass with fine shaved ice, stir or shake well, and dress with fruit in season; serve with a straw.

Bartender's Manual, *Harry Johnson, 1882*

This is the less common ***Knickerbocker*** cocktail — unless ***'Special'*** is clearly stated, people are usually referring to the *'á la Monsieur'* version.

K

KNICKERBOCKER SPECIAL

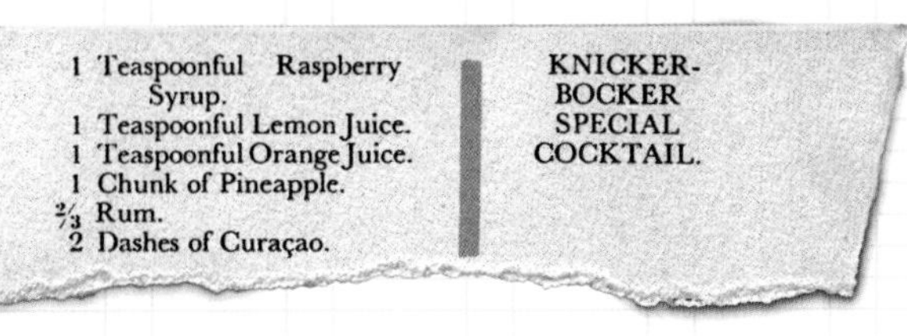

1 Teaspoonful Raspberry Syrup.
1 Teaspoonful Lemon Juice.
1 Teaspoonful Orange Juice.
1 Chunk of Pineapple.
⅔ Rum.
2 Dashes of Curaçao.

KNICKERBOCKER SPECIAL COCKTAIL.

The Savoy Cocktail Book, *Harry Craddock, 1930*

Featured in Harry Johnson's *Bartender's Manual (1882)*, as well as Harry McElhone's *Barflies and Cocktails (1927)*, both appear simply as *Knickerbocker.*

Harry Craddock borrows MacElhone's recipe for *The Savoy Cocktail Book (1930)*, changing the name to *Knickerbocker Special*, which makes it easier to differentiate this version from its sibling.

SPECS

GOLD RUM
45ML (1½ OZ)

PINEAPPLE
1 SMALL CHUNK

LEMON JUICE
5ML (1 TSP)

ORANGE JUICE
5ML (1 TSP)

RASPBERRY SYRUP
5ML (1 TSP)

PIERRE FERRAND ORANGE CURAÇAO
2.5ML (½ TSP)

METHOD

1. Muddle pineapple, add ingredients, then shake and strain into a cocktail glass.

2. Garnish with a dehydrated slice of pineapple (optional).

LAST WORD

TO

LIBERAL

CO-SPECS

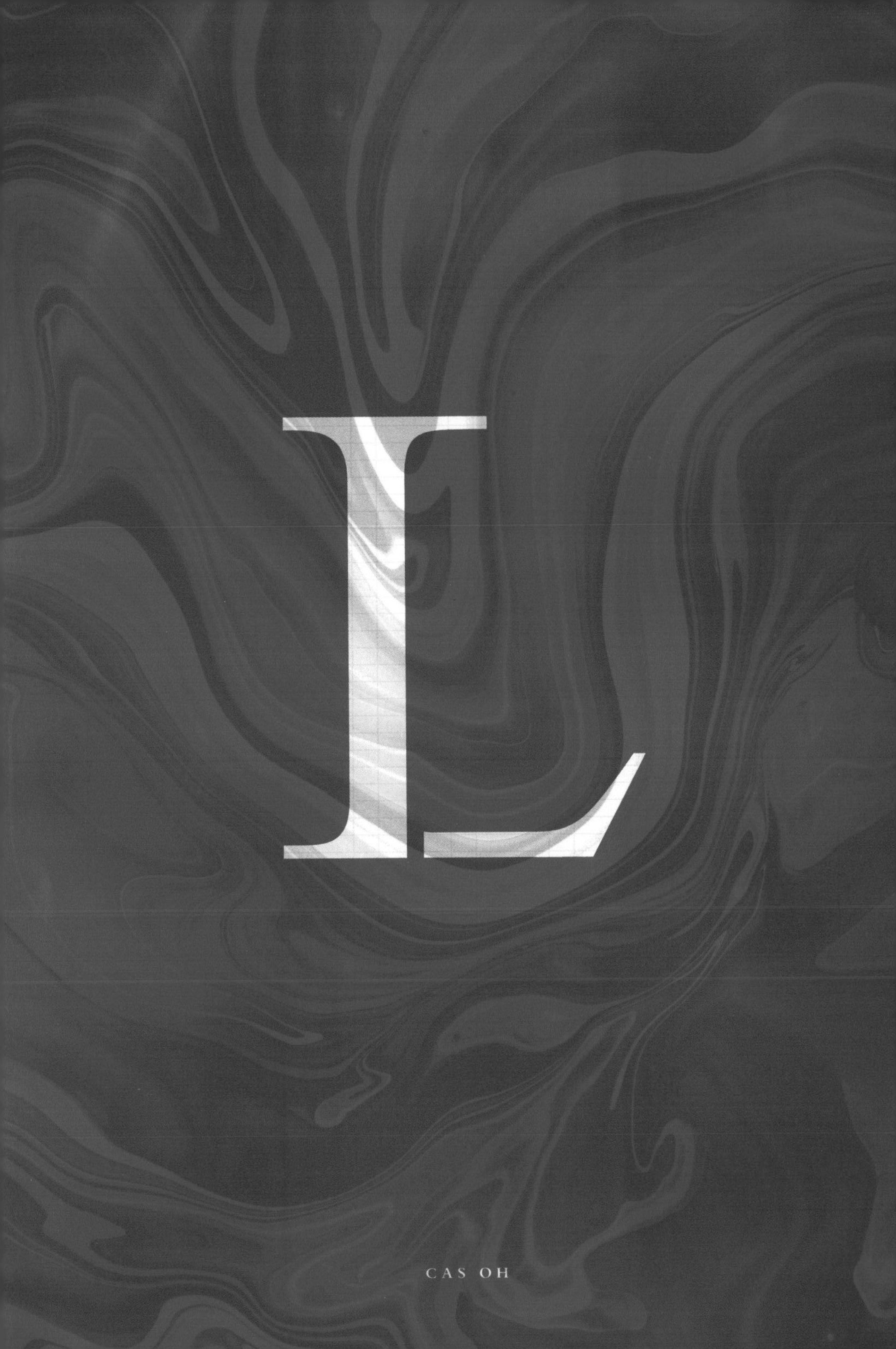
L
CAS OH

LAST WORD

L

THE LAST WORD

PERFECTLY BALANCED EQUAL PARTS RATIO COCKTAIL REVIVED BY MURRAY STENSON

SPECS

GIN
20ML (¾ OZ)

MARASCHINO
20ML (¾ OZ)

GREEN CHARTREUSE
20ML (¾ OZ)

LIME JUICE
20ML (¾ OZ)

METHOD

1. Shake and strain into a cocktail glass.
2. No garnish.

At a glance the *Last Word* seems like a modern-day invention; quite a contemporary combination of ingredients. It was actually created pre-Prohibition, and only plucked out of the turbid depths of obscurity by Murray Stenson of the Zig Zag Cafe in Seattle, when he uncovered it in Ted Saucier's *Bottoms Up (1951)*. After Stenson put the *Last Word* on his bar's menu in 2000 its popularity spread to cocktail bars around the world.

Ted Saucier's 1951 recipe calls for equal parts of the four ingredients. Although he doesn't specify which type of Chartreuse to use, it's usually made with green nowadays. In a notation above the recipe, he credits the drink to the Detroit Athletic Club, saying:

"This cocktail was introduced around here about thirty years ago by Frank Fogarty, who was very well known in vaudeville. He was called the 'Dublin Minstrel,' and was a very fine monologue artist."

A vaudeville monologist is comparable to a stand-up comedian of today.

THE

LEAP YEAR

A TOAST FOR 29TH FEBRUARY.

L

Created by Harry Craddock to celebrate the leap year of 1928, this drink first appears in his 1930 recipe collection *The Savoy Cocktail Book.*

A leap year occurs once every four years, where an extra day is added onto February to keep the calendar year synchronised with the solar-year. It's a long-held folk tradition that on a leap year women can propose to men, especially on 29th February. For the guys out there ostriching an impending walk down the aisle, keep an eye on the leap year indicator on your perpetual calendars, so you know when to book that year-long sabbatical!

LEAP YEAR COCKTAIL.

1 Dash Lemon Juice.
⅔ Gin. ⅙ Grand Marnier.
⅙ Italian Vermouth.
Shake well and serve in cocktail glass. Squeeze lemon peel on top.

This Cocktail was created by Harry Craddock, for the Leap Year celebrations at the Savoy Hotel, London, on February 29th, 1928. It is said to have been responsible for more proposals than any other cocktail that has ever been mixed.

The Savoy Cocktail Book, *Harry Craddock, 1930*

SPECS

GIN
60ML (2 OZ)

GRAND MARNIER
15ML (½ OZ)

SWEET VERMOUTH
15ML (½ OZ)

LEMON JUICE
5ML (1 TSP)

METHOD

1. Shake and strain into a cocktail glass.
2. Garnish with a lemon twist.

THE

LIBERAL

BITTER BUT HAS LOVELY DEEP HERBAL, ORANGE AND CARAMEL NOTES.

Liberal Cocktail.

Fill a mixing-glass half-full fine ice, add one dash syrup, half a jigger Amer Picon bitters, half a jigger whiskey. Mix, strain into cocktail-glass. A small piece of lemon peel on top. Serve.

Modern American Drinks, *George J. Kappeler, 1895*

The *Liberal* is one of the few cocktails that feature Amer Picon, the bitter orange liqueur from France flavoured with gentian and quinquina.

These days it's common to use only tiny amounts of Amer Picon – almost like a bitters – though I don't think it's necessary to shy away from it here.

Picon is indeed bitter but has lovely deep herbal, orange and caramel notes, and the earliest recipes called for liberal use. Amer Picon is difficult to find in the USA, so alternatives or homemade versions are sometimes used.

L

LIBERAL

LIBERAL COCKTAIL
⅓ Jigger Italian Vermouth.
⅔ Jigger Rye Whiskey.
1 Dash Amer Picon.
Stir.

Straub's Manual of Mixed Drinks, *Jacques Straub, 1913*

APPEARANCES IN PRINT

This cocktail has changed significantly over the years since the first printed recipe in George J. Kappeler's *Modern American Drinks (1895),* which was simply equal parts whiskey and Amer Picon.

Italian vermouth had been added by the time it was printed in Thomas Stuart's *Stuart's Fancy Drinks and How to Mix Them (1904);* that recipe calls for ⅓ of each, with three or four dashes of absinthe. It settles close to the modern recipe by the time we see it in Jacque Straub's *Manual of Mixed Drinks (1913),* with a 2:1 ratio and the Amer Picon reduced to a dash. The addition of orange bitters is finally seen in Albert Stevens Crockett's *Old Waldorf Bar Days (1931).*

As with the *Last Word,* it's Murray Stenson from the Zig Zag Cafe in Seattle who can be credited with bringing this drink back to the attention of modern bartenders.

SPECS

RYE WHISKEY
60ML (2 OZ)

SWEET VERMOUTH
30ML (1 OZ)

AMER PICON
15ML (½ OZ)

ORANGE BITTERS
1 DASH

METHOD

1. Stir and strain into a cocktail glass.

2. Garnish with a lemon twist.

MAI TAI

TO

MULATA DAIQUIRI

CO-SPECS

M

CAS OH

THE MAI TAI

"ANYBODY WHO SAYS I DIDN'T CREATE THIS DRINK IS A DIRTY STINKER."

The History of the ***Mai Tai*** is contentious and convoluted. Thankfully two authors – Jeff Berry and Martin Cate – have gone to great lengths to unravel the history of this cocktail for us, in their books *Beachbum Berry Remixed (2009)* and *Smuggler's Cove (2016)*, respectively. Of the two main characters that feature in the ***Mai Tai's*** story, the first is Trader Vic:

TRADER VIC

Victor Bergeron is said to have invented the ***Mai Tai*** in 1944 at his restaurant in Oakland when two Tahitian friends, Eastham and Carrie Guild visited him. He used Wray & Nephew 17-year-old Jamaican rum, mixed it with orange curaçao from Holland, and added some French orgeat, rock candy syrup and lime. When Carrie tried it she's said to have exclaimed "Mai Tai-Roa Aé!" which translates as "out of this world – the best". Naturally, Vic promptly named it the ***Mai Tai***. His original recipe is transcribed as: *2 oz Wray & Nephew 17yr, ½ oz Holland DeKuyper orange curaçao, ½ oz French Garnier orgeat syrup, ¼ oz Trader Vic's rock candy syrup, Juice of 1 fresh lime.*

The drink spread rapidly; it was so popular that by 1950, the world's supply of Wray & Nephew 17 year had run completely dry. Vic saw fit to replace it with the 15 year, but this too was already drying up just a few years later in the early '50s. In response to the shortage, he divided the base spirit (rum) into:

- 1 part: Wray & Nephew 15yr to
- 1 part: a blend of Red Heart & Coruba *(both of which are full-bodied, lightly aged Jamaican rums with lots of colouring added).*

M

MAI TAI

SPECS

SMITH & CROSS JAMAICAN RUM
30ML (1 OZ)

APPLETON 12
30ML (1 OZ)

LIME JUICE
30ML (1 OZ)

ORANGE CURAÇAO (PIERRE FERRAND)
15ML (½ OZ)

ORGEAT
15ML (½ OZ)

METHOD

1. Shake and strain over crushed ice into a double rocks glass.

2. Garnish with a spent half of lime (dome up) and a mint sprig.

By the mid-1950s the Wray & Nephew 15 year was also exhausted, leading to Vic bottling his own private label 8 and 15 year Jamaican rums, under the Trader Vic brand.

He mixed this with Martinique rum to try and replicate the original rum flavour present when he had invented the drink.

Martin Cate makes a compelling case that the Martinique style rum Vic was talking about was not the AOC rhum agricoles we assume from Martinique (made with pressed sugar cane juice), but rather molasses based 'rhum traditionnels'. He points to the disparity between Trader Vic and Donn Beach's description of Martinique rums on their menus, compared to how agricoles are normally described. They use terms like 'heavy bodied', 'burnt flavour of the Demerara', 'coffee coloured' and 'nutty', none of which fit with agricole – known instead for being synonymous with grassy flavours.

Continued on next page...

In fact, there are no agricole rums on Donn's menus and only one (St James) on Vic's; the rest are all molasses based. Although Vic does name St James, Martin Cate makes the point that Vic was a known penny pincher, and it would have been too expensive to use as part of the standard specs.

By the early 1960s, Vic had bottled a *Mai Tai* blend rum, consisting of rums from Puerto Rico, Martinique, Jamaica and Guinea.

By the time the *Mai Tai* makes its first formal appearance in print in 1972 (in Trader Vic's *Bartender's Guide)* it has been tweaked from the original described above, to this modified version:

2 oz Trader Vic Mai Tai rum or 1 oz dark Jamaica rum & 1 oz Martinique rum, 1 lime, ½ oz orange Curaçao, ¼ oz orgeat, ¼ oz rock candy syrup.

Shaken, and served over shaved ice in a double old fashioned glass; garnished with a spent lime shell, and a sprig of mint.

DON THE BEACHCOMBER (DONN BEACH)

The only name better than his adopted pseudonym 'Don the Beachcomber' is his actual name – Ernest Raymond Beaumont-Gantt. Sounds like he lined up four film noir detectives from the 1940s, and assumed all their names at once.

Donn is the man responsible for starting the Tiki movement, and it was a visit to his restaurant in 1937 that inspired Victor (Trader Vic) Bergeron to open a Polynesian restaurant of his own.

In her 2002 book, *Hawaii Tropical Rum Drinks & Cuisine by Don The Beachcomber*, Donn's widow Phoebe Beach puts forth the claim that Donn invented a drink called the *'Mai Tai Swizzle'* in 1933, which if correct would predate Trader Vic's. Shaken with crushed ice and poured unstrained into a double old-fashioned glass, the recipe is listed in the book as: *Mai Tai Swizzle, 1 ½ oz Myer's Plantation rum, 1 oz Cuban rum, ½ oz Cointreau, ¼ oz falernum, 1 oz grapefruit juice, ¾ oz lime juice, 6 drops (1/8 teaspoon) Pernod, Dash Angostura bitters, Garnished with 4 mint sprigs.* Phoebe Beach says it wasn't one of his favourites, which might explain why it doesn't appear on any of his restaurant's menus during these years.

Berry obtained a 1937 recipe book from waiter Dick Santiago, who worked for Donn Beach; there is no ***Mai Tai*** or ***Mai Tai Swizzle*** to be found, meaning Vic couldn't have nicked Donn's recipe when he first visited the restaurant that year. Berry suspects the ***Mai Tai Swizzle*** was probably invented sometime in the 1950s.

Continued on next page…

Another twist to the story is that a man who worked with Donn Beach for over ten years, Edward 'Mick' Brownlee, says that Donn never claimed Vic stole the ***Mai Tai*** from him, but that he based it on another cocktail of his called the ***Q.B. Cooler.***

Berry shows us the recipe for this in *Beachbum Berry Remixed* (2009):

Q.B. Cooler, 1 oz gold Jamaican rum, 1 oz light Puerto Rican rum, ½ oz Demerara rum, ½ oz honey mix (1:1), ½ oz falernum, 1 oz orange juice, ½ oz lime juice, ½ teaspoon ginger syrup, 2 dashes Angostura bitters, 1 oz soda water.

This is blended with crushed ice, poured directly into a double old fashioned glass, and garnished with mint sprigs.

The *Mai Tai Swizzle* has no similarity to Trader Vic's Mai Tai at all, whereas the *Q.B. Cooler* does have a more similar flavour profile.

As an interesting aside: 'Q.B.' stands for Quiet Birdmen, a secretive all-male pilot fraternity formed in 1921 by WW1 aviators.

In *Trader Vic's Bartender's Guide* (1972), after describing how the cocktail was invented, Vic ends by saying:

"Anybody who says I didn't create this drink is a dirty stinker." Shots fired.

So both men may or may not have independently come up with their own ***Mai Tai*** cocktail, but we do know that it was Vic that first came up with the ***Mai Tai*** as we presently know it, and did so in 1944; his is by far the superior version.

Notes: Rock candy syrup is merely a super-concentrated sugar syrup. Trader Vic described the spent lime shell and a mint garnish of his Mai Tai as like a small desert island with a palm tree.

THE

MAIDEN'S BLUSH

FALSE ACCUSATION BLUSH, AND TYRANNY.

57—MAIDEN'S BLUSH.

Fill a tumbler with chipped ice; put in half a teaspoonful of powdered sugar, a teaspoonful of raspberry syrup; squeeze half a lemon in; add half a teaspoonful of absinthe, half a wine glassful of Old Tom gin; shake well and strain off into a coloured glass, putting a slice of lemon on top.

American and Other Drinks,
Charlie Paul, 1884

The ***Maiden's Blush*** makes its first known print appearance in Charlie Paul's *American and Other Drinks* (1884). It then appeared in Louis Fouquet's Bariana shortly afterwards, in 1896. Both recipes are similar, except that Fouquet one-ups Paul (in true French fashion) by adding 30ml of white absinthe to his recipe.

Many have mistakenly credited this cocktail to Harry Craddock, author of *The Savoy Cocktail Book*, however, as we saw from Charlie Paul, the drink is at least 45 years older than the 1930 print of Craddock's book.

M

MAIDEN'S BLUSH

Craddock lists a No.1 version, with dry gin (instead of Old Tom), the absinthe replaced by curaçao, and the raspberry syrup replaced with grenadine.

His No.2 is a copy of Harry MacElhone's earlier *Maiden's Blush* recipe from *Barflies and Cocktails (1927)*, consisting of ⅔ gin, ⅓ absinthe, and one teaspoon grenadine.

The best modern version – which is actually pretty similar to Charlie Paul and Fouquet's recipes – is from W.J. Tarling's 1937 *Café Royal Cocktail Book:*

½ Dry gin, ¼ Lemon juice, ⅛ Absinthe, tsp powdered sugar, 3 dashes Raspberry syrup, Lemon slice garnish.

SPECS

OLD TOM GIN
45ML (1 ½ OZ)

LEMON JUICE
15ML (½ OZ)

RASPBERRY SYRUP
5ML (1 TSP)

SUGAR SYRUP
5ML (1TSP)

ABSINTHE
2.5ML (½ TSP)

METHOD

1. Shake and strain into a cocktail glass.

2. Garnish with a lemon twist.

THE

MAMIE TAYLOR

WHISKY GINGER.

Not sure if this is Mayme Taylor, or Oscar Wilde after an argument with the hairdresser.

Named after Broadway opera singer Mayme Taylor, it was, for a very short period at the very beginning of the 20th century, one of the most popular cocktails in America.

The reason for the difference in spelling is unclear, but the supposed tale of its invention is as described by Eric Felton of *The Wall Street Journal* (see opposite).

M

MAMIE TAYLOR

"The story goes that in the summer of 1899 Mayme went sailing on Lake Ontario. Returning to shore, the actress and her friends went looking for refreshments. At a hotel, she asked for a Claret Lemonade but was mistakenly served Scotch and ginger ale."

"On tasting it," recounted her flack, "Miss Taylor found it much to her liking, but asked to have the flavour softened with a piece of lemon peel." The addition of citrus was such a success that the barman declared the drink would thereafter be called a *"Mamie Taylor."*

– Eric Felton, *The Wall Street Journal, 2008*

SPECS

BLENDED SCOTCH
50ML (2 OZ)

LIME JUICE
15ML (½ OZ)

GINGER ALE
TO TOP

METHOD

1. Build over ice in a highball glass.

2. Garnish with a lime wedge.

NOTES

The ginger ale back then would have been spicier than most brands today, so use the best brand you can find – it is also sometimes made with ginger beer.

THE

MANHATTAN

ON THE MOUNT RUSHMORE OF WHISKY COCKTAILS.

MANHATTAN COCKTAIL.

(Use large bar glass.)

Two or three dashes of Peruvian Bitters;
One to two dashes of gum syrup;
One-half wine glass of whiskey;
One-half wine glass of Vermouth;
Fill glass three-quarters full of fine shaved ice, mix well with a spoon, strain in fancy cocktail glass and serve.

How to Mix Drinks: Bar Keeper Handbook, *George Winter, 1884*

HISTORY

*The oft-repeated story of the **Manhattan** is that it was invented at a banquet held at the Manhattan Club, in November 1874.*

Hosted by Jennie Jerome, mother to Winston Churchill, the event was held in honour of Samuel Tilden, who had been elected as governor. Enter the doyen of myth-busting, David Wondrich, with his book *Imbibe!*. He deflated this story with the revelation that in November 1874 Jennie Jerome was actually at Blenheim Palace in Oxfordshire, giving birth to baby Winston Leonard Spencer-Churchill.

MANHATTAN

Manhattan Cocktail, No. 1.

(A small wine-glass.)

1 pony French vermouth.
½ pony whisky.
3 or 4 dashes Angostura bitters.
3 dashes gum syrup.

Manhattan Cocktail, No. 2.

2 dashes Curacoa.
2 " Angostura bitters.
½ wine-glass whisky.
½ " Italian vermouth.
Fine ice ; stir well and strain into a cocktail glass.

The Modern Bartender, *O. H. Byron, 1884*

SPECS

RYE WHISKEY
6oML (2 OZ)

SWEET VERMOUTH
3oML (1 OZ)

ANGOSTURA BITTERS
2 DASHES

METHOD

1. Stir and strain into a cocktail glass.
2. Garnish with a cherry.

Although the timeline for the story above clearly isn't true, the evidence does suggest it was invented at the Manhattan Club sometime in the late 1870s to early 1880s. Several newspaper articles from the late 19th to early 20th-century point the finger in that direction, including the club's official history (an account from 1915) which states: "The celebrated *Manhattan* cocktail was inaugurated at the club."

Another interesting theory comes from William F. Mulhall, a bartender at the Hoffman House from 1882 to 1915. When he was interviewed in 1922 he said: "The *Manhattan* cocktail was invented by a man named Black, who kept a place ten doors below Houston Street on Broadway in the sixties".

Continued on next page...

When Wondrich investigated this claim, he did find a George Black in the city directory who operated a bar at 493 Broadway below Houston, from 1874 to 1881 which, interestingly, was called The Manhattan Inn.

The popularity of the *Manhattan* was widespread from the mid-1880s and has never stopped.

APPEARANCE IN PRINT

The first time the Manhattan appears in print is in the September 1882 newspaper *Olean Democrat*, New York: *"It is but a short time ago that a mixture of whiskey, vermouth and bitters came into vogue... It went under various names - Manhattan cocktail, Turf Club cocktail, and Jockey Club cocktail. Bartenders at first were solely puzzled what was wanted when it was demanded. But now they are fully cognizant of its various aliases and no difficulty is encountered."*

Manhattan Cocktail.

(Use small bar-glass.)

Take 2 dashes of Curaçoa or Maraschino.
1 pony of rye whiskey.
1 wine-glass of vermouth.
3 dashes of Boker's bitters.
2 small lumps of ice.

Shake up well, and strain into a claret glass. Put a quarter of a slice of lemon in the glass and serve. If the customer prefers it very sweet use also two dashes of gum syrup.

61. MANHATTAN COCKTAIL.

(Use a large bar glass.)

Fill the glass up with ice;
2 or 3 dashes of Gum Syrup;
1 or 2 dashes of Bitters; (Boker's genuine only);
1 dash of Curaçoa (or absinthe if required);
1/2 wine glass of Whiskey·
1/2 wine glass of Vermouth;
stir up well, strain into a fancy cocktail glass, squeeze a piece of lemon peel on the top, and serve; leave it for the customer to decide whether to use Absinthe or not. This drink is very popular at the present day.

Bar-Tender's Guide, *Jerry Johnson, 1887*
Bartender's Manual, *Harry Johnson, 1888*

It makes its first cocktail book appearance in two books in 1884: George Winter's *How to Mix Drinks: Bar Keeper's Handbook*, as well as O.H. Byron's *The Modern Bartender.* Both of the recipes call for equal parts whiskey to vermouth, which is also how it was served at the Manhattan club. Winter adds dashes of gum syrup and calls for Peruvian bitters, but that's very probably because they were a sponsor. Byron lists two recipes – a No.1 which uses dry vermouth and a bit of gum syrup, and a No.2 with Italian vermouth with dashes of orange curaçao. When it appears in Jerry Thomas' 1887 *Bar-Tender's Guide*, the mysterious editor of that edition switches the ratios to make it one part whiskey to two parts vermouth, as well as adding curaçao and maraschino.

23. Manhattan Cocktail.

Half a tumblerful of cracked ice,
2 dashes of gum,
2 dashes of bitters,
1 dash of absinthe,
⅔ drink of whiskey,
⅓ drink of vino vermouth.
(A little maraschino may be added.)
Sttir this well, strain, and serve.

The Flowing Bowl, *A. William Schmidt, 1892*

He specifies Boker's bitters and garnishes it with a quarter slice of lemon. In the 1888 edition of his *Bartender's Manual*, Harry Johnson sticks to the equal parts whiskey to vermouth ratio, adding curaçao "or absinthe if required", Boker's bitters and gum syrup. He notes that "This drink is very popular at the present day."

The first time we see the modern standard ratio of two parts whiskey to one part vermouth is in William "The only William" Schmidt's *The Flowing Bowl,* in 1891. This is the ratio that most *Manhattans* are made with today. Schmidt also adds gum syrup, a dash of absinthe, and notes that a little maraschino may be added. The recipe from the Manhattan Club itself, recorded in 1916 in Henry Watterson's *History of the Manhattan Club: A Narrative of the Activities of Half a Century,* is: *"equal portions of vermouth and whiskey, with a dash of orange bitters."*

My preference is for rye whiskey (as opposed to bourbon) in my *Manhattans,* especially the higher proof ryes. For me, there is only one type of *Manhattan,* and that's one made with sweet vermouth. Dry *Manhattan?* No Dry *Manhattan* for you!

"It pays to keep an open mind, but not so your brains fall out."

– *Carl Sagan*

21

THE

MARGARITA

'MARGARITA, MORE THAN A GIRL'S NAME...' ALSO THE REASON MANY CHILDREN ARE CONCEIVED.

No other classic cocktail has as many claimants putting their hand up shouting 'I'm Spartacus!' than the ***Margarita.***

EARLY APPEARANCES IN PRINT

The first time we see a printed recipe for the *Margarita* (in composition at least) is rather surprisingly in England – W.J. Tarling's *Café Royal Cocktail Book (1937)* included a drink called the ***Picador,*** with the unmistakably familiar ingredients: *¼ fresh Lime or Lemon Juice, ¼ Cointreau, ½ Tequila.*

David Wondrich cites a recipe from a 1939 book titled *Cotton Club Cocktail Book,* by Charlie Connolly. Called the ***Tequila,*** it's also the same as a ***Picador,*** but with a salt rim – certainly a ***Margarita*** in all but name.

The first known print mention under the modern name – ***Margarita*** – is in the December issue of Esquire Magazine in 1953, where it was the featured cocktail of the month.

The article says *"She's from Mexico, Señores, and her name is the* ***Margarita Cocktail*** *– and she is lovely to look at, exciting and provocative."* It goes on to list the recipe as: *1 oz of tequila, a dash of triple sec and the juice of half a lemon or lime.*

M

MARGARITA

SOME OF THE COMMON STORIES BANDIED AROUND:

• *Danny Negrete:* said to have created it while working as a manager at the Garci Crespo Hotel in Puebla, Mexico in 1936, for his sister-in-law... Margarita, as a wedding present. In 1944 he began working at the famous Agua Caliente Racetrack, leading some to speculate it may have been named after Rita Hayworth who performed at the track as a teenager, her real name being Margarita Cansino.

• *Carlos 'Danny' Herrera:* the owner of the Rancho La Gloria restaurant/bar in Rosarito, Mexico. In 1938, or 1947/48 depending on the source, he claims he invented it for an actress who used to come in called Marjorie King; she said she was allergic to all spirits except tequila. Carlos was obviously not allergic to bullshit.

• *Francisco 'Pancho' Morales:* 4th July 1942, at Tommy's Place in Ciudad Juarez, Mexico... Someone asked for a Magnolia cocktail – he didn't know how to make it, and made this instead.

Note: Magnolia is a brandy, curaçao, egg yolk, sugar and champagne drink found in the late 19th century to early 20th-century cocktail books.

Continued on next page...

SPECS

TEQUILA
50ML (2 OZ)

COINTREAU
25ML (1 OZ)

LIME JUICE
25ML (1 OZ)

METHOD

1. Shake and strain into a cocktail glass which has been half rimmed with salt.

2. If your glasses are kept in a freezer, use the condensation to line the glass with salt, otherwise wet it with a lime wedge. Wipe out any salt inside the glass.

238. Whiskey Daisy.

Prepared in the same manner as Brandy Daisy, substituting whiskey for the brandy.

239. Gin Daisy.

Made in the same way as Brandy Daisy, but using gin instead of brandy.

240. Rum Daisy.

Mixed with the same ingredients as Brandy Daisy, but using rum instead of brandy.

Bar-Tender's Guide, *Jerry Thomas, 1876*

• *Santos Cruz:* invented in the 40s at a studio in Galveston, Texas for legendary jazz singer Peggy Lee (Fever; Why Don't You Do Right). He says he simply made a Sidecar, but with tequila. Peggy's real name was Margaret, so her guitarist husband Dave Barbour named it *'Margarita'* after her.

• *Margaret 'Margarita' Sames:* American socialite from Texas; she claims she invented it at a Christmas party in her holiday home in Acapulco in 1948. Apparently Tommy Hilton was at the party, and soon put the drink on the menu at all of his Hilton Hotels.

• *John Durlesser:* head bartender at the Tail o' the Cock restaurant in Los Angeles, Durlesser says he invented it in 1936 when tequila first started becoming available in LA. In the mid-1950s, Vern Underwood was the Cuervo tequila distributor for America, and at some point, he noticed that the Tail o' the Cock was using more tequila than all of his accounts combined. When he investigated, he found that it was due to the *Margarita.* Underwood soon put full page Cuervo magazine adverts out across the country, with the tagline: *'Margarita, more than a girl's name...'.*

237. Brandy Daisy.

(Use small bar glass.)

3 or 4 dashes gum syrup.
2 or 3 do. orange cordial.
The juice of half a lemon.
1 small wineglass of brandy.
Fill glass half full of shaved ice.
Shake well and strain into a glass, and fill up with Seltzer water from a syphon.

Bar-Tender's Guide, *Jerry Thomas, 1876*

THE DAISY THEORY

Another theory is that the *Margarita* was just the old-school late 19th century *Daisy,* with a spirit-switch for tequila. Prohibition led to an exodus of Americans looking for a legal drink, jumping ship to major cities in Europe, Cuba, and across the border to Mexico.

By the 1920s, the *Daisy* was already a well-known drink, so it is possible that it was just a logical iteration of an already popular staple, remade with the local spirit. Giving this theory another leg up is the fact that the Spanish word for *Daisy* is in fact, *Margarita.*

An Irishman named Henry Madden, who worked at the Turf Bar in Tijuana, claims precisely that. He claims that during the 1920s someone came in and asked for a *Gin Daisy,* and he mistakenly grabbed the wrong bottle.

Thankfully the customer loved it, ordered another, and soon the good word spread. Simon Difford points out that the first mention of a *Tequila Daisy* was in the Moville Mail on 23rd July 1936, in a piece titled 'Graham's Sightseeing'; in it Henry Madden is interviewed, and relays the story above.

Continued on next page...

POPULARITY STATESIDE

By the 1960s the *Margarita* was everywhere, and people had already started blending it. But the moment it went nuclear was in 1971... Dallas restaurateur Mariano Martinez took a soft serve ice cream machine, and modified it to serve slushy versions of the *Margarita*. People went nuts for his boozy slushies, and versions of this machine spread nationwide, notching the *Margarita's* recognition level up from 3 to 11.

WHODUNNIT?

In honesty, there's more chance of building a house of cards in the dark than determining which of the invention stories we should believe. Could it be one of the many claimants mentioned above? Or was it just a simple twist on a *Sidecar* or *Daisy?* Perhaps it was just the *Picador* given a new name? Pass.

A GOOD POINT

Naren Young makes a good point in his article in *Imbibe* magazine saying that although it could have been invented in Mexico, he finds it difficult to believe a Mexican created this drink as there has never been a cocktail culture in Mexico – in fact, the locals don't drink *Margaritas* to this day.

Note: The original Margarita Machine can be found in the Smithsonian's National Museum of American History.

"Very interesting experiments happen and it's not always a good thing, but learning from doing it – all the beautiful mistakes – and accidentally coming up with something I love is the real fun."

– *DJ QBert*

THE MARGUERITE

THE LESSER-KNOWN RELATION TO THE DRY MARTINI.

Marguerite Cocktail.

HALF a mixing-glass full of fine ice, three dashes of orange bitters, one-half jigger of Plymouth gin, one-half jigger of French vermouth. Mix, strain into cocktail-glass. Place an olive in the bottom of glass and serve.

Bitters
Plymouth Gin
French Vermouth

Cocktails... How to Make Them, *Livermore & Knight Co., 1898*

The ***Marguerite*** *cocktail is considered the forerunner to the* ***Dry Martini.***

Originally made with equal parts Plymouth gin and dry vermouth (with dashes of orange bitters), over time the *Marguerite* became drier and more gin-heavy as tastes changed.

Although it is the precursor to the *Dry Martini* there wasn't a direct switch from one to the other – instead, it was a gradual transition. In fact, they often appeared alongside each other in the cocktail books from the beginning of the 20th century; their differentiating point being that the *Marguerite* always called for Plymouth gin, whereas the *Dry Martini* used London Dry.

M

MARGUERITE

MARGUERITE COCKTAIL.

(Use a large bar glass.)

Fill glass ¾ full of fine-shaved ice;
2 or 3 dashes of orange bitters;
2 or 3 dashes of anisette;
½ wine glass of French vermouth;
½ wine glass of Plymouth gin;
Stir up well with a spoon, strain into a cocktail glass, putting in a cherry, squeeze a piece of lemon peel on top and serve.

Bartender's Manual, *Harry Johnson, 1900*

SPECS

PLYMOUTH GIN
45ML (1 ½ OZ)

DRY VERMOUTH
45ML (1 ½ OZ)

ORANGE BITTERS
2 DASHES

METHOD

1. Stir and strain into a cocktail glass.
2. No garnish.

The *Marguerite's* first appearance in print is in *Cocktails... How to Make Them*, published by Livermore & Knight co. in 1898: *"Half a mixing-glass full of fine ice, three dashes of orange bitters, one-half jigger of Plymouth gin, one-half jigger of French vermouth. Mix, strain into cocktail-glass. Place an olive in the bottom of glass and serve."*

It then appears two years later in Harry Johnson's *Bartender's Manual* (1900), still with equal parts Plymouth and dry vermouth, though Johnson adds in anisette to the recipe, which wasn't typical.

Continued on next page...

MARGUERITE COCKTAIL

Take two dashes of orange bitters,
One dash of Maraschino,
One liqueur-glass of French Vermouth, and
Two liqueur-glasses of Plymouth gin.

Fill the mixing-glass with ice; stir well and strain into a cocktail-glass.

Louis' Mixed Drinks, *Louis Muckensturm, 1906*

We see the change in preference to a more gin-heavy recipe in Thomas Stuart's *Stuart's Fancy Drinks and How to Mix Them (1904): ⅔ Plymouth gin, ⅓ French vermouth, 1 dash of orange bitters.*

As the popularity of the *Dry Martini* increased, that of the *Marguerite* waned. In time the *Marguerite* was relegated to the hinterland of forgotten cocktails, watching the continued ascent of the *Dry Martini* from the sidelines.

THE
MARMALADE COCKTAIL

M

MARMALADE COCKTAIL

USE A HIGH-QUALITY MARMALADE WITHOUT CHUNKS FOR THE BEST RESULTS.

MARMALADE COCKTAIL.
(6 people)

By its bitter-sweet taste this cocktail is especially suited to be a luncheon aperitif. Place the following mixture in the shaker:
2 Dessertspoonsful Orange Marmalade.
The Juice of 1 big or 2 small Lemons.
4 Glasses Gin.
Shake carefully and pour out, squeezing a piece of orange rind into each glass.

The Savoy Cocktail Book, *Harry Craddock, 1930*

Until relatively recently this was thought to have been the invention of Harry Craddock around the 1920s, and first appearing in print in *The Savoy Cocktail Book* (1930). However, thanks to Martin Doudoroff we now know that it first appears in *Drinks - Long & Short* by Nina Tote & A.H. Adair some five years earlier, in 1925. They note that it's *"Sweet and slightly bitter, this cocktail is distinctly a luncheon apéritif."* The recipe given is: *"Two tablespoons of marmalade (Cooper's Oxford Marmalade), the juice of one large juicy lemon or two small ones, and four glasses of gin are the ingredients of this cocktail. Shake well, and pinch a piece of fresh orange peel over each glass."*

SPECS

GIN
60ML (2 OZ)

LEMON JUICE
15ML (½ OZ)

ORANGE MARMALADE
2 TBSP

METHOD

1. Add marmalade and gin to a shaker; press the marmalade with a spoon and stir to dissolve.

2. Add lemon juice, shake and strain into cocktail glass.

3. Garnish with an orange twist.

THE

MARTINEZ

A CLOSE RELATION OF THE MANHATTAN AND MARTINI.

Manhattan Cocktail, No. 1.

(A small wine-glass.)

1 pony French vermouth.
½ pony whisky.
3 or 4 dashes Angostura bitters.
3 dashes gum syrup.

Martinez Cocktail.

Same as Manhattan, only you substitute gin for whisky.

The Modern Bartender, *O. H. Byron, 1884*

The first appearance of the *Martinez* is in O.H. Byron's *The Modern Bartender (1884)*, where it's included as a simple note stating *"Same as Manhattan, only you substitute gin for whisky."* Somewhat confusingly then, he lists two *Manhattans:* one using sweet vermouth and the other dry, and both with different ratios of spirit to vermouth.

The other noteworthy early appearance is in Jerry Thomas' *Bar-Tender's Guide (1887)*, which was published two years after his death. Thomas' name is often thrown into the ring as the possible inventor of the *Martinez* cocktail – the story being that he created it while working in San Francisco during the early 1860s, for a visitor bound for the East Bay town of Martinez, CA. It doesn't appear in his 1862 book however, and as such this story is now widely thought to be untrue.

Thomas' recipe is also somewhat nebulous, citing 'vermouth' without specifying which kind (sweet or dry). It's quite likely he meant sweet vermouth, as that was far more prevalent in America during that time, and indeed, sweet vermouth in a *Martinez* is considered standard today. Interestingly though, if you look at the ten or so recipes for this cocktail spanning from 1884 to 1946, the majority specify the use of a dry vermouth. The original gin used for the *Martinez* would likely have been genever – the predominant style exported to America in the 19th century. This would seem to fit with it being a *Manhattan* variation, as the Dutch spirit genever has a similar flavour profile to whiskey. By the late 1880s, genever had fallen out of favour, giving way to Old Tom gin, and eventually London Dry.

Note: Personally, I think using Old Tom or genever makes for a far more interesting drink. The recipe I've listed, with double the vermouth to gin, is based on the Jerry Thomas 1887 recipe. It is far more common to find it two parts gin to one part sweet vermouth these days, or even equal parts. They are all good; go with whichever way your preferences sway you.

Martinez Cocktail.

(Use small bar-glass.)

Take 1 dash of Boker's bitters.
2 dashes of Maraschino.
1 pony of Old Tom gin.
1 wine-glass of Vermouth.
2 small lumps of ice.

Shake up thoroughly, and strain into a large cocktail glass. Put a quarter of a slice of lemon in the glass, and serve. If the guest prefers it very sweet add two dashes of gum syrup.

Bar-Tender's Guide, *Jerry Thomas, 1887*

M MARTINEZ

SPECS

SWEET VERMOUTH
60ML (2 OZ)

OLD TOM GIN (OR GENEVER TO REPLICATE ORIGINAL)
30ML (1 OZ)

MARASCHINO
5ML (1 TSP)

BOKER'S BITTERS (OR ANGOSTURA)
1 DASH

METHOD

1. Stir and strain into a cocktail glass.

2. Garnish with a lemon twist.

"It's much better down there."
– Enzo Mollinari

THE MARTINI

"HE KNOWS JUST HOW I LIKE MY MARTINI – FULL OF ALCOHOL".

DRY MARTINI COCKTAIL.

A LA CHARLIE SHAW, LOS ANGELES, CAL.

Into a mixing-glass place some cracked ice, two dashes of Orange bitters, half a jigger of French vermouth and half a jigger of dry English gin (any good brand); stir well until thoroughly chilled, strain into a stem cocktail-glass, squeeze a piece of lemon peel over the top and serve with an olive.

Martini Cocktail—No. 1.

HALF a mixing-glass full fine ice, three dashes orange bitters, one-half jigger Tom gin, one-half jigger Italian vermouth, a piece lemon peel. Mix, strain into cocktail-glass.

Bitters
Gin
Italian Vermouth
Lemon peel

Martini Cocktail—No. 2.

Bitters
Tom Gin
Italian Vermouth
Sherry
Lemon peel

FILL mixing-glass half-full fine ice. Add two dashes Boker's bitters, one-half jigger Tom gin, one-half jigger Italian vermouth, half a teaspoonful sherry, piece of lemon peel. Mix, and strain into cocktail-glass.

Top: The World's Drinks and How to Mix Them, *William Boothby, 1908*
Middle & Bottom: Cocktails... How to Make Them, *Livermore & Knight Co., 1898*

The popular theory is that the *Martini* developed from the *Martinez,* and indeed that may be the case, though the evolution is not so linear as to be clear cut.

The same time as the *Martinez* made its first print appearance, another cocktail called the *Turf Club* also made its print debut, sharing similarities with the *Martinez* whilst also possessing the essential DNA of a *Martini*.

M

MARTINI

SPECS

GIN
60ML (2 OZ)

DRY VERMOUTH
15ML (½ OZ)

METHOD

1. Stir and strain into a cocktail glass.
2. Garnish with a lemon twist or olive.

NOTE

For an extensive chronological breakdown, Simon Difford does a great job of tracking the timeline of the Martini on his website.

A few years later, the *Marguerite* – a precursor to the *Dry Martini* – also shows up, illustrating the plethora of different drinks with similar ingredients that played a part in the evolution of the *Martini* as we know it. Let's start by looking at the *Martini* and the *Dry Martini,* and how they progressed over the years.

MARTINI

It's important to note that the original *Martini* was always a sweet vermouth drink. More specifically, it was always made with Old Tom gin and an equal amount of vermouth, then generally garnished with a lemon peel. Outside of those three staples, different recipes added dashes of a variety of new ingredients, including things like curaçao, maraschino, gum syrup, and orange/Angostura/Boker's bitters. The *Dry Martini* – most prevalent today – was simply a dry vermouth variant of the sweet vermouth based *Martini;* the word 'dry' was an indication of the type of vermouth in this case, not the amount used.

Continued on next page…

EARLY COCKTAIL BOOK APPEARANCES FOR THE MARTINI

The first recipe printed as *Martini Cocktail* was in the 1888 edition of *Harry Johnson's Bartenders Manual.* It was comprised of equal parts Old Tom gin and vermouth, with typical Harry Johnson additions of curaçao, Boker's bitters and gum syrup – this was stirred and garnished with a lemon peel. He also lists a *Bradford a la Martini,* which is actually more *Martini*-like than his *Martini,* being equal parts Old Tom and vermouth, with orange bitters and lemon peel, shaken and garnished with an olive.

George J. Kappeler's *Modern American Drinks (1895)* gives a concise, definitive version of the old-school *Martini:* equal parts Old Tom and sweet vermouth, three dashes of orange bitters and lemon peel garnish.

A year later Louis Fouquet includes a *Martini* in his French cocktail manual *Bariana (1896),* adding a Gallic twist. It roughly translates as equal parts gin and sweet vermouth, with four dashes of orange bitters, two dashes of absinthe, three dashes of curaçao, three dashes of creme de noyaux (a French liqueur made with dried apricot kernels) and brandy. This was garnished with a lemon peel.

Tim Daly, in *Daly's Bartenders' Encyclopedia* lists two recipes, *Martini Cocktail,* and a *Bottle of Martini Cocktail.* The *Martini Cocktail* is the same specs as Kappeler's, but interestingly it's garnished with an olive.

The 'bottle' version uses dry vermouth, showing an early move to a 2:1 ratio of gin to vermouth. This 2:1 ratio is also used by Louis Muckensturm in Louis' *Mixed Drinks* (1906).

Robert Vermeire's recipe from *Cocktails and How to Mix Them* (1922) again shows the 2:1 ratio, this time specifying Martini Rosso as the vermouth, as well as orange bitters and a lemon twist.

When Harry Craddock included it in *The Savoy Cocktail Book* (1930), it has lost the bitters and is simply London dry gin and sweet vermouth, in a 2:1 ratio.

BOTTLE OF MARTINI COCKTAIL.

Use bar shaker for mixing.

1 pony glass of orange bitters.
½ pony glass of maraschino.
Half fill the shaker with fine ice.
1-3 bottle of French vermuth.
2-3 bottle of Tom gin.
Mix well with spoon, strain into a full quart bottle, cork and label.
Always use a dark-colored bottle when mixing cocktails for a party.
This is supposed to be a very dry cocktail.
Ice should always be used in making bottled cocktails.

MARTINI COCKTAIL.

Use a mixing glass.

Half fill with fine ice.
2 dashes of orange bitters.
½ wine glass of Tom gin.
½ wine glass of vermuth.
Spoon well and strain into a cocktail glass; put in an olive, and serve.

Daly's Bartender Encyclopaedia, *Tim Daly, 1903*

DRY MARTINI

The *Dry Martini* emerged in the late 1890s, as taste preferences were starting to shift toward drier cocktails. An interview with a bar owner in *The New York Herald* from 1897 shows the shifting tide:

"When a customer comes in and orders a sweet drink,...I know at once that he's from the country. In all my acquaintance with city men, I know not more than half a dozen who can stand sweet things...People are beginning to realize that their stomachs are not of cast iron. They want everything dry, the drier the better."

EARLY COCKTAIL BOOK APPEARANCES FOR THE DRY MARTINI

The *Dry Martini* soon followed the *Martini,* offering a dry vermouth variant to the standard version made with sweet vermouth. The first appearance of this iteration is in a French cocktail book called *American Bar (1904)* written by Frank P. Newman, a bartender at the Ritz in Paris. The recipe translates from French as equal parts gin and dry vermouth, three dashes of Angostura or orange bitters, garnished with lemon zest, cherry or olive.

In the same year *Applegreen's Bar Book,* by John Applegreen, lists a *Martini Cocktail* made with equal parts Old Tom gin and Italian vermouth, with two dashes of orange bitters and a dash of syrup. Under it his *Martini Cocktail,* Dry is listed as: *"[the] Same as above except to omit the syrup."*

The first listing of a *Dry Martini,* named as such and printed in an English language book, is in Louis Muckensturm's *Louis' Mixed Drinks* (1906). His recipe is two parts dry gin to one part French vermouth, with two dashes of orange bitters, and a dash of curaçao, garnished with a lemon peel.

William Boothby opts for equal parts Plymouth gin to dry vermouth, with a dash of orange bitters in *The World's Drinks and How to Mix Them (1908).*

By 1916, the two parts dry gin to one part vermouth pattern had become the norm, as seen in *Recipes for Mixed Drinks* by Hugo R. Ensslin. Harry Craddock's *Dry Martini* in *The Savoy Cocktail Book (1930)* also uses the 2:1 ratio, but importantly the bitters is now gone; this is also true of the recipe in Lucius Beebe's *The Stork Club Bar Book (1946).*

Continuing the trend for the *Martini* to grow ever drier, Ted Saucier's *Bottom's Up! (1951),* lists a *Martini* (extra dry) that's four parts dry gin to one part dry vermouth. Around the 50s and 60s, the *Martini* reached the zenith of dryness, with vermouth being used in ever more scant amounts, sometimes administered by an atomiser, sometimes not at all. In the era of the three-martini lunch, less vermouth was the el primero choice.

OLD SCHOOL MARTINI RECIPE

30ml Old Tom gin
30ml sweet vermouth
two dashes of orange bitters,
lemon twist garnish.

OLD SCHOOL DRY MARTINI RECIPE

30ml dry gin,
30ml dry vermouth,
one dash of orange bitters,
lemon twist garnish.

N° 79

Dry Martini Cocktail

Verre n° 5

Prendre le verre à mélange n° 1, mettre quelques morceaux de glace :

3 traits d'angostura ou orange bitter.

Finir avec gin et vermouth sec, quantités égales, remuer, passer dans le verre n° 5, servir avec un zeste de citron, une cerise ou une olive, au goût du consommateur.

MARTINI COCKTAIL (DRY)

⅔ Dry Gin
⅓ French Vermouth
1 dash Orange Bitters

Stir well in a mixing glass with ice, strain and serve, with olive in glass.

American Bar, *Frank P. Newman, 1904*
Recipes for Mixed Drinks, *Hugo R. Ensslin, 1917 (2nd Edition)*

VODKA MARTINI

Vodka arrived in the United States in the early 1900s and was pretty widespread by the late '30s. By the end of the 1960s vodka had taken over as the spirit of choice in the *Dry Martini,* and as the decades wore on *Gin Martinis* fell by the wayside. This was helped in part by an introduction to a wide public audience in the 1962 James Bond movie Dr No. In the film, Sean Connery takes his *Vodka Martini "Shaken, not stirred".* This would become a catchphrase repeated throughout the Bond franchise, and unfortunately became ingrained into the public's perception of the *Martini* as well. David Embury in *The Fine Art of Mixing Drinks (1948)* refers to the *Vodka Martini* as a *Kangaroo.* It's printed for the first time as a *Vodkatini* in Ted Saucier's *Bottoms Up,* in 1951; *4 parts Smirnoff vodka to 1 part dry vermouth, stirred and garnished with a lemon peel.*

HOW DID THE MARTINI GET ITS NAME?

We don't know for sure, but there are many theories. Suggestions include: a judge called Martine, the Martini-Henry rifle, a riff of the *Martinez,* businessman Frank Martine, or the Martinez restaurant on 14th street. It could be any, or none, of these. One plausible theory is that it takes its name after the famous brand of vermouth Martini & Rossi, which was marketed heavily at the time.

57 MARTINI COCKTAIL.

(Use a large bar glass.)

Fill the glass up with ice;
2 or 3 dashes of Gum Syrup;
2 or 3 dashes of Bitters; (Boker's genuine only.)
1 dash of Curaçoa;
1/2 wine glassful of Old Tom Gin;
1/2 " " " Vermouth;
stir up well with a spoon, strain it into a fancy cocktail glass, squeeze a piece of lemon peel on top, and serve. (See Illustration, Plate No. 13.)

Martini Cocktail.

Half a mixing-glass full fine ice, three dashes orange bitters, one-half jigger Tom gin, one-half jigger Italian vermouth, a piece lemon-peel. Mix, strain into cocktail-glass. Add a maraschino cherry, if desired by customer.

Bartender's Manual, *Harry Johnson, 1888*
Modern American Drinks, *George J. Kappeler, 1895*

NOTES ON TEMPERATURE

Unless you're making it *Naked* as they do in Dukes Bar, don't keep your spirit in the freezer – dilution is a crucial aspect of the *Martini;* frozen spirits won't allow the ice to dilute the drink enough. Temperature is vitally important to this drink. An ice-cold *Martini* is like the first sip of water for a desert strandee – nectar from the Gods; a warm one is a human rights violation and tastes more like Bear Grylls' regular drink of choice.

It should be cold to the last drop, so use smaller cocktail glasses, not something resembling an upturned traffic cone. Everyone has a preferred ratio; Hemingway liked his Montgomery style 15:1, Churchill went sans vermouth, others like Bernard DeVoto, who wrote *The Hour: A Cocktail Manifesto* in 1948, are more esoteric with a 3.7 to 1 preference (no Bernard).

VARIATIONS

Montgomery: A 15:1 ratio ***Martini,*** named after British Field Marshal Bernard Montgomery, who would only attack if he had a 15 to 1 advantage.

Buckeye: A ***Dry Martini*** garnished with a black olive.

Naked Martini: An undiluted ***Martini,*** with the spirit poured straight into the glass from the freezer.

Dirty Martini: With the addition of olive brine.

Roosevelt Martini: A ***Dry Martini*** garnished with two olives. Named for U.S president, Franklin D. Roosevelt.

French Martini: Shake vodka, Chambord and pineapple juice with ice, then strain into the trash.

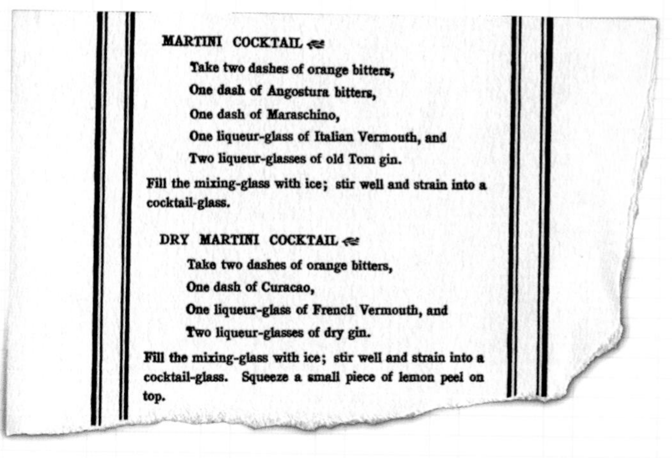

MARTINI COCKTAIL

Take two dashes of orange bitters,
One dash of Angostura bitters,
One dash of Maraschino,
One liqueur-glass of Italian Vermouth, and
Two liqueur-glasses of old Tom gin.

Fill the mixing-glass with ice; stir well and strain into a cocktail-glass.

DRY MARTINI COCKTAIL

Take two dashes of orange bitters,
One dash of Curacao,
One liqueur-glass of French Vermouth, and
Two liqueur-glasses of dry gin.

Fill the mixing-glass with ice; stir well and strain into a cocktail-glass. Squeeze a small piece of lemon peel on top.

Louis' Mixed Drinks, *Louis Muckensturm, 1906*

NOTES ON EXECUTION

Always stir a ***Martini,*** it should be limpid, liquid silk – not aerated and light from shaking. Don't pour vermouth over ice and discard before stirring; the surface area of the ice is different every time, so you have no control over the final proportions. Instead add the vermouth as you would any other ingredient, measured.

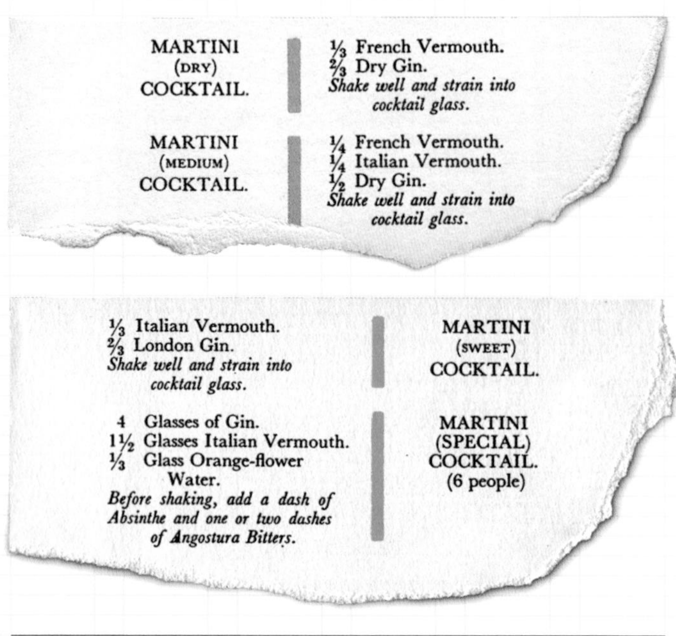

MARTINI (DRY) COCKTAIL.

1/3 French Vermouth.
2/3 Dry Gin.
Shake well and strain into cocktail glass.

MARTINI (MEDIUM) COCKTAIL.

1/4 French Vermouth.
1/4 Italian Vermouth.
1/2 Dry Gin.
Shake well and strain into cocktail glass.

MARTINI (SWEET) COCKTAIL.

1/3 Italian Vermouth.
2/3 London Gin.
Shake well and strain into cocktail glass.

MARTINI (SPECIAL) COCKTAIL. (6 people)

4 Glasses of Gin.
1 1/2 Glasses Italian Vermouth.
1/3 Glass Orange-flower Water.
Before shaking, add a dash of Absinthe and one or two dashes of Angostura Bitters.

The Savoy Cocktail Book, *Harry Craddock, 1930*

What David Embury calls *"the most perfect of aperitif cocktails"* is truly that. A few of these before dinner, and you'll be hungry enough to eat the feet off a low flying duck.

FAMOUS MARTINI QUOTES

"I never go jogging, it makes me spill my Martini."
– George Burns

"Martinis are the only American invention as perfect as a sonnet."
– H.L. Mencken

"I should have never switched from scotch to Martinis."
– Humphrey Bogart

"He knows just how I like my martini – full of alcohol."
– Homer Simpson

"The elixir of quietude."
– E.B. White

"Martinis should always be stirred, not shaken, so that the molecules lie sensuously one on top of the other."
– W. Somerset Maugham

THE

MARY PICKFORD

TAKE IT EASY ON THE MARASCHINO AND GRENADINE FOR THIS ONE.

This drink is often miscredited to bartender Eddie Woelke but was actually invented by his colleague Fred Kaufman during the 1920s, at Hotel Sevilla in Cuba. He named it after the silent movie star Mary Pickford, who was known as 'America's Sweetheart'.

Pickford was in Cuba at the time filming a movie with her husband Douglas Fairbanks and Charlie Chaplin.

The earliest recipe can be found in Leon Pujol and Oscar Muniz's *Manual del Cantinero (1924)*. Interestingly it features gin instead of rum, so perhaps that was the original base. A few years later, when it's mentioned in Basil Woon's *When It's Cocktail Time in Cuba (1928)*, rum is specified. This is the standard way a ***Mary Pickford*** is made today.

*"The **Mary Pickford,** invented during a visit to Havana of the screen favourite by Fred Kaufman, is two-thirds pineapple-juice and one-third Bacardi, with a dash of grenadine."*
– When It's Cocktail Time in Cuba, Basil Woon, 1928.

M

MARY PICKFORD

MARI PICKFORD

1 Vasito Gordon Gin.

1 Cucharadita Jugo Piña.

1/2 cucharadita marrasquino.

1/2 cucharadita granadina

Bátase bien frape y sirvase en copa de Clover.

TRANSLATION

1 cup Gordon's Gin

1 teaspoon pineapple juice

½ teaspoon maraschino

½ teaspoon grenadine

Serve in a Clover glass.

Manual del Cantinero,
Leon Pujol & Oscar Muniz, 1924

SPECS

WHITE RUM
60ML (2 OZ)

PINEAPPLE JUICE
30ML (1 OZ)

MARASCHINO
5ML (1 TSP)

GRENADINE
5ML (1 TSP)

METHOD

1. Shake and strain into a cocktail glass.
2. No garnish.

THE

METROPOLITAN & METROPOLE

MCDONALD'S, MCDOWELL'S.

SPECS

METROPOLITAN

COGNAC
45ML (1½ OZ)

DRY VERMOUTH
45ML (1½ OZ)

SUGAR SYRUP (2:1)
5ML (1 TSP)

ANGOSTURA BITTERS
3 DASHES

METHOD

1. Stir and strain into a cocktail glass.
2. Garnish with a lemon twist.

These are two very similar cocktails – in name and ingredients – and both are named after hotels.

METROPOLITAN

The *Metropolitan Cocktail* is similar to a dry brandy *Manhattan*, with a bit of sugar. It first appears in O.H. Byron's *The Modern Bartender (1884)* with two parts dry vermouth to one part brandy, and then a few years later pops up again in George J. Kappeler's *Modern American Drinks (1895)* – here the ratio has changed to equal parts.

Metropolitan Cocktail.

(A small wine-glass.)

½ pony brandy.
1 " French vermouth.
3 dashes Angostura bitters.
3 " gum syrup.

The Modern Bartender, *O. H. Byron, 1884*

M

METROPOLITAN & METROPOLE

How the *Metropolitan* got its name is a bit unclear. There were numerous venues called the Metropolitan at the time, and no accompanying details as to exactly which of these it takes its name from. However, according to David Wondrich, it was most likely Jerry Thomas' bar at the Metropolitan Hotel, New York.

METROPOLE

Above Kappeler's *Metropolitan* recipe, the *Metropole* makes its first appearance. Starting with the same foundation of brandy, dry vermouth and sugar, a few simple switches have been made: the Angostura has been replaced with Peychaud's and orange bitters, and the garnish changed to a cherry instead of lemon.

The *Metropole* we know was the house cocktail of the Hotel Metropole which stood on 42nd and Broadway in NYC. The adjoining Café Metropole had an all-night license, which meant its crowd comprised of some of the shadier denizens of the night. It is famous as the place where Herman Rosenthal, owner of several New York gambling houses, was shot dead in 1912 (as mentioned in the *Jack Rose* story); this was a week before the hotel went bankrupt.

Continued on next page...

SPECS

METROPOLE

COGNAC
50ML (2 OZ)

DRY VERMOUTH
25ML (1 OZ)

SUGAR SYRUP (2:1)
2.5ML (½ TSP)

PEYCHAUD'S BITTERS
2 DASHES

ORANGE BITTERS
1 DASH

METHOD

1. Stir and strain into a cocktail glass.
2. Garnish with a lemon twist.

Metropole Cocktail.

Two dashes gum-syrup, two dashes Peyschaud bitters, one dash orange bitters, half a jigger brandy, half a jigger French vermouth, a mixing-glass half-full fine ice. Mix, strain into cocktail-glass, add a maraschino cherry.

Metropolitan Cocktail.

Two lumps of ice in a small wine-glass, add three dashes gum-syrup, two dashes Angostura bitters, one pony brandy, one pony French vermouth. Mix, take out the ice, add a small piece twisted lemon-peel.

Modern American Drinks, *George J. Kappeler, 1895*

Considering the stark similarity of the two cocktails, it seems likely that when the Hotel Metropole opened, it took the established ***Metropolitan Cocktail*** and made a few minor tweaks to come up with their own 'house cocktail'.

THE

MILK PUNCH – BRANDY

M

MILK PUNCH - BRANDY

A BRUNCH TIME STAPLE IN NEW ORLEANS.

22. Milk Punch.

(Use large bar glass.)

1 table-spoonful of fine white sugar.
2 do. water.
1 wine-glass of Cognac brandy.
½ do. Santa Cruz rum.
⅓ Tumblerful of shaved ice.
Fill with milk, shake the ingredients well together, and grate a little nutmeg on top.

The Bon Vivant's Guide or How to Mix Drinks,
Jerry Thomas, 1862

This single-serve *Milk Punch* is one of several *Milk Punch* recipes listed in Jerry Thomas' *The Bon Vivant's Guide or How to Mix Drinks (1862).* With a split base of cognac and rum, this version is presented as a drink that could be served hot or cold.

BRANDY MILK PUNCH (NEW ORLEANS STYLE)

Cognac 45ml (1 ½ oz), whole milk 60ml (2 oz), cream 60ml (2 oz), sugar syrup (2:1) 15ml (½ oz), vanilla extract (½ tsp).

Shake and strain into a double rocks glass over crushed ice. Garnish with grated nutmeg over the drink.

Another variant that has gained much popularity in New Orleans is the *Brandy Milk Punch* (shown above), which has become a brunch-time staple.

SPECS

COGNAC
60ML (2 OZ)

GOLD RUM
30ML (1 OZ)

SUGAR SYRUP (2:1)
15ML (½ OZ)

WHOLE MILK
60ML (2 OZ)

METHOD

1. Shake and strain into a double rocks glass over crushed ice.
2. Garnish with grated nutmeg over the drink.

THE

MILK PUNCH – ENGLISH

ONE OF THE BEST DRINKS AROUND.

24. English Milk Punch.

Put the following ingredients into a very clean pitcher, viz.:

The juice of six lemons.
The rind of two do.
1 lb. of sugar.
1 pine-apple, peeled, sliced and pounded.
6 cloves.
20 coriander seeds.
1 small stick of cinnamon.
1 pint of brandy.
1 do rum.
*1 gill of arrack.
1 cup of strong green tea.
1 quart of boiling water.

The boiling water to be added last; cork this down to prevent evaporation, and allow these ingredients to steep for at least six hours; then add a quart of hot milk and the juice of two lemons; mix, and filter through a jelly-bag; and when the punch has passed bright, put it away in tight-corked bottles. This punch is intended to be iced for drinking.

The Bon Vivant's Guide or How to Mix Drinks,
Jerry Thomas, 1862

By 1862 – the time Jerry Thomas' *The Bon Vivant's Guide or How to Mix Drinks* was printed – ***Milk Punches*** had already been around for well over a hundred years, the earliest documented version we know of being Mary Rockett's recipe from 1711 *(see recipe).*

As the milk interacts with the acid it curdles, and once the casein-rich curds are strained out, just whey remains in the mixture. The milk essentially acts as a filter, softening the cocktail and adding a unique velvety feel on the palate. Use raw milk if you can find it. Otherwise, unpasteurised whole milk is your best bet.

This is the greatest of all *Milk Punches.* **Admittedly this drink is a bit of a ball-ache to make, but worth the effort. A well made** *English Milk Punch* **is one of the best drinks around.**

Continued on next page...

THE MILK PUNCH-ENGLISH

PHASE 1

ZEST OF LEMONS 6

CASTER SUGAR 300G

LEMON JUICE
JUICE OF 6 LEMONS
270ML (9 OZ)

GRENADINE
5ML (1 TSP)

PINEAPPLE
1 WHOLE SLICED

STAR ANISE 6

CLOVES 20

CORIANDER SEEDS
40 (1 TSP)

CINNAMON STICKS 4

COGNAC
750ML (25 OZ)

SMITH & CROSS RUM
375ML (12½ OZ)

EL DORADO 12YR RUM
375ML (12½ OZ)

BATAVIA ARRACK
300ML (10 OZ)

SENCHA GREEN TEA
250ML (8 OZ)

ANGOSTURA BITTERS
10ML (2 TSP)

BOILING WATER
375ML (12½ OZ)

METHOD 1

1. In a large container, make oleo-saccharum (oil sugar) by muddling the zest of six lemons into caster sugar to extract the oils, making sure any white pith is cut away from the zests. Leave for a few hours until the sugar is dissolved.

2. To this mixture add muddled pineapple, coriander seeds (that have been crushed with a pestle and mortar), cinnamon sticks, star anise, cloves and lemon juice.

3. Add to this the spirits, green tea and boiling water, stir the mixture and seal the container. Leave for 48 hours.

PHASE 2

LEMON JUICE
90ML (3 OZ)

UNPASTEURISED WHOLE MILK
1 LITRE

METHOD 2

1. Pour the mixture from phase one (that's been left for 48 hours) through a large mesh strainer to remove all fruit, spices and other bits.

2. In a separate container add the milk which has been brought to a boil. Add the juice of two lemons to the punch mixture and pour this over the milk. The mixture will immediately curdle. Seal this airtight and leave for 24 hours.

3. Strain the mixture through a muslin cloth to remove the curds and any other remaining bits. This can now be clarified by further straining the mixture through filter coffee paper. Repeat until it is transparently clear. It should have a translucent yellow clarity.

4. Bottle and serve on the rocks. Will keep almost indefinitely. Makes approximately 25 to 30 servings.

CAS OH

THE

MILK PUNCH – MARY ROCKETT'S

THE OLDEST MILK PUNCH RECIPE.

David Wondrich's *Punch* (2010) brings to our attention the oldest known recipe for ***Milk Punch,*** which comes from the recipe book of a housewife named Mary Rockett, and was believed to have been from 1711.

We know about Mary Rockett and her recipe because it features in a 1914 biography of British writer Aphra Behn, penned by Montague Summers (and referenced by Wondrich, as noted above). Behn (1640-1689) was the very first woman to earn her living from writing, and as such, she is considered a pioneer and an inspiration for female authors who came after her.

It is a classic 'bowl' or 'bottle' style ***Milk Punch,*** whereby hot milk is added to a mixture containing citrus, which curdles the milk. The liquid is then strained through a tightly woven cloth to lift out the milk solids, leaving only the whey in the drink. This renders a uniquely silky texture and rounds out the citrus and spirits nicely.

As Wondrich points out the milk in 1711 would have been unpasteurised, so use raw milk if available, or unpasteurised whole milk if not.

M

MILK PUNCH - MARY ROCKETT'S

'Old Mr. John Bowman, the player, told me that Mrs. Behn was the First Person he ever knew or heard of who made the Liquor call'd Milk Punch.'-Oldys: MS. note in Langbaine. In a tattered MS. recipe book, the compilation of a good housewife named Mary Rockett, and dated 1711, the following directions are given how to brew this tipple. 'To make Milk Punch. Infuse the rinds of 8 Lemons in a Gallon of Brandy 48 hours then add 5 Quarts of Water and 2 pounds of Loaf Sugar then Squize the Juices of all the Lemons, to these Ingredients add 2 Quarts of new milk scald hot stirring the whole til it curdles, grate in 2 nutmegs, let the whole infuse 1 hour then refine through a flannel bag.'

A Memoir of Mrs. Behn,
Montague Summers, 1914

MARY'S RECIPE / QUARTERED

PHASE 1

ZEST OF 2 LEMONS

COGNAC
900ML (30 OZ)

METHOD

1. In a large container, add the zest of two lemons to brandy, making sure any white pith is cut away from the zests. Seal and leave at room temperature for 48 hours.

PHASE 2

CASTER SUGAR
225G

LEMON JUICE
90ML (3 OZ)

WATER (MINERAL OR FILTERED)
1 LITRE

HOT MILK
½ LITRE

NUTMEG
½

METHOD

1. Add the sugar, water and juice of two lemons to the brandy and lemon zest mixture. Pour into a container containing hot milk brought to the boil; the mixture will curdle straight away. Grate in the nutmeg and leave for 24 hours.

2. Strain the mixture through a muslin cloth to remove the curds and peels. Strain the mixture again through filter coffee paper until clear; bottle and serve straight up or with ice. Will keep almost indefinitely. Makes approximately 14 servings.

THE

MILLIONAIRE

WHICH ONE DO YOU MEAN?

MILLIONAIRE COCKTAIL I.
⅓ Jamaica Rum
⅓ Apricot Brandy
⅓ Sloe Gin
1 dash Grenadine
Juice of 1 Lime
Shake well in a mixing glass with cracked ice, strain and serve.

MILLIONAIRE COCKTAIL II.
⅔ Dry Gin
⅓ White Absinthe
White of 1 Egg
1 dash Anisette
Shake well in a mixing glass with cracked ice, strain and serve.

Recipes for Mixed Drinks, *Hugo R. Ensslin, 1917 (2nd Edition)*

If ever a cocktail had you asking "which one?" when someone orders it, it would be the *Millionaire.* So many wildly different drinks exist under the *Millionaire* moniker that it can be rather confusing...

The three main recipes are:

• The **Millionaires** *1 and 2,* as printed in the 1917 edition of Hugo R. Ensslin's *Recipes for Mixed Drinks*;

• The *Millionaire* made with rye, curaçao, grenadine and orange bitters, that featured in Jacque Straub's *Drinks (1914).*

The most common version cited today is probably the *Millionaire No.1,* which would also be my preferred version. As well as the three shown, there are versions with gin, Italian vermouth, grenadine, pineapple and egg white (Trader Vic), as well as one with rye, Pernod, grenadine and egg white (Frank Meier).

M

MILLIONAIRE

Millionaire Cocktail
1 dash orange bitters.
6 dashes curaçao.
¾ jigger rye whiskey.
2 dashes grenadine syrup.
1 white of egg.
Stir well. Serve in claret glass.

Drinks, *Jacques Straub, 1914*

SPECS

MILLIONAIRE

RYE WHISKEY
60ML (2 OZ)

ORANGE CURAÇAO (PIERRE FERRAND)
10ML (2 TSP)

GRENADINE
2.5ML (½ TSP)

ORANGE BITTERS
1 DASH

1 EGG WHITE

METHOD

1. Dry shake, then shake with ice and strain into a cocktail glass.

SPECS

MILLIONAIRE NO.1

JAMAICAN RUM (APPLETON 12)
20ML (¾ OZ)

APRICOT BRANDY
20ML (¾ OZ)

SLOE GIN
20ML (¾ OZ)

LIME JUICE
20ML (¾ OZ)

GRENADINE
2.5ML (½ TSP)

METHOD

1. Shake and strain into a cocktail glass.

SPECS

MILLIONAIRE NO.2

GIN
50ML (1 ½ OZ)

WHITE ABSINTHE
25ML (¾ OZ)

ANISETTE
2.5ML (½ TSP)

1 EGG WHITE

METHOD

1. Dry shake, then shake with ice and strain into a cocktail glass.

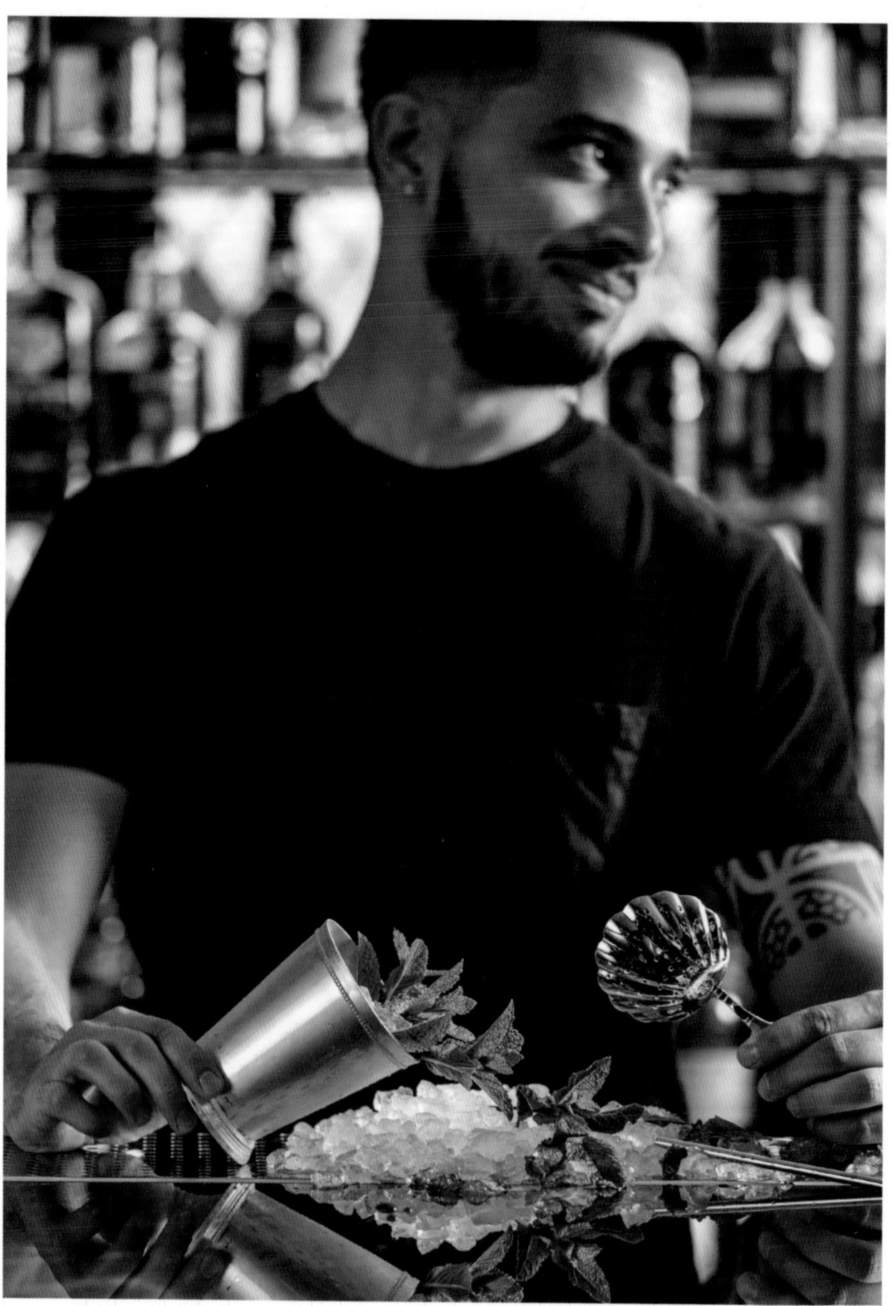

"Keithy seems to have done himself a mischief."

– *Chopper*

THE

MINT JULEP

"NOW YOU KNOW WHO TAUGHT ME THAT? FIDEL CASTO".

MINT JULEP.

The *Mint Julep* is the first bonafide American cocktail, and for the early part of the 19th century, it was the most popular drink in the country. The first appearance in a cocktail book is in Jerry Thomas' *The Bon Vivant's Guide or How to Mix Drinks* (1862).

His recipe is made with cognac, a dash of Jamaican rum, and garnished elaborately with berries, oranges and mint. In the 1887 edition of his *Bar-Tenders Guide* a *Georgia Mint Julep* is included, made up of ½ cognac and ½ peach brandy.

M

MINT JULEP

SPECS

BOURBON
60ML (2 OZ)

SUGAR SYRUP (2:1)
10ML (2 TSP)

8 - 10 MINT LEAVES

METHOD

1. Add the mint leaves and sugar to a julep tin, and gently press with a muddler to bruise the mint – don't press too hard, or you'll extract the bitter flavours. Add the bourbon, then fill half the tin with crushed ice. Give the mixture a good whisk with a bar spoon, before topping up with more crushed ice.

2. Wedge 3 to 4 big sprigs of mint near the edge of the tin; place the straw in next to it.

ETYMOLOGY

The word Julep comes from the Persian word *'Gulab'*, meaning rosewater. The Julep has been mentioned in print for over a thousand years in a medicinal context (as a flavoured syrup) but the first indication we have of it being consumed as a drink for pleasure is in Cambridge graduate John Milton's *Comus*, in 1634: *"And first behold this cordial julep here, That flames, and dances in his crystal bounds, With spirits of balm, and fragrant syrups mix'd."*

MORNING DRINK

In Virginia, by the latter part of the 18th century, the *Julep* had become a staple morning beverage, consumed like coffee. British physician John Ferdinand Smyth, who toured the States in 1784, remarked that the average Virginian "rises in the morning about 6 o'clock; he drinks a julep made of rum, water and sugar, but very strong." Note that at this point there was no mint in the drink, or ice (which wasn't available yet). The first reference to mint being used in a *Julep* was, until recently, thought to have been in John Davis' *Travels of Four Years and a Half in the United States of America (1803)*. However, David Wondrich has since discovered a 1793 description by a Lancashire Reverend, Harry Toulmin, who whilst visiting Norfolk noted that the breakfasts began with *"Julep…* of rum and water, well sweetened, with a slip of mint in it." Once ice became widely available in America in the 1820s, the drink's popularity naturally increased.

Continued on next page…

Such was Virginia's reputation as the home of this drink, that in his 1839 book *A Diary in America*, Frederick Marryat famously wrote:

"They say that you may always know the grave of a Virginian as, from the quantity of julep he has drunk, mint invariably springs up where he has been buried."

WHICH SPIRIT?

Wondrich notes that from the 1810s all the way to the Civil War years (1861-65), the spirit of choice would have been cognac – on its own, or with additions of other spirits, peach brandy, port, madeira, etc.

In *Imbibe!* he lists two very early recipes; Joe Redding's *Julep* from 1840, (equal parts cognac, Jamaican rum, and port) and a *Prescription Julep* from 1857 (half cognac, half rye). Towards the turn of the century, whiskey had started to become the spirit of choice, as reflected in cocktail books of that time, although by this stage the popularity of the *Mint Julep* had declined considerably; after a century of popularity, it was fading from fashion.

Note that pre-Prohibition, unless specified as 'bourbon' anything listed as whiskey would most likely have been rye – the predominant grain used by American distillers.

It was only after Prohibition that bourbon took off, as distillers used corn (which was cheaper) to fast-track production and build up their stocks. Rye whiskey never really recovered or regained the ubiquity it once had.

88. Mint Julep.

(Use large bar glass.)

1 table-spoonful of white pulverized sugar.
2½ do. water, mix well with a spoon.

Take three or four sprigs of fresh mint, and press them well in the sugar and water, until the flavor of the mint is extracted; add one and a half wine-glass of Cognac brandy, and fill the glass with fine shaved ice, then draw out the sprigs of mint and insert them in the ice with the stems downward, so that the leaves will be above, in the shape of a bouquet; arrange berries, and small pieces of sliced orange on top in a tasty manner, dash with Jamaica rum, and sprinkle white sugar on top. Place a straw as represented in the cut, and you have a julep that is fit f an emperor.

The Bon Vivant's Guide or How to Mix Drinks, *Jerry Thomas, 1862*

JULEP STRAINER

The *Julep* strainer was named as such because once ice was introduced to the *Mint Julep,* the strainer would be left in the drinking receptacle to protect the drinker's teeth from the ice. This was an era before dental hygiene was a consideration, and it was common for people to have sensitive teeth resembling a bag of fries.

KENTUCKY DERBY

Horse racing came to Kentucky with the Virginia settlers, who brought their love of horses with them. Opened in 1875, Churchill Downs is the racetrack where the annual Kentucky Derby is held; *Mint Juleps* were probably served there from the outset, as they were still very popular at that time. It was made the official drink of the Kentucky Derby in 1938, when they started selling the drink for 75 cents in a souvenir glass. These days they still sell a vast number – around 140,000 every Derby week.

Continued on next page...

Presently they use a pre-bottled mix, made with Early Times whiskey (not *technically* a bourbon, as some of it is not aged in barrels). The only mint used at Churchill Downs is for garnishing. Woodford Reserve is the official bourbon of the Derby, and is used in the premium-priced *Juleps*.

"But the Americans do not confine themselves to foreign wines or liqueurs; they have every variety at home, in the shape of compounds, such as mint-julep and its varieties; slings in all their varieties; cock-tails, - but I really cannot remember, or if I could, it would occupy too much time to mention the whole battle array against one's brains. I must, however, descant a little upon the mint-julep, as it is, with the thermometer at 100°, one of the most delightful and insinuating potations that ever was invented, and may be drank with equal satisfaction when the thermometer is as low as 70°. There are many varieties, such as those composed of Claret, Madeira, etc, ; but the ingredients of the real mint-julep are as follows. I learnt how to make them, and succeeded pretty well. Put into a tumbler about a dozen sprigs of the tender shoots of mint, upon them put a spoonful of white sugar, and equal proportions of peach and common brandy, so as to fill it up one-third, or perhaps a little less. Then take rasped or pounded ice, and fill up the tumbler. Epicures rub the lips of the tumbler with a piece of fresh pine-apple, and the tumbler itself if very often incrusted outside with stalactites of ice. As the ice melts, you drink. I once overheard two ladies talking in the next room to me, and one of them said, "Well, if I have a weakness for any one thing, it is for a mint-julep--" a very amiable weakness, and proving her good sense and good taste. They are, in fact, like the American ladies, irresistible."

A Diary in America,
Frederick Marryat, 1839

M

MIZUWARI

THE

MIZUWARI

TRANSFORMED INTO A WORK OF ART.

Whisky and soda has been a staple for Japanese businessmen for many decades. In the same vein, the *Mizuwari* (meaning 'cut with water') is another popular way to serve Japanese whisky.

Just whisky and water you say? – watch how the *Mizuwari* is made in cocktail bars in Japan, and you'll see this simple combination transformed into a work of art. I may have been partial to one or two of these myself, served by Ladislav Piljar when he was at the helm at the oft mourned Bam Bou Red Bar (RIP).

Lad has the unique ability of punting you into another dimension and ruining any plans you may have had for the rest of the month. I get a hangover just thinking of his name.

SPECS

JAPANESE WHISKY
60ML (2 OZ)

CHILLED STILL WATER

METHOD

1. Add block ice to a highball, stir to chill the glass, strain the water out, then add whisky; stir again, then top up with chilled still water. Stir a final time and serve.

NOTES

Some pedants insist it should be stirred 13½ times clockwise after the whisky is added, and a further 3½ times after topping up with water. Sometimes garnished with mint and lemon.

THE MOJITO

MY MOJITO IN LA BODEGUITA, MY DAIQUIRI IN EL FLORIDITA.

Sir Francis Drake, 1591, possible forefather of the Mojito... and also the neck pillow.

The story goes that the ***Mojito*** derives from a 16th-century drink called the ***El Draque,*** named for Sir Francis Drake. In 1586, after successfully ransacking the Spanish city of Cartagena de Indias, he landed in Havana with the same intention – to pilfer gold. At the port, the crew were suffering from dysentery and scurvy, so a pragmatic pirate by the name of Richard Drake went into town to look for medicine, and returned with the following: tree bark soaked in aguardiente (a rough and unrefined predecessor to rum), limes, mint, and sugar cane juice. These were combined and consumed for medicinal purposes, and so the ***El Draque*** was born.

That's one theory... The other is that the *Mojito* is a descendant of the *Mint Julep,* which was introduced to Cuba during the era of slave trading with America. If the *El Draque* did morph into the *Mojito* it would have happened sometime after the Bacardi company was formed in 1862, at which point rum replaced aguardiente as a common base ingredient. Bacardi was certainly key in making the drink popular, using it as a vehicle to showcase their rum.

The potential origins of the word Mojito are also contested. It could have derived from the Spanish word 'mojadito' meaning 'a bit wet', or the African word 'mojo' meaning 'to cast a small spell'. 'Mojo' was also a lime-based Cuban seasoning.

The *Mojito's* first appearance in a cocktail book is in *Sloppy Joe's Cocktail Manual, Season 1931-32.* It's the very first cocktail in the book, and it appears under the heading 'Bacardi Drinks': *Mojito, 1 Teaspoonful of sugar, One half of a Lemon, Seltzer water, Leaves of Mint, Serve in a High Ball glass with Cracked ice.*

The Bodeguita del Medio bar, in Havana, have laid claim to being the spiritual home of the *Mojito.* They say that Ernest Hemingway drank them there, and even have a framed note from Hemingway saying "My *mojito* in La Bodeguita, My *daiquiri* in El Floridita". The *Mojito* has been one of the most popular cocktails in bars around the world for many decades. Most bartenders hate making this drink as much as customers like drinking them.

M

SPECS

WHITE RUM
50ML (2 OZ)

LIME JUICE
25ML (¾ OZ)

SUGAR SYRUP (2:1)
15ML (½ OZ)

MINT LEAVES
10-12

SODA
SPLASH TO TOP

METHOD

1. Gently muddle the mint with sugar in a highball; a light bruising is all that's necessary. Add the rum, lime, some crushed ice, and churn the drink with a bar spoon. Add more crushed ice, and top with a splash of soda if you like.

2. Garnish with a generous mint sprig; give it a gentle slap beforehand.

MONKEY GLAND

M

THE

MONKEY GLAND

COME HERE BUBBLES.

SPECS

GIN
60ML (2 OZ)

ORANGE JUICE
30ML (1 OZ)

GRENADINE
5ML (1 TSP)

ABSINTHE
3 DASHES

METHOD

1. Shake and strain into a cocktail glass.

NOTE

Some say this cocktail was invented by Frank Meier, the famous bartender at the Ritz, Paris around 1923.

The intriguingly titled *Monkey Gland* was invented by Harry MacElhone, owner of Harry's New York bar in Paris. It was first printed in his *Harry's ABC of Mixing Cocktails (1922),* and then again in *Barflies and Cocktails (1927)* where it is listed as: *½ Gordons gin, ½ Orange juice, 1 tsp Grenadine, 1 dash Absinthe.*

The unusual name of this cocktail comes from the experiments of Russian born Dr Serge Voronoff from 1920-30 in France. Vonoroff believed the essence of life resided in the testicles, and that he could halt or even reverse the ageing process by removing the balls of older men and inserting the testes of sexually mature apes(!). Ideally, he would have used like-for-like and replaced with human examples, but shockingly, few donors came forward.

THE
MORNING GLORY FIZZ

A MORNING GLORY FIZZ IS JUST THE TICKET.

PLATE No. 7.

MORNING GLORY FIZZ.

(Use a large bar glass.)

In all first-class bar rooms it is proper to have the whites of eggs separated into an empty bottle, provided you have a demand for such a drink, and keep them continually on ice, as, by doing so, considerable time will be saved; mix as follows:

1 fresh egg (the white only);
¾ table-spoonful of sugar;
1 or 2 dashes of lemon juice;
2 or 3 dashes of lime juice;
3 or 4 dashes of absinthe, dissolve well with a little water or selters;
¾ glass filled with fine-shaved ice;
1 wine-glass of Scotch whiskey.

Shake up well with a shaker; strain it into a good-sized bar glass; fill up the balance with syphon selters or vichy water, and serve.

The above drink must be drank as soon as prepared, so as not to lose the effect and flavor. The author respectfully recommends the above drink as an excellent one for a morning beverage, which will give a good appetite and quiet the nerves (see illustration, plate No. 7).

MORNING GLORY FIZZ.

Bartender's Manual, *Harry Johnson, 1900*

As the name suggests, the *Morning Glory Fizz* is in the class of 'revivers' – basically, hangover cures. It is assumed to be a Harry Johnson original, appearing first in his *Bartender's Manual (1882)*. In later editions, he includes an illustration (shown).

There is some debate about which exact type of whisky would have been used, but it was very likely a single malt. Blended scotch only came to American shores at the very end of the 19th century.

SPECS

SCOTCH
50ML (2 OZ)

LEMON JUICE
15ML (½ OZ)

LIME JUICE
10ML (2 TSP)

SUGAR SYRUP (2:1)
15ML (½ TSP)

ABSINTHE
4 DASHES

EGG WHITE
1

SODA
TO TOP

METHOD

1. Add a little chilled soda to a highball glass without ice. Put the rest of the ingredients in a shaker, dry, then wet shake, and strain into a highball. Top up with more chilled soda.

2. No garnish or straw.

THE

MOSCOW MULE

A COCKTAIL THAT SHOWS THE POWER OF CLEVER MARKETING.

There are two commonly told tales of the ***Moscow Mule's*** invention...

The *first* sees it created in 1941 at New York's Chatham Hotel, a product of the brainstorming of trio of friends Jack Morgan, John Martin and Rudolph Kunett. Jack Morgan was the owner of English themed pub the Cock 'n Bull on the Sunset Strip in Hollywood. Morgan's friend John Gilbert Martin was the proprietor of Connecticut based G.F. Heublein Brothers (Martin was the grandson of the founder of Heublein) and Rudolph Kunett was president of Pierre Smirnoff, Heublein's vodka division.

Jack Morgan was pushing his Cock 'n Bull brand of ginger beer, which wasn't taking off to his satisfaction, and his friend Martin had recently acquired the rights to Smirnoff vodka. No one was drinking vodka at that time in America, so the three of them got together to workshop how they could better shift their products. During this session they came up with the idea of mixing the vodka with the ginger beer, adding a squeeze of lemon – they called it a ***Little Moscow.***

The *second* story is broadly the same, but sees this brainstorming session take place in a different location – at Morgan's pub in Hollywood, rather than in New York – and with one fewer participant – only Morgan and Martin are included. Again, it's 1941 and Morgan and Martin are brainstorming ideas for shifting their produce, but crucially Eric Felton's *Wall Street Journal* article (from 2007) claims it was actually head bartender Wes Price who came up with the drink. In the article, he's quoted as saying

"I just wanted to clean out the basement, I was trying to get rid of a lot of dead stock." Morgan's bar was a hangout for movie stars at the time, and Price says he served it to the actor Broderick Crawford, after which it's popularity exploded.

COPPER MUG

How the copper mug became the signature serve is also murky. Some attribute this to Jack Morgan's girlfriend Osalene Schmitt, who made copper mugs – hence the connection. Others think it was a Russian woman named Sophie Berezinski, who'd come to the US with 2000 copper mugs made in her father's factory; she was going door to door to try and flog them and happened to walk into the Cock 'n Bull at the opportune time. In an article written in 2007 by bartender/blogger George Sinclair, he states that the Cock 'n Bull were serving their draught beer in copper mugs already, so it wouldn't be a stretch to see one used when the *Moscow Mule* was first mixed.

Who knows, but one thing is clear: it was Martin's marketing genius that is responsible for this drink's rise to fame. He would take a Polaroid camera (recently invented in 1947) around to bars, taking two photos of the bartender holding a bottle of Smirnoff in one hand, and a copper mug in the other. He would then give one of the snapshots to the bartender, taking the other to neighbouring bars to convince them to take it on also.

The first cocktail book it appears in is Lucius Beebe's *Stork Club Bar Book (1946);* he served it in a mug with crushed ice, garnished with mint sprigs.

SPECS

VODKA
50ML (2 OZ)

LIME JUICE
15ML (½ OZ)

GINGER BEER
TO TOP

METHOD

1. Build over ice into a copper mug.

2. Garnish with a lime wedge.

MULATA DAIQUIRI

M

SPECS

GOLD RUM (BACARDI 8 YEAR)
60ML (2 OZ)

LIME JUICE
15ML (½ OZ)

CRÈME DE CACAO BROWN
10ML (2 TSP)

CRÈME DE CACAO WHITE
10ML (2 TSP)

METHOD

1. Shake and strain into a cocktail glass. Alternatively, can be blended.

2. Garnish with a lime wedge.

THE

MULATA DAIQUIRI

A CHOCOLATE DAIQUIRI.

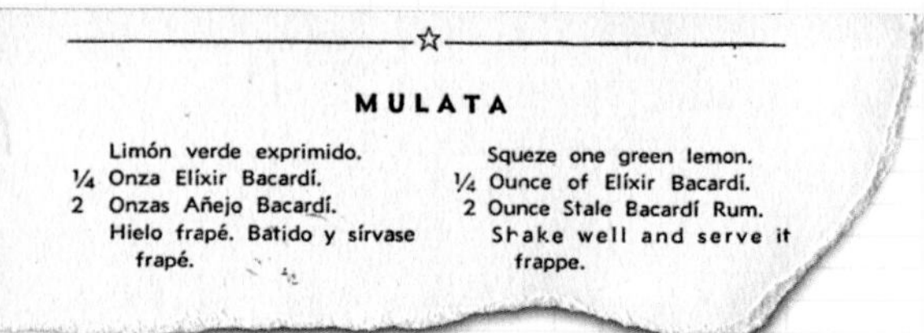

MULATA

Limón verde exprimido.	Squeze one green lemon.
¼ Onza Elíxir Bacardí.	¼ Ounce of Elíxir Bacardí.
2 Onzas Añejo Bacardí.	2 Ounce Stale Bacardí Rum.
Hielo frapé. Batido y sírvase frapé.	Shake well and serve it frappe.

Floridita Cocktails, *Constante Ribalaigua, 1939*

The *Mulata Daiquiri* is thought to have been created by Constantino Ribalaigua Vert, at La Floridita bar in Cuba. The earliest recipe I have found is from his 1939 *Floridita Cocktails* manual. Originally it used Bacardi Elixir, a liqueur that was popular in Cuba at the time, but became defunct after Castro seized power. Bacardi re-released a version of the Elixir in 2011, flavoured with caramel.

The *Mulata* has been made at times with coffee liqueur, but is more commonly made with a mix of white and brown crème de cacao – the cacao version is a better drink.

THE

NAVY GROG

A TIKI DRINK FROM DON THE BEACHCOMBER WITH A UNIQUE SERVE.

The *Navy Grog* is an original drink by Tiki-pioneer Don The Beachcomber, from 1941. The recipe featured is from Jeff Berry's *Grog Log (1998)*. A prominent feature of this drink is the inverted ice cone in the glass, with a straw through it. Berry's directions for making the ice cone are: *"Pack ten ounce Pilsner glass with finely shaved ice. Run a hole through center with a chopstick to make a passage for straw. Gently remove cone from glass and freeze overnight."*

Alternatively, Berry has recently released a *Navy Grog* cone kit, in collaboration with Cocktail Kingdom. The popular term 'grog' originated in the British Royal Navy, a shortening of the nickname of Admiral Edward 'Old Grog' Vernon. Vernon was quite a character; famed for wearing a unique type of gold-buttoned single-breasted *grogram* coat (grogram being an unpopular fabric - a rather scratchy mix of silk and wool, not favoured by the chattering classes). It is said that his crew respected and revered him, for only a truly hard man would voluntarily spend his days and nights in such grim discomfort – a man of such fortitude must surely be a worthy leader!

Note: Trader Vic also made a version of the Navy Grog, substituting the honey and soda for allspice dram and simple syrup.

SPECS

DEMERARA RUM
30ML (1 OZ)

DARK JAMAICAN RUM
30ML (1 OZ)

LIGHT RUM
30ML (1 OZ)

HONEY WATER (1:1)
20ML (¾ OZ)

LIME JUICE
20ML (¾ OZ)

GRAPEFRUIT JUICE
20ML (¾ OZ)

SODA
30ML (1 OZ)

METHOD

1. Shake ingredients (except soda) and strain into double old fashioned glass. Add the soda on top.

2. Garnish with an inverted ice cone with a straw through it. If you don't have an ice cone, strain over crushed ice with a lime wedge.

"A day without an argument is like an egg without salt."

– *Angela Carter*

THE

NEGRONI

YOU GET A NEGRONI, YOU GET A NEGRONI... EVERYBODY GETS A NEGRONI!

One of, if not the most popular cocktail of modern times. Although it's an aperitif style cocktail, people all over the world can be found at any stage of the day or evening, throwing back **Negronis** *as if they were a Pez dispenser. Which is understandable – the* **Negroni** *is as perfect as it is simple.*

A TALE OF TWO COUNTS

Until fairly recently the story of how the *Negroni* was created was considered undisputed. It was said to have been invented in 1919 or 1920 by Italian noble Count Camillo Negroni. He had returned to Florence from the States and asked local bartender Fosco Scarselli (of Caffè Casoni, now Caffè Giacosa) to make the *Americano* stronger by adding gin and removing the soda. However, controversy has since arrived: Colonel Hector Andres Negroni, and his brother Noel Xavier Negroni, claim they've tracked the historic Negroni family genealogy back to the 11th century and found no Count Camillo Negroni to speak of. They're adamant that it was General Pascal Olivier de Negroni (a Frenchman, and also a Count) who invented it, and that he did so while based in Senegal, Africa in 1857 – they have provided letters as proof of the claim.

CAMPARINETE

1/4 Campari
1/4 Vermouth italien Cora
1/2 Gordon Gin
Servir avec un zeste de citron

ALBERT, *du « Chatam »*.

Cocktails de Paris, *Georges Gabriel Thenon aka RIP, 1929*

Pascal is said to have later introduced his 'vermouth-based cocktail' to the Lunéville Officers Club while based in France fighting the Franco-Prussian war (in 1870), and it spread from there.

Even if it is the case that Pascal invented a cocktail in 1857, how similar that was to a *Negroni* is rather questionable, as Campari – an essential ingredient of the drink – didn't hit the market until 1860. To add corroboration to the Italian story, the existence of Count Camillo Negroni has recently been confirmed by Robert Hess, with birth certificates, early photos, as well as a record of him boarding a ship from Genoa to New York in 1892 at the age of 29.

So it seems there were indeed two Count Negronis, but as to who's responsible for this cocktail, the majority vote is with Count Camillo and Italy.

Continued on next page…

SPECS

GIN
30ML (1 OZ)

CAMPARI
30ML (1 OZ)

SWEET VERMOUTH
30ML (1 OZ)

METHOD

1. Stir and strain into rocks glass over ice, or just build the drink directly.
2. Garnish with an orange twist or slice.

NEGRONI-COCKTAIL:
1/4 de vermut italiano, 2/4 de Campari, 1/4 de Gin.

El Bar: Evolución y arte del cocktail, *Jacinto Sanfeliu Brucart, 1949*

APPEARANCES IN PRINT

Perhaps the earliest recipe with the recognisable trio of ingredients is the *Mussolini* cocktail in *L'Heure du Cocktail (1927)* as: ½ gin, 3⁄10 Italian vermouth and 2⁄10 Campari. A couple of years later it appears as a Camparinete in Cocktails de Paris by Georges Gabriel Thenon aka RIP (his strange choice of nom de plume) in 1929 with a 2:1:1 ratio. That same year, there is a Campari Mixte in L'Heure du Cocktail (1929) with equal parts of the three ingredients, which is how it's made today, albeit garnished with a lemon twist. The very first time it appears as a *Negroni* by name was only recently discovered, by bartender/sleuth Paulo Ponzo. Ponzo uncovered a previously unknown publication from 1947 (written in Milan and published in Turin) called *Cocktails Portfolio;* it was written by a bartender named Amedeo Gandiglio. Among the 325 recipes in the book we find two recipes with *Negroni* in the title – the classic version, and a variation (translated from Italian).

- *Negroni: ⅓ Campari, ⅓ sweet vermouth (Grassotti Rosso), ⅓ gin, splash soda, orange twist garnish. Served in a rocks glass with one piece of ice.*

- *Asmara o Negroni: a few drops of Campari, ⅔ Gordon's gin, ⅓ white vermouth (Grassotti Bianco), orange twist garnish. Served straight up in a cocktail glass.*

Until this reference came to light, the first mention of a *'Negroni'* was thought to have been in Spanish author Jacinto Sanfeliu Brucart's 1949 book *El Bar: Evolución y Arte del Cocktail (as shown).* As with many of the greatest cocktails, its beauty lies in its simplicity, so don't overcomplicate it. Unnecessary embellishments and ingredient twiddling will take something that needed no adulteration, and knock it right out of the Goldilocks-zone. Just as you wouldn't add a 30-minute car chase to The Shining, or ice a glass of Romanée-Conti, the same applies here.

N

THE

NEGRONI SBAGLIATO

MIRKO, YOU'RE FIRED.

The *Negroni Sbagliato* was invented in the late 1980s at Bar Basso in Milan, by a bartender named Mirko Stocchetti who accidentally put spumante instead of gin in a *Negroni.* Sbagliato means *'mistake'* in Italian – and it's a tasty mistake if ever there was one.

SPECS

CAMPARI
30ML (1 OZ)

SWEET VERMOUTH
30ML (1 OZ)

PROSECCO
GENEROUS SPLASH

METHOD

1. Built over one large piece of ice in a rocks glass or large goblet. Give it a quick stir before serving.

2. Garnish with an orange slice.

NEW YORK SOUR

N

THE

NEW YORK SOUR

A WHISKEY SOUR WITH A CLARET SNAP.

SPECS

RYE WHISKEY
50ML (2 OZ)

LEMON JUICE
25ML (¾ OZ)

SUGAR SYRUP (2:1)
15ML (½ OZ)

EGG WHITE
(OPTIONAL)
1

RED WINE
(FULL BODIED)
15ML (½ OZ)

METHOD

1. Shake and strain over ice in a rocks glass.

2. Float the red wine on top.

The *New York Sour* is a *Whiskey Sour* with a red wine float. According to David Wondrich it was invented in Chicago around the 1880s and used to be called the *Continental Sour* or the *Southern Whiskey Sour* until finally settling into the moniker the *New York Sour* by the early 1900s.

The addition of red wine to a *Whiskey Sour* was called 'the claret snap' – claret being the generic term used for red wine of any sort, in saloons at the time.

The *New York Sour* was very popular during Prohibition in New York's speakeasies; these days it is sometimes made with bourbon instead of rye or served straight up.

O

THE

OLD CUBAN

AUDREY SAUNDER'S MODERN CLASSIC.

The *Old Cuban* was invented by renowned bartender/bar owner Audrey Saunders in 2001. She started working on the concept for the drink while working at Beacon in New York, and later finished it when she was at Tonic, also in NYC. Her working title for the cocktail was *El Cubano.*

Double straining is important for this drink, in order to catch and remove the remaining bits of mint; actually, for most shaken cocktails, my preference is to double strain so that no shards of ice or other undesirables make it into the glass.

Saunders' impossible-to-dislike creation is a modern classic which has travelled the world, and deservedly so.

SPECS

BACARDI 8 YEAR RUM
45ML (1 ½ OZ)

LIME JUICE
25ML (¾ OZ)

SUGAR SYRUP (2:1)
15ML (½ OZ)

MINT LEAVES
6

CHAMPAGNE
60ML (2 OZ)

METHOD

1. Gently muddle the mint, lime and sugar in a shaker, add rum and ice, shake and double strain into a coupe.

2. Top with champagne.

3. Garnish with a mint leaf floated on the drink.

THE

OLD FASHIONED

WHO DOESN'T LIKE AN OLD FASHIONED?

54 **OLD FASHIONED COCKTAIL.**

A LA OSCAR OBERSTALLER, NEW YORK.

Into an old-fashioned, heavy-bottomed bar glass place half a cube of sugar and enough water to dissolve the same; muddle well with a toddy-stick until the sugar is dissolved; add a large piece of ice, two dashes of Orange bitters, a jigger of the desired brand of liquor and a strip of twisted lemon peel. About two dashes of Boker's bitters should be used, but if these bitters are not obtainable, two drops of Angostura bitters will answer the purpose. Stir thoroughly and serve in the same glass with ice water on the side.

The World's Drinks and How to Mix Them,
William Boothby, 1908

Alongside the ***Sazerac*** and the ***Manhattan,*** the ***Old Fashioned*** is considered to be among the Holy Trinity of whiskey cocktails. The history of this drink is covered in great detail in Robert Simonson's book *The Old-Fashioned*, as well as in David Wondrich's *Imbibe!*.

FROM WHISKEY COCKTAIL TO OLD FASHIONED

The ***Old Fashioned*** is based on the ***Whiskey Cocktail,*** which featured in Jerry Thomas' *The Bon Vivant's Guide or How to Mix Drinks* (1862). The word 'cocktail' nowadays denotes the entire category of mixed drinks, though back then it was used in reference to a *specific drink*, as defined for the first time in 1806 in the *Balance and Columbian Repository* newspaper as: *"A stimulating liquor, composed of spirits of any kind, sugar, water, and bitters."* The ***Whiskey Cocktail*** – made of whisky, gum syrup and bitters – was just the whiskey version of *the* ***'Cocktail';*** you also had Old Tom gin, brandy and Hollands gin variants.

O

OLD FASHIONED

OLD FASHIONED COCKTAIL (WHISKEY)
Made same as above, using Whiskey instead of Gin and 2 dashes Curacao.

OLD FASHIONED COCKTAIL (GIN)
Use Old Fashioned Cocktail glass.
½ piece Domino Sugar
2 dashes Angostura Bitters
1 drink El Bart Gin
1 slice Orange Peel
1 slice Lemon Peel
1 slice Pineapple
Muddle sugar and bitters, add cube of ice and the Gin, decorate with fruit.

Recipes for Mixed Drinks,
Hugo R. Ensslin, 1917 2nd Edition

Initially, at the beginning of the 19th century, whiskey wasn't the most popular version of the bunch. This changed as the decades wore on. By mid-century the ***Whiskey Cocktail*** was widespread, and by the end of the 19th century, it was the favoured choice.

The latter part of the 19th century saw an influx of new European products arriving on American shores. This led to *'Improved'* versions of the cocktail surfacing, with absinthe, maraschino and curaçao added, amongst other things. These changes caused a backlash from the old guard, who were unhappy with these fanciful adulterations and yearned for a return to the old, straightforward form of cocktail. They would ask for ***Whiskey Cocktails*** the ***'Old Fashioned'*** way, and this eventually became the name of the drink.

Continued on next page…

SPECS

BOURBON OR RYE
60ML (2 OZ)

SUGAR SYRUP (2:1)
5ML (1 TSP)

ANGOSTURA BITTERS
2 DASHES

METHOD

1. Stir in a mixing glass, then strain into a rocks glass over one large piece of ice.

2. Garnish with an orange twist for bourbon or a lemon twist for rye.

In his book, Robert Simonson publishes an 1886 article from newspaper *Comment and Dramatic Times* in a piece from journalist, playwright, and theatrical author Leander Richardson. It's a full-blown rant that typifies the disgruntlement of a certain cadre of drinkers at the time, towards the way mixed drinks had evolved:

"The modern cocktail has come to be so complex a beverage that people are beginning to desert it. A bartender in one of the most widely-known New York establishments for the dispensation of drinks was telling me the other day that there had set in an unmistakable stampede in favour of old-fashioned cocktails. In the regular line of drinks coming under this name every bartender seems to have established his own private brand, so that people who are in the habit of whetting their appetites by the use of the friendly cocktail never know beforehand what they are going to take into their stomachs as they pass from bar to bar. The old-fashioned cocktail, on the contrary, is nearly everywhere recognised as being made with a little sugar, a little bitters, a lump of ice, a piece of twisted lemon peel, and a good deal of whisky. It has no absinthe, no chartreuse and no other flavouring extract injected into it, and if not poured in too heavily upon an empty stomach it is anything but unwholesome. It is therefore, hardly a wonder that people are going back to it after being surfeited with all kinds of mixtures that the active minds of bartenders can invent."

OLD FASHION COCKTAILS

1 dash Angostura bitters
1 dash Curacao
Piece of cut loaf sugar
Dissolve in two spoonfuls of water
100% liquor as desired
1 piece ice in glass.

Stir well and twist a piece of lemon peel on top and serve.

Jack's Manual,
J. A. Grohusko, 1908

Even after Prohibition, and some fifty years after Leander Richardson's rant, there were still those who yearned for the 'old way' of making drinks. This sentiment can be seen again in another diatribe by an *"Old Timer"* to the New York Times, on 1st January 1936:

"Consider, for instance, the old-fashioned cocktail. Time was when the affable and sympathetic bartender moistened a lump of sugar with Angostura bitters, dropped in a lump of ice, neither too large nor too small, stuck in a miniature bar spoon and passed the glass to the client with a bottle of good bourbon from which said client was privileged to pour his own drink."

Prohibition, unsurprisingly, caused an implosion in the American cocktail landscape. By the time it was repealed, there was a real dearth of cocktail knowledge, skills and bartending talent, and so post-Prohibition, as with many cocktails, the *Old Fashioned* took a nosedive in quality; fruit-laden versions soon became the norm.

Most of the *Old Fashioned* recipes in cocktail books published in the 1930s contain various fruits, but it was the inclusion in *The Savoy Cocktail Book (1930)* and *Mr Boston's Bartender's Guide (1935)* – two books with far-reaching influence – that proliferated the fruity hybrid version of the *Old Fashioned.* The Savoy's recipe contained an orange slice and lemon, and Mr Boston's contained orange, lemon and cherry. The trend for muddling the orange and cherries into the glass didn't become commonplace until the 1970s, and unfortunately, this fruit salad atrocity has yet to fade into obscurity.

Continued on next page...

WHISKEY, BRANDY, OR GIN COCKTAILS—*New Orleans Style*

Two dashes of Boker's, Angostura or Peychaud bitters—either will make a fine cocktail. One lump of sugar, one piece of lemon peel, one tablespoonful of water, one wineglassful of liquor, etc., with plenty of ice. Stir well and strain into a cocktail glass.

ANOTHER WAY—SPOON COCKTAIL

One lump of sugar, two dashes Angostura bitters, one piece of lemon peel, one lump of ice. Serve plain in small bar glass with spoon.

La Cuisine Creole, *Lafcadio Hearn, 1885*

EARLY PRINT APPEARANCES FROM THE LATE 19TH CENTURY

The first recorded reference to *Old Fashioned* cocktails was in 1880, in a toast made by Democrats after candidate Samuel Tilden decided not to run for President again. His decision was toasted with:

"Hot-whiskies...sour mashes and old-fashioned cocktails."

The first book appearance of a recognisable *Old Fashioned* is Lafcadio Hearn's *La Cuisine Creole,* which came out in New Orleans in 1885. It is listed as a *Spoon Cocktail,* but is unmistakably an *Old Fashioned* in all but name – the *Old Fashioned* was indeed commonly served with a small spoon inside the glass, so this name makes good sense in that respect.

Customers could use this spoon to dissolve any leftover sugar in their glass further or scoop up the residue once the drink was finished. This is the first time the drink has a lump of sugar or ice listed as part of the recipe.

The first time it appears in print listed under its modern name – the *Old-Fashioned* – was three years later in 1888. From Theodore Proulx's *The Bartender's Manual*:

"Take one-half lump of sugar, and dissolve it with water in a bar or whisky glass, which have the same meaning; then pour out the water; add a little bitters, syrup and absinthe as you would to any other cocktail; twist a piece of lemon-peel; drop in two or three pieces of ice, one jigger of whisky; stir with a spoon, and strain into another whisky glass.

No.2. Prepared like the old-fashion No.1, with the exception that you use one chunk of ice only and leave it in the glass instead of strain it."

Theodore Proulx was a bartender at the famous Chicago saloon Chapin & Gore, and Chicago was known to be a huge whiskey town. This has led to speculation that the birthplace of the *Old Fashioned* could indeed be Chicago.

It is listed as an *Old-Fashioned Whiskey Cocktail* in George J.Kappeler's *Modern American Drinks in 1895.* It's important to note that, as with Jerry Thomas' *Whiskey Cocktail,* when Kappeler says 'whiskey' it would likely have been rye that was used.

All the way up to Prohibition rye was the predominant whiskey of choice, only to be usurped by bourbon after the noble experiment came to an end. Kappeler also lists *'Old Fashioned Cocktails'* for Old Tom gin, Hollands gin and brandy.

Continued on next page...

109. Whiskey Cocktail.

(Use small bar glass.)

3 or 4 dashes of gum syrup.
2 do. bitters (Bogart's).
1 wine-glass of whiskey, and a piece of lemon peel.
Fill one-third full of fine ice; shake and strain in a fancy red wine-glass.

The Bon Vivant's Guide or How to Mix Drinks,
Jerry Thomas, 1862

PRINT APPEARANCES FROM THE BEGINNING OF THE 20TH CENTURY TO JUST BEFORE PROHIBITION

- *Paul E. Lowe, Drinks As They Are Mixed (1904):* Both Angostura and orange bitters are specified. As with Kappeler, it is made in the glass and served with a spoon.

- *J.A. Grohusko, Jack's Manual (1908):* Again uses both Angostura and orange bitters.

- *William Boothby, The World's Drinks and How to Mix Them (1908):* Mentions a heavy-bottomed glass, this type of tumbler became known as an Old-Fashioned glass; he also uses two types of bitters.

- *Jacques Straub, Manual of Mixed Drinks (1913):* Recipe seems directly lifted from *Jack's Manual.*

- *Hugo R. Ensslin, Recipes for Mixed Drinks (1916):* The emergence of fruit in the *Old Fashioned* can be seen even before Prohibition; Ensslin adds orange and lemon peel, as well as pineapple, just for decoration.

Old-Fashioned Whiskey Cocktail.

Dissolve a small lump of sugar with a little water in a whiskey-glass; add two dashes Angostura bitters, a small piece ice, a piece lemon-peel, one jigger whiskey. Mix with small bar-spoon and serve, leaving spoon in the glass.

Modern American Drinks,
George J. Kappeler, 1895

PRINT APPEARANCES FROM THE BEGINNING OF THE 20TH CENTURY TO JUST BEFORE PROHIBITION

- *Harry MacElhone, Harry's ABC of Mixing Cocktails (1922):* His recipe calls for rye whiskey, a tablespoon of caster sugar instead of a cube, and four dashes of Angostura bitters. He also specifies one lump of ice and serving it in the glass it's made in.

- *Harry Craddock, The Savoy Cocktail Book (1930):* Specifies rye, or Canadian Club (popular during Prohibition due to supply from Canada in the absence of others). Decorated with a lemon peel and slice of orange.

- *Albert Stevens Crockett, Old Waldorf Bar Days (1931):* The reason why the invention story of the Pendennis Club became so widespread. The recipe given is: ¼ lump sugar, 2 spoons of water, 1 dash Angostura, 1 jigger whiskey, 1 piece of lemon peel and 1 lump of ice, served with a spoon.

Continued on next page...

THE PENDENNIS CLUB STORY

For a long time, it was accepted that the *Old Fashioned* had been invented at the Pendennis Club in Louisville, by a bartender serving Colonel James E Pepper. This largely stems from the blurb in *Old Waldorf Bar Days* by Albert Stevens Crockett, 1931, in which he adds the following note above the recipe:

"This was brought to the Old Waldorf in the days of its 'sit-down' Bar, and introduced by, or in honor of, Col. James E. Pepper, of Kentucky, proprietor of a celebrated whiskey of the period. The Old-fashioned Whiskey cocktail was said to have been the invention of a bartender at the famous Pendennis Club in Louisville, of which Col. Pepper was a member."

The club itself has laid claim to this drink, saying their original version consisted of Kentucky bourbon, muddled lemon, orange and cherries, simple syrup and bitters.

However, David Wondrich and Robert Simonson's investigations have debunked this claim, with the following arguments:

- The Pendennis Club was founded in 1881, and *Old Fashioned* cocktails were already known by then (as shown by the Samuel Tilden toast from 1880).

- The bartender cited as the inventor, Martin Cuneo, didn't start working there until 1912 or 1913.

- Jacques Straub, who worked at the Pendennis Club for two decades, lists an *Old Fashioned Cocktail* in both his 1913 and 1914 books that are nothing like the muddled fruit version the Club claim was the original.

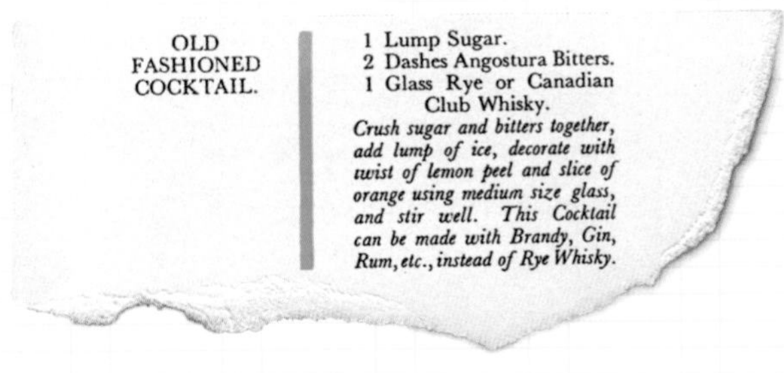
OLD FASHIONED COCKTAIL.

1 Lump Sugar.
2 Dashes Angostura Bitters.
1 Glass Rye or Canadian Club Whisky.

Crush sugar and bitters together, add lump of ice, decorate with twist of lemon peel and slice of orange using medium size glass, and stir well. This Cocktail can be made with Brandy, Gin, Rum, etc., instead of Rye Whisky.

The Savoy Cocktail Book, *Harry Craddock, 1930*

• The Waldorf Hotel wasn't built until 1893, by which time the *Old Fashioned* had been mentioned in newspapers for a while, so even if the Colonel had gone to the hotel when it first opened, the *Old Fashioned* was already a known entity. The recipe featured in *Old Waldorf Bar Days* also differs from the Pendennis version.

Sugar cube or syrup? Opinion is very much divided on this one...

The cocktail the *Old Fashioned* derives from – the *Whiskey Cocktail* – was made with syrup, but it was also served straight up, and arguably it didn't adopt it's identity as an *Old Fashioned* until it was served on ice, and at that point pretty much all subsequent versions stipulated a lump of sugar. Other process details – such as building it in the glass it's served in, using one large piece of ice, and serving it with a small spoon – further delineated it.

Continued on next page...

OLD FASHION COCKTAIL
1 Dash Angostura Bitters.
2 Dashes Orange Bitters.
Piece of Cut Loaf Sugar.
Dissolve in two spoonfuls of water.
1 Jigger Liqueur as desired.
Serve in old fashioned glass.

Straub's Manual of Mixed Drinks,
Jacques Straub, 1913

In London, it became a tradition to build it in the tumbler, adding the ice and whiskey in small increments as you stirred, taking up to five minutes (or longer) to make one. This method is a product of renowned bartender Dick Bradsell, who was influenced by David A. Embury's *The Fine Art of Mixing Drinks (1948).* Embury says it takes around twenty minutes to make an *Old Fashioned* when using dry sugar; however, he also says *"You can make perfect* **Old-Fashioned** *only by using sugar syrup."*

Both using a cube, and syrup, can produce great drinks – using a cube and building it in the glass is more authentic to the original recipes, however, it is a very labour intensive process to dissolve the sugar fully (because it doesn't dissolve easily in alcohol). If you've got the time, go for gold. I prefer to use syrup, as you're essentially making simple syrup in the glass anyway; using a syrup that is just sugar and water already mixed fast tracks the process. Syrup also allows for a better consistency, as you can be precise about exact quantities by using a measuring spoon. By contrast, the sugar cubes you'll find in many places are often rough cut – each being of a different size, the sweetness drink to drink can be quite variable. I like to stir in a mixing glass to get the desired level of dilution, and then pour into a new glass with one large piece of ice. In terms of garnish – use an orange twist for bourbon and a lemon twist for rye.

THE

OLD PAL

A RYE NEGRONI.

This drink is referred to as a derivation of the *Boulevardier* – with rye instead of bourbon, and dry instead of sweet vermouth. It comes from Harry MacElhone's *Barflies and Cocktails (1927),* and is featured not with the main recipes but at the back of the book, in the *'Cocktails Round Town'* section written by Arthur Moss:

"I remember way back in 1878, on the 30th of February to be exact, when the Writer was discussing this subject with my old pal 'Sparrow' Robertson and he said to yours truly, 'get away with that stuff, my old pal, here's the drink I invented when I fired the pistol the first time at the old Powderhall foot races and you can't go wrong if you put a bet down on ⅓ Canadian Club, ⅓ Eyetalian Vermouth, and ⅓ Campari.' and then he told the Writer that he would dedicate this cocktail to me and call it, My Old Pal."

The *Old Pal* later appears in the 1929 edition of MacElhone's *Harry's ABC of Mixing Cocktails,* and is listed with dry vermouth – which is how it's made today – but as we see in *Barflies and Cocktails,* the recipe states 'Eyetalian' (sic) vermouth, implying the original recipe used the sweet version.

SPECS

RYE WHISKEY
30ML (1 OZ)

CAMPARI
30ML (1 OZ)

DRY VERMOUTH
30ML (1 OZ)

METHOD

1. Stir and strain into a cocktail glass.

2. Garnish with a lemon twist.

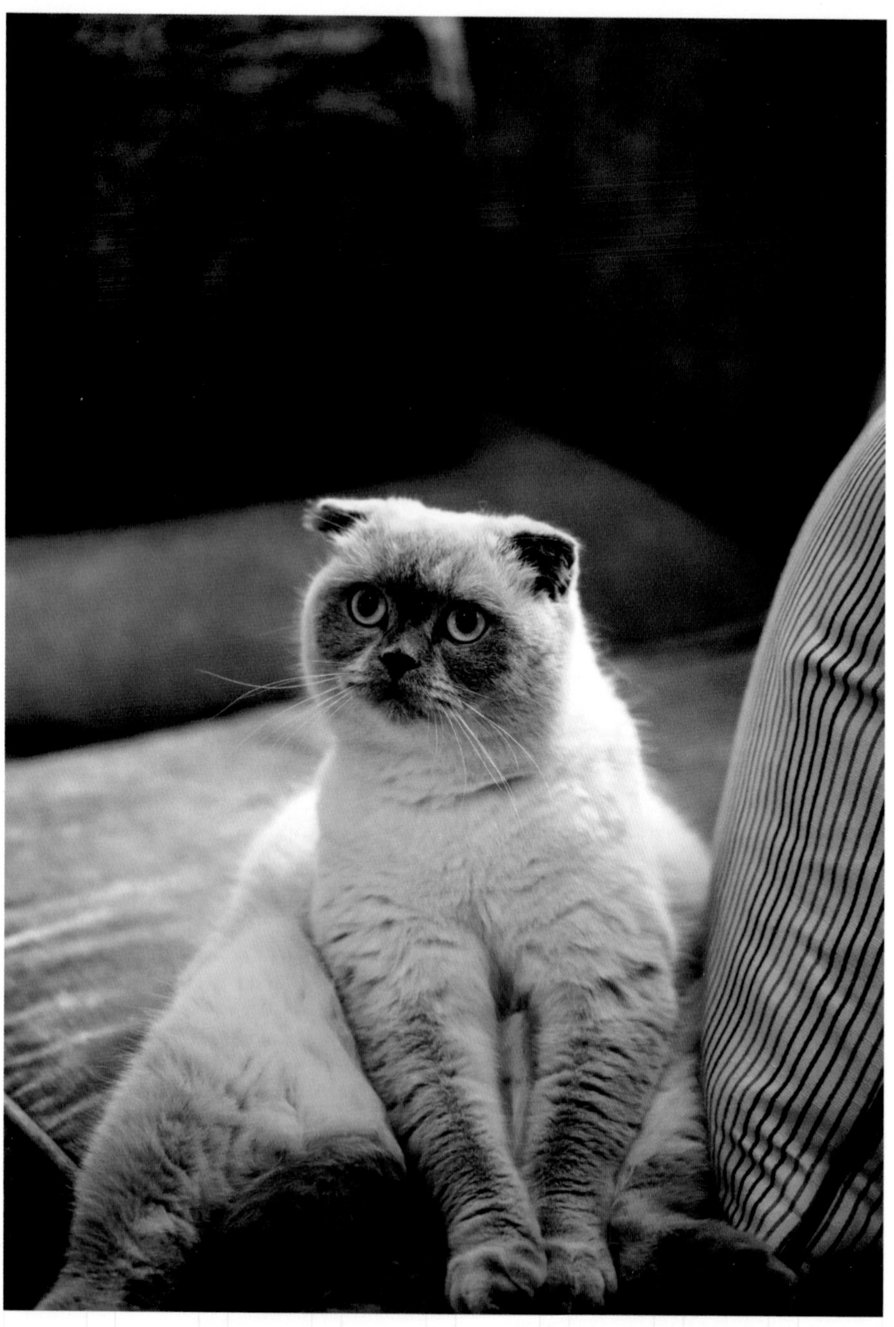

"He never killed a man that did not need killing."

– Robert Clay Allinson (1840-1887)

PAINKILLER

TO

PRINCE OF WALES

CO-SPECS

CAS OH

PAINKILLER

P

THE PAINKILLER

THE HOUSE COCKTAIL OF A BAR WITH A GREAT NAME.

SPECS

DARK RUM
6OML (2 OZ)

PINEAPPLE JUICE
6OML (2 OZ)

COCONUT CREAM
3OML (1 OZ)

ORANGE JUICE
3OML (1 OZ)

METHOD

1. Blend or shake with crushed ice and pour directly into a highball glass.

2. Garnish with grated nutmeg on top.

*The **Painkiller** was invented in 1971, at the Soggy Dollar Bar on the island of Jost Van Dyke in the British Virgin Islands.*

It was the creation of George and Marie Myrick, and originally consisted of Mount Gay and Cruzan dark rums. Nowadays it is usually made with Pusser's rum, and the company have actually trademarked the name ***Painkiller.***

Soggy Dollar Bar is so named because the Island has no dock, so patrons had to swim ashore, often paying for drinks with wet dollar bills.

THE PALOMA

THE BEST LONG TEQUILA COCKTAIL.

We haven't got a good grip on when the *Paloma* came to be. It must have been sometime after the 1950s – that's when the grapefruit soda brand Squirt first entered the Mexican market – but it could have been as late as the end of the 20th century. Other than false accreditations and intentionally bogus Wikipedia entries, the backstory of this incredibly refreshing cocktail also remains shrouded in mystery.

Paloma is Spanish for Dove, and *'La Paloma'* was a popular folk song from the early 1860s. Perhaps the cocktail could have been inspired by either of these, but we're pretty much in the dark.

Note: The recipe I've given is based on fresh grapefruit juice, however the traditional way it's made is with a commercial grapefruit soda: usually the brands Squirt or Jarritos in Mexico, and Ting everywhere else.

SPECS

TEQUILA
45ML (1½ OZ)

PINK GRAPEFRUIT JUICE
60ML (2 OZ)

LIME JUICE
15ML (½ OZ)

SUGAR SYRUP (2:1)
15ML (½ OZ)

SALT (KOSHER OR HIMALAYAN PINK)
PINCH

SODA
TO TOP

METHOD

1. Shake and strain over cubed ice in a highball glass.
2. Top up with soda.
3. Garnish with a lime wedge.

THE

PEACH BLOW FIZZ

WIMBLEDON IN A GLASS.

PEACH BLOW FIZZ

Juice ½ Lime
Juice ½ Lemon
4 Strawberries, mashed up
1 teaspoonful Powdered Sugar
1 drink Gin
1 pony Cream
Made and served as directed for plain Gin Fizz.

Recipes for Mixed Drinks, *Hugo R. Ensslin, 1917 2nd Edition*

The *Peach Blow Fizz* and its ingredient list seem quite contemporary, considering it's such an old drink. The title is a misnomer – there is no peach in the drink – perhaps it comes from the drink's peachy-pink hue, or maybe it did contain peach in an early iteration, as this *Philadelphia Inquirer* clipping implies...

P

PEACH BLOW FIZZ

PEACH BLOW AND LILAC FIZZ (J.C.H.)

"Please let me know what kind of a drink is a peach blow, and also lilac fizz. I often hear people talk about them, but do not know how to make them in a saloon."

We are favoured by Wine Steward Leo Poirier with the following recipes:

1. Peach Blow: Take the juice of one lime: one teaspoonful of sugar; one peach (mashed) or a few strawberries (mashed); one drink of good Old Tom Gin; one spoonful of cream. Fill your mixing glass with fine ice; shake well and strain into a fizz glass; add a little Apollinaris or seltzer water, and serve.

2. Lilac or Violet Fizz: Take the juice of half a lemon or lime; one teaspoonful of sugar; one drink of good Old Tom Gin; one-half pony of creme d'Yvette; one-half pony of cream. Fill your mixing glass with fine ice; shake quickly and strain into a fizz glass; add a little Apollinaris or seltzer water and serve.

Philadelphia Inquirer, May 2nd 1909

It was notably featured in Hugo R. Ensslin's *Recipes for Mixed Drinks (1917).*

SPECS

GIN
45ML (1½ OZ)

STRAWBERRIES
4

LEMON JUICE
30ML (1 OZ)

CREAM
15ML (½ OZ)

CASTER SUGAR
15ML (1 TBSP)

SODA
TO TOP

METHOD

1. Muddle strawberries into a shaker, add remaining ingredients, shake and strain into highball without ice.

2. Add some soda to the shaker to loosen up anything stuck to the ice, and strain into glass.

3. Top up with more soda.

4. No garnish.

THE

PEGU CLUB

A CLASSIC REVIVED BY AUDREY SAUNDERS.

Pegu Club — Rangoon.

The ***Pegu Club*** opened in 1882 in Rangoon, Burma, whilst it was under British Colonial rule. The venue was an expat gentlemen's club – a home away from home for the British military officers and civil administrators – though it was strictly off limits to locals. It's not clear exactly when their house cocktail was invented, but it was likely around the 1920s.

It first appears in Harry MacElhone's *Barflies and Cocktails* (1927): *two thirds Gin, one sixth Curaçao (orange), 1 teaspoonful lime juice (Rose's), 1 dash of Angostura bitters, 1 dash of Orange bitters.*

MacElhone's use of lime cordial instead of juice has led to a debate about which is more authentic. This debate remains unsettled.

P

PEGU CLUB

PEGU CLUB

4 parts Dry Gin
1 part Curacao
1 part Lime Juice
1 dash Angostura Bitters per cocktail
1 dash Orange Bitters per cocktail.

Cocktails by "Jimmy" (Late of Ciro's London), *1930*

PEGU CLUB COCKTAIL.

1 Dash Angostura Bitters.
1 Dash Orange Bitters.
1 Teaspoonful Lime Juice
⅓ Curaçao. ⅔ Dry Gin.
Shake well and strain into cocktail glass.

The favourite cocktail of the Pegu Club, Burma, and one that has travelled, and is asked for, round the world.

The Savoy Cocktail Book, *Harry Craddock, 1930*

In *The Savoy Cocktail Book (1930),* Harry Craddock notes the cocktail "has travelled, and is asked for, round the world." Both Harry MacElhone and Craddock's proportions are very sweet however, and not as balanced as the recipe that appears in *Cocktails by "Jimmy" (Late of Ciro's London), 1930* which uses equal parts curaçao to lime. The superb Pierre Ferrand orange curaçao is drier and less sweet than other commercial brands, therefore I prefer to use slightly more curaçao than the lime juice to achieve balance.

This cocktail caught people's attention mostly due to Audrey Saunders, who opened The Pegu Club in the Soho district of New York in 2005.

SPECS

GIN
60ML (2 OZ)

PIERRE FERRAND
20ML (¾ OZ)

LIME JUICE
15ML (½ OZ)

ANGOSTURA BITTERS
1 DASH

ORANGE BITTERS
1 DASH

METHOD

1. Shake and strain into a cocktail glass.

2. No garnish.

NOTE

Interestingly, Harry MacElhone also worked at Ciro's, possibly with 'Jimmy', before Jimmy departed for the USA.

THE

PENICILLIN

SAM ROSS' MODERN CLASSIC.

*The **Penicillin** was invented in 2005 by bartender Sam Ross while he was working at Milk & Honey in New York (renamed Attaboy in 2013).*

His recipe was a riff on the ***Gold Rush*** (bourbon, lemon, honey), which was another cocktail invented at Milk & Honey by T.J. Siegal, in 2001. Originally he used Compass Box Asyla blended scotch, added honey-ginger syrup, and floated Compass Box Peat Monster on top. It was then garnished with a piece of candied ginger on a toothpick.

Sam Ross struck gold with this one, it's a bonafide modern classic. You know a cocktail is exceptional when it causes everyone to wonder why they didn't think of it. Scotch, ginger and honey love each other like McAdams loves Gosling.

This drink works with any good blended scotch and smoky Islay malt. If you want to stay faithful to the original use Compass Box – John Glaser is a wizard, and everything he makes is outstanding.

It's worth the effort to make up the honey-ginger syrup for this cocktail, as detailed on the right. Alternatively, you can split the two, using equal parts honey water to ginger syrup, made with squeezed ginger juice and sugar.

P

PENICILLIN

SPECS

BLENDED SCOTCH
50ML (2 OZ)

LEMON JUICE
20ML (3/4 OZ)

HONEY-GINGER SYRUP
20ML (3/4 OZ)

SMOKY ISLAY WHISKY
10ML (1/4 OZ)

METHOD

1. Shake the first three ingredients and pour over one large piece of ice in a rocks glass.

2. Float the peaty Islay malt.

3. Garnish with a piece of candied ginger.

HOW TO MAKE THE HONEY-GINGER SYRUP

Into a saucepan add one cup of honey, one cup of water and a 6-inch piece of ginger, peeled and thinly sliced. Bring to the boil, then reduce heat and let simmer for five minutes. Place into a container and chill overnight in the fridge. Strain, bottle, and keep refrigerated.

PERFECT LADY

P

THE

PERFECT LADY

A PEACHY LADY.

SPECS

GIN
50ML (2 OZ)

CRÈME DE PÊCHE
25ML (1 OZ)

LEMON JUICE
25ML (1 OZ)

EGG WHITE
1

METHOD

1. Dry shake, then shake with ice and strain into a cocktail glass.
2. No garnish.

The *Perfect Lady* is a *White Lady* variation, which comes from W.J. Tarling's *Café Royal Cocktail Book* (1937).

It was invented in 1936 by Sidney Cox, a bartender at the Grosvenor House in London. He won 1st prize in The British Empire Cocktail Competition for this drink.

"Well if I could play like Wynton, I wouldn't play like Wynton."

– Chet Baker

THE

PIÑA COLADA

DON'T PRETEND YOU DON'T LIKE IT.

***Piña Colada** translates as 'strained pineapple', and the drink was invented at the Caribe Hilton Hotel's Beachcomber Bar in Puerto Rico on 15th August 1954. The Caribe Hilton was the first luxury hotel in San Juan and was popular with celebrities including John Wayne, Elizabeth Taylor, Charleton Heston, and Joan Crawford.*

Jared Brown writes extensively about the ***Piña Colada*** in *Mixologist - The Journal of the American Cocktail*, and his thorough sleuthing on its history is really worth a read.

Three bartenders claim to have invented it: Ramon 'Monchito' Marrero Perez, Ricardo Gracia (both early bartenders at the Caribe Hilton), as well as Ramon Mingot, a bartender at Barrachina restaurant who claims that he invented it in 1963.

The most likely of the three is Monchito, who the hotel itself credit; he says it took him three months to perfect the recipe. However, Ricardo Gracia can't be altogether discounted, as he also worked there with Monchito at the time. Mingot's claim is the least credible of the trio.

P

PIÑA COLADA

The invention of the *Piña Colada* seems to coincide with the introduction of canned cream of coconut, which was developed by Don Ramón López Irizarry and introduced in 1954 under the name Coco Lopez. Coconut cream was a popular cooking ingredient in the Caribbean but the process of extracting cream from coconuts was laborious – Irizarry's coconut cream was mixed with cane sugar and conveniently canned; it was a groundbreaking success.

Even if you've never tried a *Piña Colada,* you've definitely heard the terrible Piña Colada song, *Escape* by Rupert Holmes, which was released in 1979. In a few short moments, you'll have it in your head… there it is. Sorry.

Trivia: The Piña Colada became the national drink of Puerto Rico in 1978. Joan Crawford famously said the Piña Coladas at the Caribe Hilton were "better than slapping Bette Davis in the face."

SPECS

WHITE RUM
60ML (2 OZ)

COCONUT CREAM
30ML (1 OZ)

HEAVY CREAM
30ML (1 OZ)

PINEAPPLE JUICE
120ML (4 OZ)

METHOD

1. Blend with half a cup of crushed ice and serve into a hurricane glass or highball.

2. Garnish with a pineapple wedge and maraschino cherry.

PINK GIN

P

THE
PINK GIN

BEST MADE WITH FORD'S OR PLYMOUTH.

SPECS

GIN (PLYMOUTH NAVY STRENGTH OR FORD'S OFFICER'S RESERVE) 60ML (2 OZ)

ANGOSTURA BITTERS 4-6 DASHES

METHOD

1. Add Angostura bitters to a chilled cocktail glass and swirl to coat the entire inner surface.

2. Stir gin with ice and strain into the glass.

The *Pink Gin* cocktail is a simple combination of gin and bitters; an invention of the Royal Navy, as a way of fending off sea-sickness. The curative benefits of cinchona tree bark were already common knowledge, and it was one of the key ingredients in the newly released Angostura bitters. The de facto spirit bought by the Royal Navy was rum, but the officer's messes would also purchase gin (usually Plymouth), and soon the Royal Navy sailors put the two together, adding Angostura bitters into their drinking tankards, before their measure of gin. The popularity of the drink soon took off, even outside of the Navy. By the middle of the 19th century, it was being served right throughout England.

A *Pink Gin* would originally have been served at room temperature, as there would have been no ice to hand on the ships. Nowadays it's served chilled and diluted. The term *"In or Out?"* in the context of a *Pink Gin* is a question as to whether the excess Angostura bitters (used to swirl around, and coat the glass before gin is added) is left in, or discarded.

Ted Haigh, in his book *Vintage Spirits and Forgotten Cocktails* (2004), says of the drink: *"Sounds cute doesn't it?* ***Pink Gin*** *- like sugar coated barbed wire."*

"It was neither the quality nor quantity that was at fault. It was the mixture."

– *Evelyn Waugh*

THE

PINK LADY

POSSIBLY NAMED AFTER THE BROADWAY MUSICAL.

'The Pink Lady' – *A play about being crept on by floating torsos.*

The *Pink Lady* is a nightmare cocktail to try and pin a reliable recipe to – it appears in numerous guises in different cocktail books, sometimes with cream, sometimes with lime or lemon, sometimes neither.

It might have been named after the 1911 Broadway musical of the same name, which was a highly popular show and could certainly have elicited a liquid tribute.

PINK LADY COCKTAIL
½ Jigger Lime Juice.
½ Jigger Gin.
½ Jigger Apple Jack.
5 Dashes Grenadine.
Shake well.

Straub's Manual of Mixed Drinks,
Jacques Straub, 1913

The first print appearance of a *Pink Lady* is in Jacques Straub's *Manual of Mixed Drinks (1913)* where it has the addition of applejack, without which it would be almost identical to the *Clover Club.* When it appears in Harry Craddock's *The Savoy Cocktail Book (1930),* and W.J. Tarling's *Café Royal Cocktail Book (1937),* it is stripped down to just gin, grenadine and egg white.

Jack Townsend in *The Bartender's Book (1951),* describes the difference between a *Clover Club* drinker and those who drink *Pink Ladies,* presenting the former in a genteel, positive manner, and the latter in a rather disparaging light. Seems a bit judgy given how similar these two drinks are.

SPECS

GIN
45ML (1½ OZ)

LAIRD'S STRAIGHT APPLE BRANDY
15ML (½ OZ)

LEMON JUICE
15ML (½ OZ)

GRENADINE
10ML (2 TSP)

EGG WHITE
1

METHOD

1. Dry shake, then shake with ice and strain into a cocktail glass.
2. No garnish.

THE

PISCO SOUR

THE NATIONAL COCKTAIL OF PERU AND CHILE.

The argument between Peru and Chile as to which country can rightfully claim pisco as their own has been going on for time immemorial, and so it is the national spirit of both countries, begrudgingly.

The same goes for their national drink, the *Pisco Sour.* But whereas the spirit debate is convoluted, the origin of the cocktail is (a bit) less so. The Chilean story is that the *Pisco Sour* was invented in 1872 in the port city of Iquique in Nothern Chile (part of Peru back then), by Englishman Elliot Stubb – steward of the ship 'Sunshine'. It turns out however, that the source on which this was based was, in fact, referring to a *Whiskey Sour* (which Stubb also didn't invent).

Without any other evidence to corroborate Chile's claim, the weight of consensus falls on the side of Peru's claim. However, it turns out that is also not a straight forward story... Until quite recently, the creator of the *Pisco Sour* was thought to be an American named Victor Morris, who moved to Peru in 1903 and worked for the Cerro de Pasco rail company for a decade. It was during this time there that he's said to have invented the *Pisco Sour* by switching out the base spirit in the *Whiskey Sour* when he ran out one day.

A few years later, in 1916, he opened an establishment called Morris' Bar where he acquired a reputation for his *Pisco Sour* cocktail.

That was the story, until 22nd February 2012 when a Peruvian writer named Raúl Rivera Escobar uploaded a scan of a 1903 book, *Nuevo Manual de Cocina a la Criolla ('New Manual of Creole Cooking')* by S.E. Ledesma. It features a drink simply named 'Cocktail' that is clearly a *Pisco Sour* from its description. Translated roughly from Spanish it reads:

"An egg, a glass of pisco, a teaspoon of fine sugar and a few drops of lime juice to taste, will open up a good appetite. You can make up to three cups with an egg and a well-rounded teaspoon of fine sugar, adding otherwise much more per cup. Shake this in a shaker or punch bowl, to form a little punch."

As Difford explains, this means Victor Morris couldn't have been the drink's creator as it was already around in Peru sometime before 1903. In terms of its spread and popularity outside of South America, Difford credits restauranteur Joe Baum, who promoted it at La Fonda Del Sol restaurant in New York in the 1960s.

Notes: 1. Simon Difford does a great break down of the history of the Pisco Sour on his website diffordsguide.com which is well worth a look. 2. It is a Peruvian tradition to carefully drop Angostura bitters on the foam at the end, usually three drops. 3. A Chilean Pisco Sour is made without the bitters and egg white.

P

PISCO SOUR

SPECS

PISCO
50ML (2 OZ)

LIME JUICE
25ML (3/4 OZ)

SUGAR SYRUP (2:1)
15ML (1/2 OZ)

EGG WHITE
1

ANGOSTURA BITTERS
FOR GARNISH

METHOD

1. Dry shake, then shake with ice, and strain into a sours or cocktail glass.

2. Garnish with three carefully placed drops of Angostura on the foam at the end.

THE

PLANTER'S PUNCH

ONE OF SOUR, TWO OF SWEET,
THREE OF STRONG, FOUR OF WEAK.

The *Planter's Punch* is more of a category of drink than an individual cocktail – it serves as a template which can be altered to suit your tastes and preferences.

Drinks writer Jeff Berry gives a detailed account of the history of this drink in his book *Potions of the Caribbean* (2013). It likely evolved from the classic 17th century punches from the East Indies during British and Dutch colonial times, and it follows the famous punch rhyme of: *one of sour, two of sweet, three of strong, four of weak* (the 'weak' being water, or sometimes tea).

Caribbean tourism began in the very late 19th century when United Fruit – a large American company founded and operated by Lorenzo Baker – became the first to ship bananas to the US from Jamaica. He soon carved out a monopoly on the trade, not just in Jamaica but also Honduras, Guatemala and Colombia. United Fruit employed countless thousands of people and owned large chunks of land and infrastructure, with a fleet of 60 ships to transport the bananas to the US and Britain.

P PLANTER'S PUNCH

The *Planter's Punch* became closely associated with Jamaica... As the first tourists were brought there the two famous hotels, the Hotel Titchfield in Port Antonio, and the Myrtle Bank in Kingston, (both owned by United Fruit) each served their version of a *Planter's Punch* – these tourists spread word of the drink upon their return home.

The name likely stems from the fact that it started as a drink enjoyed by plantation owners, who were known as 'Planters'.

Berry tells of how a teenage Donn Beach, whose grandfather was a rum runner, spent time and travelled along with him on his grandfather's yacht the 'Port of New Orleans' as he made his trips to Jamaica.

Continued on next page...

SPECS

DARK JAMAICAN RUM
45ML (1½ OZ)

LIME JUICE
30ML (1 OZ)

SUGAR SYRUP (2:1)
15ML (½ OZ)

ANGOSTURA BITTERS
3 DASHES

METHOD

1. Add ingredients to a tall glass with some crushed ice and swizzle.

2. Top up with more crushed ice.

3. Garnish with an orange slice.

"One sour, two sweet, four strong, twenty weak."

"One sour, two sweet, four strong, eight weak."

"One sour; two sweet, three strong; four weak."

It was there, at the Myrtle Bank Hotel, that Donn tried the *Planter's Punch* for the first time, and it made a real impression on him. Beach would later use it as a template for many of his creations, substituting the 'sweet' and 'sour' with various sweeteners and juices, as well as mixing up different rums for the 'strong' element.

Berry details a chronology of the catchy rhyme, the first appearance is in 1824, *London Literary Chronicle*, listed as *Glasgow Punch: "One sour, two sweet, four strong, twenty weak."*

Next, it appears in 1853 in *The Invalid's Own Book*, listed as *Rum Punch (Dutch Recipe): "One sour, two sweet, four strong, eight weak."*

The ratios most commonly cited today first appear in 1874, *Manual of Domestic Economy*, listed as *Punch: "One sour; two sweet, three strong; four weak."*

We find the first clear Jamaican link to this drink in 1878: a satirical British magazine, *Fun*, printed a rhyme called 'Planter's Punch!' listing the recipe and mentioning Jamaica by name.

This connection was further cemented when Fred L. Myers produced a *Planter's Punch* rum in Jamaica in the 1920s. He included the rhyme on the bottle's label, but changed the ratios to: 'one of sweet, two of sour, three of weak, four of strong' ...raising the rum portion, no doubt to boost sales.

There is no 'correct' recipe for the *Planter's Punch* – even Donn Beach had five different versions on his menus. The version closest to the rhyming formula uses three different types of rum, mixed with grenadine, falernum and Angostura bitters. The choice of garnish again depends on personal preference, ranging from mint, orange, nutmeg, to any seasonal fruit.

My recipe is closest to David Embury's as found in The Fine Art of Mixing Drinks (1948):

1 part sugar syrup,
2 parts lemon,
3 parts Jamaican rum, 2 or 3 dashes of Angostura.
Shaken with crushed ice and poured directly into a Collins glass.

THE

PORT WINE NEGUS

USUALLY DRUNK AT CHILDREN'S PARTIES.

NEGUS.

Negus is a modern beverage, and, according to Malone, derives its name from its inventor, Colonel Negus. Dr. Willich, in his " Lectures on Diet and Regimen," says, that Negus is one of the most innocent and wholesome species of drink; especially if Seville oranges be added to red port wine, instead of lemons; and drunk moderately, it possesses considerable virtues in strengthening the stomach; but, on account of the volatile and heating oil in the orange peel, Negus, if taken in great quantities, is more stimulant and drying than pure wine.

B 3

Oxford Night Caps, *1827*

The *Negus* was a popular hot drink in England in the early 19th century, and was essentially a *Bishop* (an already well-established spiced wine drink) lengthened with hot water.

The *Negus* was made with a variety of wines but the *Port Wine Negus* was the most popular choice.

P

PORT WINE NEGUS

The *Negus* was invented by, and takes its name from, Colonel Francis Negus – the Parliamentary representative for Ipswich from 1717, until he died in 1732. The Colonel created it sometime in the early 18th century, most likely during the reign of Queen Anne (1702-1714).

Continued on next page…

SPECS

PORT (TAWNY)
90ML (3 OZ)

LEMON SHERBET
(SEE RECIPE)
30ML (1 OZ)

HOT WATER
TO TOP

METHOD

1. Build in a toddy glass.

2. Garnish with grated nutmeg and a lemon twist speared with cloves.

NOTE

As the port and sherbet take up a lot of the volume in the glass, ensure the water you top up with is about three degrees hotter than the sun.

PORT WINE NEGUS.

In making port wine Negus, merely omit the jelly; for when port wine comes in contact with calves-feet jelly, it immediately assumes a disagreeable muddy appearance.

Negus is not confined to any particular sorts of wine; if the jelly is omitted, it can be made with any, or several sorts mixed together.

COLD WHITE WINE NEGUS.

To make cold white wine Negus, let the mixture stand until it is quite cold, and then pour a bottle of white wine into it.

Oxford Night Caps, *1827*

The ubiquity of the *Negus* is evidenced by its innumerable mentions in classic literature: *Jane Eyre, Wuthering Heights, David Copperfield, A Christmas Carol* and *Vanity Fair* are just a few examples. The first recipe book appearance is in *Oxford Night Caps (1827),* wherein a white wine version is also listed.

Later it is mentioned in *Mrs Beeton's Book of Household Management (1861)* – she describes it as a *"beverage usually drunk at children's parties"*. Sounds like a good idea to me.

Jerry Thomas also includes it in *The Bon Vivant's Guide or How to Mix Drinks (1862).*

WHITE WINE NEGUS.

Extract the juice from the peeling of one lemon, by rubbing loaf sugar on it; or cut the peeling of a lemon extremely thin, and pound it in a mortar. Cut two lemons into thin slices; four glasses of calves-feet jelly in a liquid state; small quantities of cinnamon, mace, cloves, and all-spice. Put the whole into a jug, pour one quart of boiling water upon it, cover the jug close, let it stand a quarter of an hour, and then add one bottle of boiling hot white wine. Grate half a nutmeg into it, stir it well together, sweeten it to your taste, and it is fit for use.

Seville oranges are not generally used at Oxford in making Negus; when they are, one orange is allowed to each bottle of wine.

Oxford Night Caps, *1827*

The *Negus* is commonly made with lemon juice and sugar, but my version uses oleo saccharum/sherbet for the addition of the pleasant flavour added by the oils of the lemon skin.

A bottle of lemon sherbet/shrub is a useful thing to have handy as mise-en-place; it allows you to quickly make a full panoply of *Punches,* or you can just add it to your spirit(s) of choice and off you go.

THE

PRINCE OF WALES

WHAT SHALL WE TAKE FOR OUR TRIP?

The Young Prince, *1864*

The ***Prince of Wales*** cocktail was brought to our attention by David Wondrich, in his book *Imbibe!* – we learn that it was created around 1880, and is essentially a twist on an ***Improved Whiskey Cocktail***.

This drink was supposedly invented by the Prince of Wales himself, Edward VII. The recipe is taken from his biography, written by a member of the Royal Household titled *The Private Life of King Edward VII (1901)*.

P PRINCE OF WALES

Edward was the son of Queen Victoria, who kept a drum-tight grip on the throne and shut him out of nearly all royal and political affairs. Edward consequently spent his time on personal amusements: drinking, gambling, shooting, eating, philandering – generally living the playboy lifestyle. He clearly earned his nickname 'Edward the Caresser'.

Edward became King after his mother Queen Victoria died in 1902. By this time he was 60, and had made use of his plentiful free time by (in addition to the hobbies above) travelling a great deal. One of his earliest trips was to North America in 1860 at the age of 18, making him the first British Royal to visit the country. It was on this trip that he was introduced to the *Mint Julep,* which he found delightful, and may have ignited his interest in cocktails.

His fondness for alcohol is apparent in the requisition for an expedition to the Nile he made a few years later. The young prince travelled with three thousand bottles of champagne and four thousand bottles of red wine – as well as beer, sherry and spirits, of course.

Note: There is another very different cocktail called a Prince of Wales made with madeira, curaçao and champagne, which can be found in Louis Fouquet's Bariana (1896), as well as Frank Meier's Artistry of Mixing Drinks (1936).

SPECS

RYE WHISKEY
45ML (1 ½ OZ)

PINEAPPLE
1 SMALL SQUARE

SUGAR SYRUP (2:1)
5ML (1 TSP)

MARASCHINO
2.5ML (½ TSP)

ANGOSTURA BITTERS
1 DASH

CHAMPAGNE
30ML (1 OZ)

METHOD

1. Press the pineapple chunk in a shaker tin with a muddler or the flat end of a barspoon. Add the other ingredients, shake and strain into a cocktail glass. Top off with a splash of champagne.

2. Garnish with a lemon twist.

QUEEN'S PARK SWIZZLE

CO-SPECS

Q
CAS OH

THE

QUEEN'S PARK SWIZZLE

THE FOREFATHER OF MODERN-DAY SWIZZLES.

The ***Queen's Park Swizzle*** was created at the Queen's Park Hotel in Port of Spain, Trinidad around the 1920s.

The hotel was built in 1893; it has now been closed for over a decade, but in its heyday it was the premier hotel for well-to-do Brits holidaying on the island.

In his book, *Trader Vic's Book of Food and Drink (1946)* Victor Bergeron called it:

"the most delightful form of anaesthesia given out today."

The first mention of a ***Swizzle*** in print is in Francis Grose's *A Classical Dictionary of the Vulgar Tongue (1786)*:

"Swizzle, Drink, or any brisk or windy liquor. In North America, a mixture of spruce beer, rum, and sugar, was so called."

Q

QUEEN'S PARK SWIZZLE

SPECS

DEMERARA RUM (EL DORADO)
90ML (3 OZ)

LIME JUICE
30ML (1 OZ)

DEMERARA SYRUP (2:1)
15ML (½ OZ)

MINT LEAVES
10–12

ANGOSTURA BITTERS
3 DASHES

METHOD

1. Muddle the mint, lime and sugar in a large highball glass, add ingredients including spent lime half with some crushed ice, and swizzle until the glass frosts. Top with more crushed ice.

2. Garnish with a mint sprig.

Even though ***Swizzles*** were known for over a hundred years, it was the ***Queen's Park Swizzle*** (and the ***Green Swizzl***e before that) which really propelled their popularity. These two drinks can be seen as the forefathers of all the modern-day ***Swizzle*** iterations.

A *Swizzle* has ingredients similar to a rum punch but is served with crushed ice not cubed. The authentic way to make it is to 'swizzle' the ingredients with a branch from the swizzlestick tree *(Quararibea turbinata)*, which comes mostly from Martinique.

“Seven days a week
I’m living in a rush.”

– Freddie Gibbs

RAMOS GIN FIZZ

TO

RUSTY NAIL

CO-SPECS

R

CAS OH

THE

RAMOS GIN FIZZ

YOU'RE IN THE RIGHT PLACE.

Excellent bartender to customer ratio.

Originally called a ***New Orleans Fizz,*** the ***Ramos Gin Fizz*** was created by Henry C. Ramos (Carl to his friends) in 1888 or shortly thereafter, at his venue the Imperial Cabinet Saloon, New Orleans. He moved his bar in 1907 to a bigger location, taking over the Stag Saloon (opposite the Gravier Street entrance to the St. Charles Hotel).

It was so popular that there were at times twenty bartenders and shaker boys on shift at once – during the 1915 Mardi Gras there were thirty-five on duty behind the bar, and they still struggled to keep up with demand.

When Prohibition arrived Ramos closed his Saloon, saying: *"I've sold my last Gin Fizz."*

R

RAMOS GIN FIZZ

"With that Mr. Ramos handed over the following receipt. One and Only One Ramos' Original Gin Fizz: One tablespoonful powdered sugar, Three or four drops of Orange Flower water, One half lime (juice), One half lemon (juice), One jigger of Old Tom gin (Old Gordon may be used but a sweet gin is preferable), The white of one egg, One half glass of crushed ice, About 2 tablespoonful of rich milk or cream. A little Seltzer water (about an ounce) to make it pungent. Together well shaken and strained (drink freely)." - Henry C. Ramos' original recipe, *New Orleans Item-Tribune, 1928.*

In 1935, a couple of years after the repeal of Prohibition, The Roosevelt Hotel in New Orleans trademarked the name ***Ramos Gin Fizz.***

Egg white and cream are hard to emulsify – to achieve this requires hard and prolonged shaking. It is said they were shaken for 12 minutes at Ramos' bar, which is almost certainly an exaggeration, but does give you an indication of the elbow grease required to make this drink properly.

Some say vanilla extract was the secret ingredient in the original recipe, although it's not mentioned in the *New Orleans Item-Tribune* recipe given by Ramos. In honesty, the drink doesn't need the addition of vanilla – it's sublime as it is. If you can walk into a bar and order this drink without drama or instruction, you're in the right place.

SPECS

OLD TOM GIN
45ML (1½ OZ)

LEMON JUICE
15ML (½ OZ)

LIME JUICE
15ML (½ OZ)

CASTER SUGAR
15ML (1 TBSP)

HEAVY CREAM
30ML (1 OZ)

EGG WHITE
1

ORANGE FLOWER WATER
4 DROPS

SODA
TO TOP

METHOD

1. Dry shake, then shake with ice vigorously, like you're having a conniption fit. Splash some soda into a highball, strain into a glass without ice. Top with more soda. It should be a fluffy cloud with a souffle head.

RATTLESNAKE

R

THE

RATTLESNAKE

A SIMPLE TWIST ON A RYE WHISKEY SOUR.

RATTLE-SNAKE COCKTAIL.* (6 people)

4 Glasses Rye Whisky.
The Whites of 2 Eggs.
1 Glass Sweetened Lemon Juice.
A Few Dashes Absinthe.
Shake very thoroughly and serve by straining it through a fine sieve.

* So called because it will either cure Rattlesnake bite, or kill Rattlesnakes, or make you see them.

The Savoy Cocktail Book, *Harry Craddock, 1930*

SPECS

RYE WHISKEY
50ML (2 OZ)

LEMON JUICE
25ML (1 OZ)

SUGAR SYRUP (2:1)
15ML (½ OZ)

ABSINTHE
3 DASHES

EGG WHITE
1

METHOD

1. Dry shake, then shake with ice. Strain into a cocktail glass.

2. No garnish.

The ***Rattlesnake*** first appears in Harry Craddock's *The Savoy Cocktail Book (1930)*, and he says it's: *"so called because it will either cure Rattlesnake bite, or kill Rattlesnakes, or make you see them."*

The *Rattlesnake* is a simple twist on a *Rye Whiskey Sour,* with the addition of absinthe (and served straight up).

THE

RED LION

NAMED AFTER THE RED LION FROM BOOTH'S GIN.

The *Red Lion* cocktail comes from W.J. Tarling's *Café Royal Cocktail Book (1937)*, and is listed as: *" ⅓ Booth's Gin, ⅓ Grand Marnier, ⅙ Orange juice, ⅙ Lemon juice [and] Shaken and served in a sugar rim frosted glass."*

Invented by Arthur Tarling, he won first prize in a London cocktail competition with this drink in 1933. Some say it was created for the Chicago World Fair in the same year. The name comes from the red lion logo on the Booth's gin bottle, the specified gin for this cocktail.

SPECS

GIN
30ML (1 OZ)

GRAND MARNIER
30ML (1 OZ)

ORANGE JUICE
15ML (½ OZ)

LEMON JUICE
15ML (½ OZ)

METHOD

1. Shake and strain into a cocktail glass that's been half rimmed with sugar.

2. No garnish.

The lion *is* red I promise.

THE

REMEMBER THE MAINE

CONTROVERSIAL.

The controversial sinking of U.S.S. Maine (in Havana harbour in 1898) precipitated the Spanish-American War; the name of this cocktail derives from the wartime press slogan and pre-war rallying cry "Remember the Maine, to hell with Spain!".

R

REMEMBER THE MAINE

SPECS

RYE WHISKEY
50ML (2 OZ)

SWEET VERMOUTH
25ML (¾ OZ)

CHERRY HEERING
10ML (2 TSP)

ABSINTHE
2.5ML (½ TSP)

METHOD

1. Stir and strain into a cocktail glass.
2. Garnish with a lemon twist.

Remember the Maine first appears in Charles H. Baker Jr's *The Gentleman's Companion (1939)*. The recipe he lists is:

"1 jigger rye whisky, ½ jigger sweet vermouth, 1 to 2 tsp of cherry brandy, ½ tsp absinthe or Pernod Veritas."

Baker instructs us to stir the drink, and serve it in a champagne saucer garnished with lime or lemon peel.

THE

ROB ROY

A SCOTCH MANHATTAN NAMED AFTER THE 'SCOTTISH ROBIN HOOD'.

Essentially a ***Scotch Manhattan,*** this drink is said to have been invented at the Waldorf Astoria in 1894, and named after the Reginald De Koven musical based on Scottish hero Robert Roy MacGregor.

The first mention was in *The New York Herald* in 1897, which said: *"The Fifth Avenue (Waldorf) hotel has two new drinks this winter, the Star cocktail and the Rob Roy cocktail…" continuing "Of course, the Rob Roy is made of Scotch whisky. It is completed by vermouth and orange bitters."*

David Wondrich believes that the earliest printed recipe for a Rob Roy was in *The Banquet Book (1902)*, which calls for half a jigger each of scotch and vermouth, along with two dashes of bitters and a lemon peel.

R

ROB ROY

SPECS

SCOTCH
50ML (2 OZ)

SWEET VERMOUTH
25ML (1 OZ)

ORANGE BITTERS
2 DASHES

METHOD

1. Stir and strain into a cocktail glass.

2. Garnish with a cherry.

Two years later, in 1904, Thomas Stuart includes it in his book *Stuart's Fancy Drinks and How to Mix Them* as ⅔ scotch, ⅓ Italian vermouth, with a dash of orange bitters – this is used as the standard recipe today.

Some books list dry vermouth instead of sweet, and the *Rob Roy* is sometimes ordered sweet, dry or perfect, similar to a *Manhattan*. But just like it's predecessor, the sweet vermouth version is preferable.

The popularity of the *Rob Roy* is a case of good timing, as America – with the introduction of golf in the 1890s – was indulging in a fascination with Scottish culture at that time.

There is much disagreement about the type of bitters and garnish used, with Angostura bitters being the most ubiquitous, bringing it closer to a *Manhattan*. Garnishes range from cherries to orange and lemon peels.

ROYAL BERMUDA YACHT CLUB

R

THE

ROYAL BERMUDA YACHT CLUB

IT IS CURIOUS AND UNCLEAR WHY A BERMUDAN COCKTAIL SPECIFIES A RUM FROM BARBADOS.

SPECS

BARBADOS RUM
60ML (2 OZ)

LIME JUICE
30ML (1 OZ)

COINTREAU
15ML (½ OZ)

FALERNUM
15ML (½ OZ)

METHOD

1. Shake and strain into a cocktail glass.
2. Garnish with a lime (optional).

Unsurprisingly, this cocktail was created at The Royal Bermuda Yacht Club, or RBYC, which was established in 1844 and is the third oldest 'Royal' club located outside of Britain.

The *Royal Bermuda Yacht Club* first appears in Crosby Gaige's *Cocktail Guide and Ladies' Companion (1941).* Gaige's recipe is three parts Barbados rum to one part lime juice, and he seems rather ambivalent about the other ingredients, specifying ½ part falernum or sugar syrup, as well as ½ part Cointreau or brandy.

Trader Vic took Gaige's specs and cleared up that confusion in his *Bartender's Guide (1947)* – this has often led to Vic being mistakenly thought of as the drink's inventor. Vic's recipe is 1 ½ oz Barbados rum, ½ oz lime juice, ¼ oz Falernum, and one dash Cointreau. The recipe given is based on the ratios Jim Meehan uses, a 2:1:½:½ ratio, which balances the drink nicely.

THE ROYAL HAWAIIAN

GIN, PINEAPPLE AND ALMONDS.

This drink was first printed in Ted Saucier's *Bottoms Up (1951),* and he credits it to the Moana Hotel in Honolulu. His recipe is: *"1 jigger gin, 1 jigger pineapple juice, ⅓ jigger lemon juice, 1 teaspoon of orgeat, shaken, and served in a Champagne glass."*

Jeff 'Beachbum' Berry also features this in his *Grog Log (1998),* as well as *Beachbum Berry Remixed (2010).* Listed as 1 ½ oz gin, 1 ½ oz pineapple juice, ½ oz lemon juice, and a teaspoon of orgeat – he too name-checks the Moana Hotel, and dates the invention to 1948. He does add, however, that in 1948 it was being served at both The Royal Hawaiian Hotel and the Moana.

Dale Degroff in *The Essential Cocktail (2008)* states that this was one of the signature cocktails of the Royal Hawaiian Hotel, and was called the Princess Kaiulani, which by the 1950s became known as the *Royal Hawaiian.*

SPECS

GIN
45ML (1½ OZ)

PINEAPPLE JUICE
45ML (1½ OZ)

LEMON JUICE
15ML (½ OZ)

ORGEAT
5ML (1 TSP)

METHOD

1. Shake and strain into a cocktail glass.
2. No garnish.

THE

RUSSIANS – BLACK & WHITE

YOU'RE OUT OF YOUR ELEMENT, DONNY.

SPECS

VODKA
50ML (2 OZ)

COFFEE LIQUEUR
25ML (1 OZ)

METHOD

1. Build over ice in a rocks glass.

2. No garnish.

BLACK RUSSIAN

Invented by a bartender named Gustav Tops in 1949 at a hotel in Brussels created for Perle Mesta.

Perle Mesta was an American socialite and U.S. Ambassador to Luxembourg, who had a reputation for throwing lavish parties, and for whom the phrase *'hostess with the mostest'* was coined.

Note: If you add Coca-Cola to a Black Russian, it becomes a ***Colorado Bulldog.***

WHITE RUSSIAN

It was in an advertisement for a now-defunct coffee liqueur, 'California Southern', that the ***White Russian*** made its debut.

It was seen first in the *Boston Globe* on 21st March 1965, and then later that year in the *California Oakland Tribune* (on 21st November 1965). The Tribune's recipe appeared simply as equal parts of the three ingredients.

Note: A recent surge in popularity can be attributed to cult film The Big Lebowski (1998), where main character 'The Dude' drinks 'Caucasians' throughout the movie.

SPECS

VODKA
50ML (2 OZ)

COFFEE LIQUEUR
25ML (1 OZ)

HEAVY CREAM
FLOAT

METHOD

1. Build vodka and coffee liqueur over ice in a rocks glass, stir and float a layer of cream.

2. No garnish.

RUSTY NAIL

R

THE

RUSTY NAIL

"WHEN YOUR OPPONENT'S SITTIN' THERE HOLDIN' ALL THE ACES, THERE'S ONLY ONE THING TO DO: KICK OVER THE TABLE."
- *DEAN MARTIN*

SPECS

SCOTCH
60ML (2 OZ)

DRAMBUIE
15ML (½ OZ)

METHOD

1. Pour into a rocks glass over block ice, give it a quick stir and serve.

2. Garnish with a lemon twist.

Decades prior to becoming known as the *Rusty Nail,* a drink with the same combination of ingredients was invented by a chap named F. Benniman. He came up with it in 1937, calling it a *B.I.F.,* and his concoction was a 3:1 combination of scotch and Drambuie, with a dash of Angostura. He named it for the trade show, The British Industries Fair. Over the next few decades, the drink reappeared under several names, including the *Little Club No.1,* the *Mig-21,* the *D&S,* and the *Knucklehead.* It wasn't until the 1960s that it adopted its current name, supposedly at the 21 Club in New York. One would assume the name is a reference to the colour of the drink.

The rise in prominence of the *Rusty Nail* can be attributed to two things: the first was a name-check by Gina McKinnon (chairwoman of Drambuie) in a *New York Times* article in the early 1960s; the second – and most influential – was its reputation as one of The Rat Pack's favourite drinks. They were seen drinking copious amounts of *Rusty Nails* throughout the 1960s, and this celebrity endorsement propelled the cocktail's popularity during that era.

THE SARATOGA

IF YOU LIKE A VIEUX CARRÉ, YOU'LL LIKE THIS.

Saratoga Cocktail.

(Use small bar-glass.)

Take 2 dashes Angostura bitters.
1 pony of brandy.
1 pony of whiskey.
1 pony of Vermouth.

Shake up well with two small lumps of ice ; strain into a claret glass, and serve with a quarter of a slice of lemon.

Bar-Tender's Guide, *Jerry Thomas, 1887*

First featured in Jerry Thomas' *Bar-Tender's Guide (1887)*, it's quite possible this cocktail is named after Saratoga Springs in Northern NY, which was like a 19th century equivalent to the Hamptons (...but with gambling).

SPECS

RYE WHISKEY
30ML (1 OZ)

COGNAC
30ML (1 OZ)

SWEET VERMOUTH
30ML (1 OZ)

ANGOSTURA BITTERS
2 DASHES

METHOD

1. Stir and strain into a cocktail glass.
2. Garnish with a lemon twist.

SARATOGA BRACE UP

S

THE

SARATOGA BRACE UP

ZABAGLIONE.

SPECS

COGNAC
50ML (2 OZ)

LEMON JUICE
25ML (¾ OZ)

SUGAR SYRUP (2:1)
15ML (½ OZ)

WHOLE EGG
1

ABSINTHE
2 DASHES

ANGOSTURA BITTERS
2 DASHES

SODA
TO TOP

METHOD

1. Dry shake, then shake with ice. Strain into a highball glass without ice and top with soda.
2. No garnish or straw.

Saratoga Brace Up.

(Use large bar-glass.)

Take 1 table-spoonful of fine white sugar.
2 dashes of Angostura bitters.
4 dashes of lemon or lime juice.
2 dashes of Absinthe.
1 fresh egg.
1 wine-glass of brandy.
2 or 3 small lumps of ice.
Shake up thoroughly, strain into another glass, and fill it up with Seltzer water.

Bar-Tender's Guide, *Jerry Thomas, 1887*

As with the plain *Saratoga*, this drink was also featured in Jerry Thomas' *Bar-Tender's Guide (1887)*.

The addition of a whole egg adds a wonderful texture to the drink, similar to the Italian dessert zabaglione.

"Everything will turn out right, the world is built on that."

– *Mikhail Bulgakov*

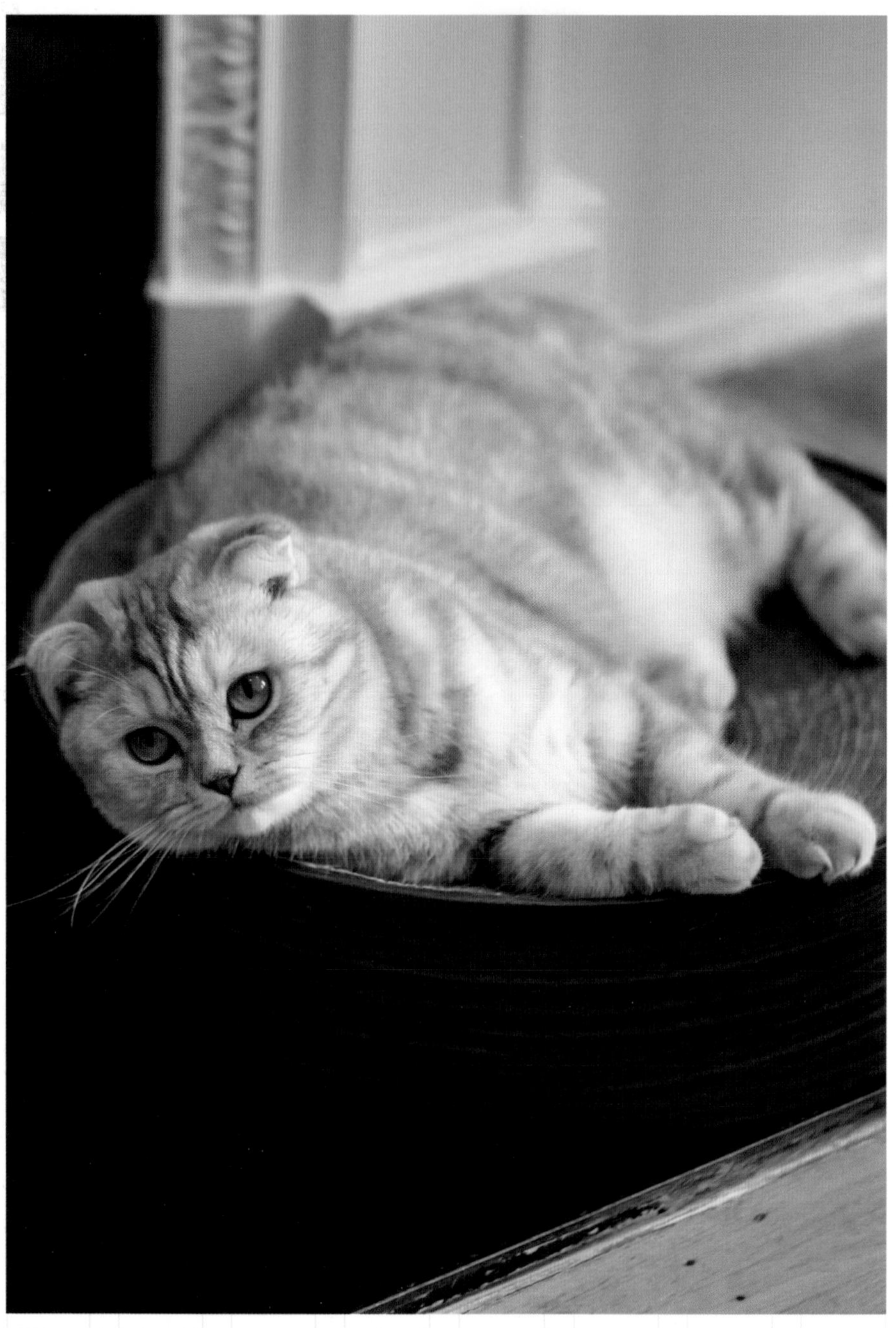

THE

SATAN'S WHISKERS

ARE YOUR WHISKERS STRAIGHT OR CURLED?

SATAN'S WHISKERS COCKTAIL. (STRAIGHT)
Of Italian Vermouth, French Vermouth, Gin and Orange Juice, two parts each; of Grand Marnier one part; Orange Bitters, a dash.
Shake well and strain into cocktail glass.

SATAN'S WHISKERS COCKTAIL. (CURLED)
For the Grand Marnier in the foregoing Cocktail, substitute the same quantity of Orange Curaçao.
Shake well and strain into cocktail glass.

The Savoy Cocktail Book, *Harry Craddock, 1930*

A variation on the *Bronx,* the *Satan's Whiskers* cocktail first appears in Harry Craddock's *The Savoy Cocktail Book (1930).* The recipe above is the *'Straight'* version – if orange curaçao is used instead of Grand Marnier, it becomes a *Satan's Whiskers (Curled).*

SPECS

GIN
20ML (1 OZ)

DRY VERMOUTH
20ML (1 OZ)

SWEET VERMOUTH
20ML (1 OZ)

ORANGE JUICE
20ML (1 OZ)

GRAND MARNIER
10ML (½ OZ)

ORANGE BITTERS
1 DASH

METHOD

1. Shake and strain into a cocktail glass.
2. No garnish.

THE

SAZERAC

THE APOTHEOSIS OF WHISKEY COCKTAILS.

SAZERAC COCKTAIL. 63

A LA ARMAND REGNIER, NEW ORLEANS, LA.

Into a mixing-glass full of cracked ice place about a small barspoonful of gum syrup, three drops of Selner bitters and a jigger of Sazerac brandy; stir well, strain into a stem cocktail-glass which has been rinsed out with a dash of absinthe, squeeze a piece of lemon peel over the top and serve with ice water on the side.

The World's Drinks and How to Mix Them,
William Boothby, 1908

Some classic cocktails have little to no recorded history to speak of, just a list of ingredients. By contrast, others have so much history and folklore that getting to the truth of things can be a bit like wading through treacle - slow and messy.

The history of the **Sazerac** *requires some effort, to parse fact from fiction. In this case we'll begin with the well-known but less-accurate story: the 'tall tale', so to speak...*

S

SAZERAC

TALE NO. 1
THE SAZERAC ACCORDING TO CLISBY ARTHUR

"A lie can travel halfway around the world before the truth can get its boots on" – This astute quote, often attributed to Mark Twain, is certainly applicable here. Of all the tall tales associated with the *Sazerac's* history the most widely spread was the account of things according to one Mr Stanley Clisby Arthur.

Clisby Arthur was a drinks writer in the 1930's, and for a long time everything we knew of the history of the *Sazerac* came from just one source – his *Famous New Orleans Drinks and How to Mix 'Em (1937)*. Being effectively the only writer on this, his account was taken as gospel on the matter for decades; it sounded plausible and was widely believed, until some recent fact checking rumbled a few key assertions.

CLISBY ARTHUR'S HISTORY OF THE SAZERAC

In 1793, a young refugee named Antoine Amedée Peychaud fled Haiti for America due to a slave uprising. He arrived with barely a possession to his name, but harbouring a secret family recipe for bitters. Born of a distinguished French family Antione was educated in New Orleans as an apothecary, and he soon opened a shop and began selling these bitters for their medicinal properties. Before long they were quite famous...

Continued on next page...

SPECS

RYE WHISKEY
60ML (2 OZ)

SUGAR SYRUP (2:1)
5ML (1 TSP)

PEYCHAUD'S BITTERS
3 DASHES

ABSINTHE
RINSE OF

METHOD

1. Stir the rye, sugar and bitters in a mixing glass; strain into a chilled rocks glass rinsed with absinthe. No ice.

2. Zest a lemon twist over the drink and discard.

Cognac had long been popular in New Orleans, so Peychaud would serve the spirit with dashes of his bitters in a double-ended egg cup, a contraption somewhat resembling a present-day jigger.

In French this was known as a 'coquetier' (pronounced *ko-k-tay*). Americans mispronounced this as *'cock-tay'* which became *'cocktail'* – the genesis of the word. Many years later, in 1859, a liquid dispensary was opened at 13 Exchange Alley (also in New Orleans) by a man named John B. Schiller.

Schiller was the local agent for the Sazerac de Forge et Fils brand of cognac, and opened his dispensary to sell the wares, naming it the 'Sazerac Coffee-house'. Schiller's *Brandy Cocktail,* made with Peychaud's bitters, was one of the most popular drinks of the day.

In 1870, Thomas H. Handy (bookkeeper to Schiller) took over the establishment and changed its name to 'Sazerac House'. Boldly, he also replaced the cognac in the cocktail with Maryland rye whiskey. As to how absinthe worked its way into the *Sazerac,* Arthur credits this to bartender Leon Lamothe, in 1858 or 1870.

This tale has all the ingredients of a story with legs – dramatic entrance of its central character; a rags to riches main character arc; a permanent stamp on the culture – the legacy around the word 'cocktail'... A story almost ripe for a movie adaptation. But is it true? *Well... not so much.*

FACT CHECKING THIS TALE WE UNCOVER THAT

Although Peychaud did flee Haiti because of the slave uprising, and did come to New Orleans, writer and historian Philip Greene discovered that he wasn't born until 1803, and that his parents were among the last of the French colonists to leave the island. Antoine would have been a wee baby at the time, not a trained apothecary clutching his family's secret bitters recipe, alongside his few belongings. For Clisby Arthur's story to fit, little Antione would have to have been slinging brandy and homemade bitters in egg cups at the age of three, or younger.

In truth, the first real mention of Antoine Amedée Peychaud (from a New Orleans print source) is in 1832, when he went into business with an F.P. Ducongé. A few years later he opened an apothecary, and it was here that he created and sold his bitters – eventually he bottled and sold them wholesale as they gained popularity.

Moving on to the claim that the word 'cocktail' first emerged from a mispronunciation of Peychaud's egg cup is also apocryphal, as the word 'cocktail' is defined for the first time in 1806 in the *Balance and Columbian Repository* newspaper as *"A stimulating liquor, composed of spirits of any kind, sugar, water, and bitters."*

With regards to Leon Lamothe being the one who added absinthe to the drink (in 1858 or 1870), drinks writer David Wondrich throws shade on this assertion in his article *Is the Sazerac a New Orleans Cocktail?*

Wondrich found an 1843 *Times-Picayune* article which makes mention of hotels serving *"brandy, sugar, absynthe (sic), bitters, and ice"* well before Lamothe was said to have come up with that tweak.

TALE NO. 2
SHORTER AND FEATURING SOME NEW CHARACTERS

This less influential tale is a shorter account, but introduced some exciting new names into the mix. This version of the *Sazerac* story is that Sewell T. Taylor, owner of the Merchant Exchange Coffee House, sold the business to Aaron Bird to start a liquor importing business. Bird then changed the name of the bar to 'Sazerac House', and began serving a *'Sazerac Cocktail'* using the brand of cognac that Taylor was importing – 'Sazerac de forge et Fils', coupled with the local bitters (from Antoine Amedée Peychaud, mentioned in the previous tale).

After changing ownership several times, Thomas H. Handy then took over, and did the switcheroo of spirits (as in the previous story).

Fact checking tale no. 2: This briefer account is also erroneous, as we see in the next section, which delves into what actually happened.

Confusingly, these three characters all appear in the *Sazerac's* history – just not playing the parts as outlined above...

THE TRUE ACCOUNT OF TAYLOR, BIRD AND HANDY

It's through the detailed research of fact-finders such as David Wondrich, Robert F Moss, and Philip Greene that we finally begin to get a clearer and more credible picture of the actual roles these characters played in the history of the *Sazerac.*

SEWELL T. TAYLOR AND AARON BIRD

It seems there were several venues called 'Exchange' at the time in question. The one Sewell T. Taylor started running in 1840 was the 'Merchant Exchange Coffee House', which he took over from a W. T. Raynall. Sometime around 1850 Taylor left the Merchant Exchange to set up a liquor importing business, located literally across the street. Handy.

Although he wasn't the first to sell the Sazerac de Forge et Fils brand of cognac in New Orleans, he quickly gained a reputation for having the most extensive selection of vintages.

When Taylor died in 1861, Aaron Bird took over his business, and shortly after moved the shop to 82 Common Street. Three years later, in 1864, Bird also died. At this point the company and all of its stock were sold at auction. That's the end of their story – there is no evidence that their business was ever called the 'Sazerac House', or that they had a house drink called the *'Sazerac'* cocktail; remember this business was not a bar, but a wholesaler/retailer of liquor.

So neither Taylor nor Bird had any part in the development of the *Sazerac* cocktail as such; what Taylor certainly did play a role in was popularising Sazerac de Forge et Fils cognac in the city.

THOMAS H. HANDY

The other character mentioned in both of the tales above, did play an essential role in the *Sazerac* cocktail, although not as described.

Thomas H. Handy was a Maryland native who moved to New Orleans with his father and started working as a clerk for Sewell T. Taylor's wholesale liquor company at 15 Royal Street, aged 23. After a stint fighting in the American Civil War (1861-65) he returned to New Orleans, and took up working for John B. Schiller – also a wholesaler in the liquor business, as well as operator of the *Sazerac* Coffee House, which was across the road from Sewell T. Taylor's establishment.

This Sazerac Coffee House was previously called the Merchant Exchange Coffee House, and was the same one that Taylor left in 1850.

Handy took over Schiller's business in 1871 and renamed it 'Thomas H. Handy & Co.', advertising the company as importers of Sazerac de Forge et Fils as well as other liquors, champagnes, wines and bitters. It's worth noting that at this point the list of bitters he sold didn't include Peychaud's.

That changed in 1873 when Handy bought out the rights to Peychaud's bitters after Antoine Amedée fell on hard times, and was forced to become an employee of Handy's. It's this link between the Thomas H. Handy Co. and the Sazerac House that would seal Peychaud's bitters as an essential ingredient in the *Sazerac* cocktail later on.

1878 to 1884 were turbulent times for Handy – he too faced financial turmoil, precipitating a bitter rivalry with one-time business partner Vincent Micas, to whom he was forced to sell his entire stake in the company. This led to years of acrimonious tit-for-tat business manoeuvring; at one point they both had venues named Sazerac located a few blocks from each other, both selling Sazerac brandy as well as Peychaud's bitters (which Handy relabelled 'Handy's Aromatic Bitter Cordial'). Micas ended up selling his liquor business in 1884, and Handy died in 1893 at the age of 54. Handy's business was taken over by his silent investor William McQuoid, who alongside bartenders Billy Wilkinson and Vincent Miret, continued to run the venue.

So we've got a clearer picture of Taylor, Bird and Handy's respective roles, but what about the *Sazerac* cocktail itself?

THE SAZERAC COCKTAIL (A CHANGE OF SPIRITS?)

As we saw earlier, Handy is often credited with changing the recipe of the *Sazerac* from cognac to rye whiskey in the early 1870s; a response to phylloxera wiping out the wine and cognac trade in France. But a crucial point to note at this stage is that by the early 1870s when Handy is said to have made the switch, there was no *'Sazerac Cocktail'* to speak of.

In his article *Is the Sazerac a New Orleans Cocktail?,* writer David Wondrich cites five separate instances between 1871 and 1885 where a mention of the *'Sazerac Cocktail'* would seem obvious – if indeed it was the famous house cocktail of the Sazerac House – yet such mentions do not occur.

The first mention of a cocktail of any sort from the Sazerac House is in the *Times-Democrat* newspaper in 1895; it praises Vincent Miret (mentioned previously, in the Handy story) for making the best whiskey cocktails in New Orleans.

Still no mention of a *'Sazerac Cocktail'* by name – this didn't come until as late as 1898, when it's mentioned in a record of the 16th biennial conference of the Alpha Tau Omega social fraternity held in New Orleans:

> "A good deal was heard at the St. James about the two mysterious articles: ***'Sazerac Cocktail'*** and an ***'Imperial Gin Fizz.'***"

The cognac cocktails served at the Sazerac House (before Handy supposedly made the base-spirit switch) would merely have been a classic *Brandy Cocktail,* as found in many places in New Orleans and other cities. This would have comprised of brandy, sugar, sometimes absinthe, and whichever bitters you had to hand – in this case, the local brand Peychaud's. If anyone mentioned a *'Sazerac Cocktail'* during that time, they likely meant a *Brandy Cocktail* made with Sazerac de Forge et Fils cognac, or any other cocktail made at the Sazerac House.

The *Brandy Cocktail* had been popular in New Orleans since the 1830s. Author Henry Didimus described it after his visit to the city in the winter of 1835-6 in *New Orleans As I Saw It.* He asks his host the difference between the city's famed *Brandy Cocktail* and a *Brandy Toddy* – he is told:

"A ***brandy toddy*** *is made by adding together a little water, a little sugar, and a great deal of brandy – mix well and drink. A brandy-cocktail is composed of the same ingredients, with the addition of a shade of Stoughton's bitters."*

By the 1870s the drinking trend had changed, and the preference for brandy shifted to the new fashionable choice – whiskey. This wasn't just due to phylloxera, but also to the increased Americanisation of New Orleans (which had been culturally more European, as a result of its French and Spanish colonial heritage).

One of the most popular cocktails at that time was the *Improved Whiskey Cocktail* (see recipe), whose ingredients are essentially the same as a whiskey-based *Sazerac* – and as mentioned earlier in the *Times-Democrat* newspaper, one of the best places to get one was the Sazerac House, made by the trusty hands of bartenders Vincent Miret and Billy Wilkinson.

As The Sazerac House's reputation for cocktails grew – thanks largely to the bartending prowess of Miret and Wilkinson – they soon began selling bottled versions of their cocktails nationwide under the Thomas H. Handy & Co. brand, labelling the product line 'Sazerac Cocktails'.

In addition to their whiskey version of the cocktail they offered several other options, including Old Tom gin, *Martini,* Holland gin, vermouth and *Manhattan.* However it was the whiskey variant the punters wanted, and it was this version that would go on to be known simply as the *Sazerac Cocktail.* So, the alternative theory is that the brandy to rye transition never happened, and they were always separate cocktails – Sazerac de Forge et Fils went into a *Brandy Cocktail,* and the *Sazerac* as we know it today was always made with rye whiskey, simply a riff on the *Improved Whiskey Cocktail.* If that is the case, then Miret and Wilkinson just took an established cocktail, perfected it and spread it to the masses, making it New Orleans' very own.

Note: 1. Stanley Clisby Arthur intentionally misquotes Didimus to say a 'shade of bitters' instead of Stoughton's to perpetuate his story of Peychaud's being the original bitters. 2. Some prefer to use both Peychaud's and Angostura bitters, as in Christopher O'Reilly's recipe; others split the spirit into equal parts of rye and cognac. I prefer just rye, Peychaud's and an absinthe rinse.

"The Sunday Mercury says that if you are at a hotel, and wish to call for a beverage compounded of brandy, sugar, absynthe, bitters and ice, called by the vulgar a cocktail, ask for une queue de chanticleer – it will be an evidence at once of your knowledge of French and of Chesterfield."

– Times-Picayune, February 1st 1843

RECIPE DEVELOPMENT

The earliest recipe of note is from Christopher O'Reilly, who worked for the Thomas H. Handy company from 1904 up to Prohibition. O'Reilly provided a recipe for the bottled version of their cocktails, and the interesting thing about the recipe is that it includes both Peychaud's and Angostura bitters, (as well as maraschino), but curiously the absinthe is missing. Chris McMillan, co-founder of the Museum of the American Cocktail, speculates that this could be because the recipe was from between 1912 and Prohibition, a period in which absinthe was banned. The first cocktail book appearance is in William "Cocktail" Boothby's *The World's Drinks and How to Mix Them (1908)*. Boothby got the recipe from someone he knew, who had worked at the Thomas H. Handy company. Everything is there as you would expect: rye, Peychaud's bitters, absinthe rinse, sugar and a lemon twist.

SAZERAC TRIVIA

- In 1934, Herbsaint (an absinthe substitute) was released, created by J. Marion Legendre to fill the gap left from the ban. From release, it's been customarily used in *Sazeracs* in New Orleans. Even though absinthe is now available in the United States many venues still use Herbsaint instead.

- In 2008, the *Sazerac* was named as the Official Cocktail of New Orleans.

- Robert Simonson points out that until the year 2000, the *Sazerac* was just a regional drink that people in New Orleans and Louisiana drank, it's only since then that its popularity has spread globally. The *Sazerac* is the apotheosis of whiskey cocktails, the ne plus ultra, nonpareil... it's very good.

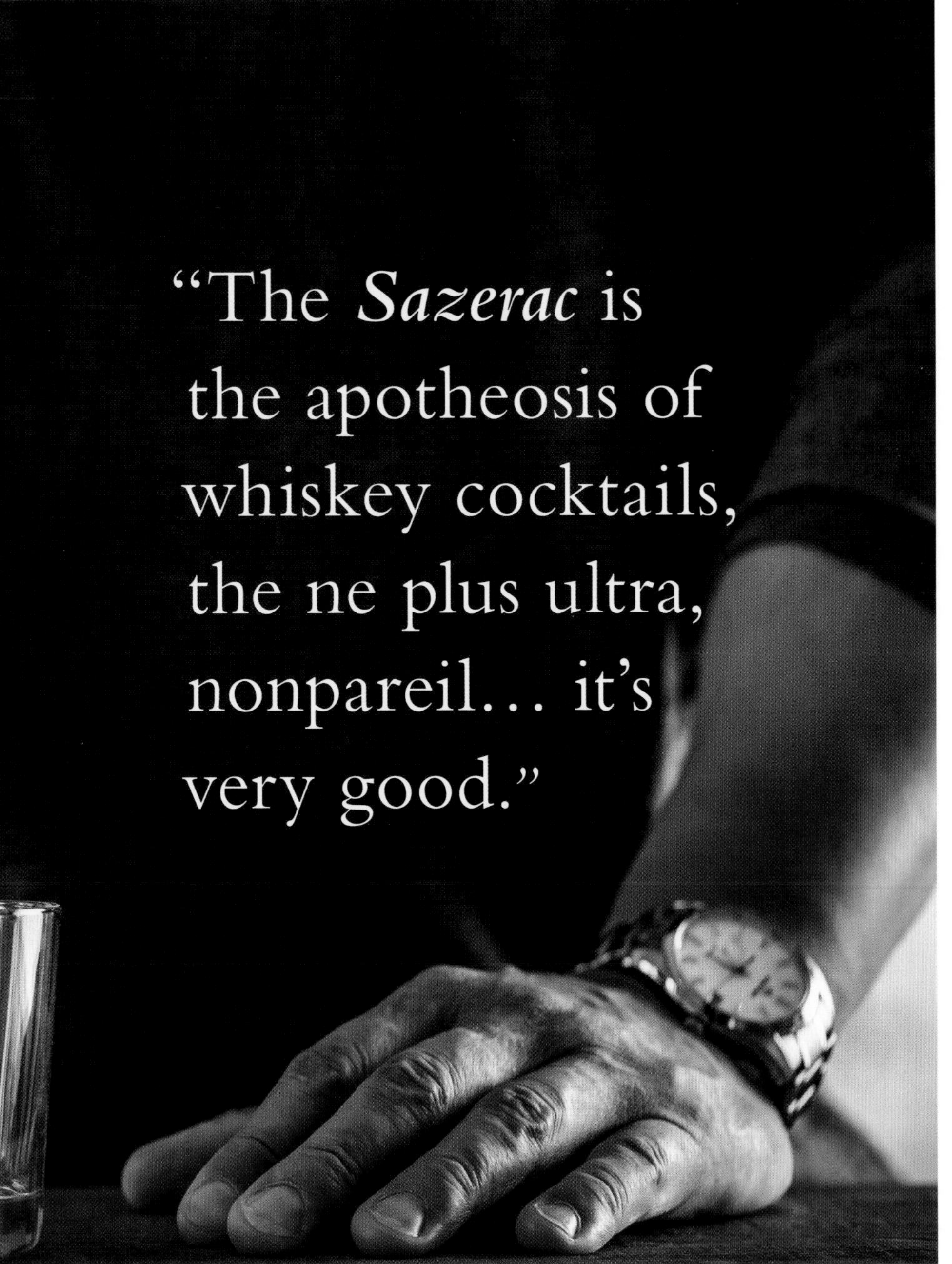
"The *Sazerac* is
the apotheosis of
whiskey cocktails,
the ne plus ultra,
nonpareil… it's
very good."

SCOFFLAW

S

THE

SCOFFLAW

A MENACE TO THE REPUBLIC ITSELF.

SPECS

RYE WHISKEY
45ML (1½ OZ)

DRY VERMOUTH
30ML (1 OZ)

LEMON JUICE
15ML (½ OZ)

GRENADINE
10ML (2 TSP)

ORANGE BITTERS
1 DASH

METHOD

1. Shake and strain into a cocktail glass.
2. No garnish.

In January 1924, four years into Prohibition, a competition was run to find a new disparaging word to describe "a lawless drinker of illegally made or illegally obtained liquor", with a prize of $200 in gold. The architect of this competition was Delcevare King – fervent supporter of the 18th Amendment, member of the Boston Republican Society, and general pious killer-of-fun. He's quoted in the *Boston Daily Globe* as saying:

"I do seek a word which will stab awake the conscience of the drinker...and stab awake the public conscience to the fact that such lawless drinking is, in the words of President Harding, 'a menace to the republic itself'" [settle down]

The winner was announced on 15th January 1924, with the prize shared by two people, Henry Irving Dale and Kate L. Butler, who came up with the term *"scofflaw"*. The term has endured, and is now used as a catchall word to describe anyone who flouts the law.

The *Scofflaw* cocktail appears in Harry MacElhone's *Barflies and Cocktails in (1927)*. MacElhone says it was invented shortly after the aforementioned competition at Harry's New York Bar in Paris, by a bartender named Jock.

THE

SCORPION

S SCORPION

THE SINGLE DRINK VERSION OF THE INFAMOUS COMMUNAL DRINK.

The *Scorpion* (also known as the *Scorpion Bowl*) was originally a communal drink, designed to be shared by several people. Served in a volcano-type Tiki bowl, it was garnished with gardenias and served with very long straws.

It's said to have been created in the 1930s in a small bar in Honolulu, Hawaii, called The Hut, though others say it was Victor 'Trader Vic" Bergeron who came up with the drink. Either way, it was certainly Vic who made it famous, when he started selling them in his restaurant in Oakland, California a decade or so later.

Vic published three different recipes for the *Scorpion* over the years, but the one from his *Trader Vic's Bartender's Guide (1972)* is considered the standard. The single drink recipe is: "*2 oz light Puerto Rican rum, 1 oz brandy, 2 oz orange juice, 1 ½ oz lemon juice, ½ oz orgeat. Blended and served in a grapefruit supreme glass – decorated with gardenia.*"

Note: A 'grapefruit supreme glass' is a stemmed bowl, shaped like an ice cream glass, with a capacity of around 18 oz.

SPECS

WHITE RUM
60ML (2 OZ)

COGNAC
30ML (1 OZ)

ORANGE JUICE
60ML (2 OZ)

LEMON JUICE
45ML (1½ OZ)

ORGEAT
15ML (½ OZ)

METHOD

1. Blend and pour into a large highball – can also be shaken and poured over cubed ice.

2. In the absence of gardenia, garnish with an orange wedge.

THE

SHERRY COBBLER

THE FOREMOST SHERRY COCKTAIL, AND FOR GOOD REASON.

97. THE COBBLER.

Like the julep, this delicious potation is an American invention, although it is now a favorite in all warm climates. The "cobbler" does not require much skill in compounding, but to make it acceptable to the eye, as well as to the palate, it is necessary to display some taste in ornamenting the glass after the beverage is made. We give an illustration showing how a cobbler should look when made to suit an epicure.

98. Sherry Cobbler.

(Use large bar glass.)

2 wine-glasses of sherry.
1 table-spoonful of sugar.
2 or 3 slices of orange.

Fill a tumbler with shaved ice, shake well, and ornament with berries in season. Place a straw as represented in the wood-cut.

The Bon Vivant's Guide or How to Mix Drinks, *Jerry Thomas, 1862*

S

SHERRY COBBLER

The *Sherry Cobbler* came about in the 1830s and was the most popular cocktail in America for most of the 19th century. The *Mint Julep* had been the previous title-holder in preceding decades until the new kid in town knocked it off its perch.

*The **Sherry Cobbler** is a seminal cocktail, not just on the American drinks scene, but in the history of cocktails as a whole. Alongside the Mint Julep, it propagated the use of ice in cocktails and can also be credited with introducing the drinking straw to the masses.*

The first known mention of the *Sherry Cobbler* was found by David Wondrich in the diary of Katherine Jane Ellice, a Canadian visiting upstate New York in 1838 – she remarks how delicious she found it.

Continued on next page…

SPECS

SHERRY (AMONTILLADO OR PALO CORTADO)
120ML (4 OZ)

GRANULATED SUGAR
2 TSP

ORANGE WHEELS
2 HALVES

METHOD

1. Add sugar and sherry to a mixing tin and stir briefly to dissolve. Add the orange slices, shake with ice and strain over crushed ice in a highball.
2. Garnish with orange slices, berries and mint

Pretty soon it had spread like wildfire coast to coast, and its popularity wasn't limited to the United States – it was a truly global phenomenon. By mid-century, there are mentions of it from locales as far-flung as Panama, Australia and France.

The name *'Cobbler'* is thought to come from the cobblestone-like appearance of the ice in the drink; at the time ice had only recently been introduced to America, shipped over from Norway.

In 1862, it was featured in the first cocktail book aimed at bartenders, Jerry Thomas' *The Bon Vivant's Guide or How to Mix Drinks.* The *Sherry Cobbler's* stranglehold is evident even toward the end of the century, as seen in Harry Johnson's Bartenders' Manual (1888) where he says: *"This drink is without doubt the most popular beverage in the country, with ladies as well as with gentlemen."*

As with many classics, its prevalence didn't survive Prohibition, but thankfully it has seen a modern-day resurgence. One point of note is that *Cobblers* originally didn't contain citrus juice, though many modern-day recipes include lemon or lime. The *Sherry Cobbler* eventually led to a fuller category of cocktails – *Cobblers* – drinks served over crushed ice in a highball or goblet, and elaborately garnished. Jerry Thomas includes several versions in his 1862 book, with a variety of wines and spirits as the base.

"Just make the jam and put it in the jar."

– Simon Barnett

THE

SIDECAR

THE PRE-EMINENT COGNAC COCKTAIL.

Dale Degroff's theory is that the name stems from bartending parlance – the practice of serving excess liquid (leftover from shaking a cocktail) in a shot glass alongside the drink – this little glass would be referred to as a *'sidecar'*.

Considered the seminal cognac cocktail, the ***Sidecar's*** first print appearance is in 1922, in both Robert Vermiere's *Cocktails: How to Mix Them* as well as Harry MacElhone's *ABC of Mixing Cocktails*. Both authors state that it was invented by Pat MacGarry, a bartender at Buck's Club in London.

In *The Fine Art of Mixing Drinks (1948)* David Embury includes the ***Sidecar*** as one of his 'Six Basic Cocktails' alongside the ***Martini***, the ***Manhattan***, the ***Old Fashioned***, the ***Daiquiri*** and the ***Jack Rose***.

He says a friend of his invented it at a bar in Paris during World War I, and named it after a Captain who used to be driven to the bistro in a motorcycle sidecar. This is a story that is commonly bandied about, though it's authenticity is uncertain.

S SIDECAR

SPECS

COGNAC
50ML (2 OZ)

COINTREAU
25ML (1 OZ)

LEMON JUICE
25ML (1 OZ)

METHOD

1. Shake and strain into a cocktail glass half rimmed with sugar.

The ratios used fall into two categories: the 'French School', which is equal parts of the three ingredients, as in Vermiere and MacElhone's recipes; and the 'English School', as found in Harry Craddock's *The Savoy Cocktail Book (1930)*, which calls for a 2:1:1 ratio. David Embury's recipe on the other hand, calls for an 8:2:1 proportion, the same as his *Daiquiri*.

*The **Sidecar** is the descendant of the **Brandy Crusta** (see recipe), with which it shares striking similarities. The difference between the two is that the **Crusta** has lesser amounts of the accompanying ingredients to the cognac base.*

Although not in the original recipes, the *Sidecar* is now commonly served with a sugar rim.

SILVER BULLET

S

THE

SILVER BULLET

"WE'RE WEREWOLVES NOT SWEARWOLVES."

SPECS

GIN
40ML (1 ½ OZ)

LEMON JUICE
20ML (¾ OZ)

KÜMMEL
20ML (¾ OZ)

METHOD

1. Shake and strain into a cocktail glass.

2. Garnish with a lemon twist.

SILVER BULLET COCKTAIL.	½ Gin. ¼ Lemon Juice. ¼ Kummel. *Shake well and strain into cocktail glass.*

The Savoy Cocktail Book, *Harry Craddock, 1930*

The *Silver Bullet* is thought to have been created around the 1920s, and it appears for the first time in Harry Craddock's *The Savoy Cocktail Book (1930).*

It's the best-known cocktail using kümmel, a liqueur flavoured with caraway seed, cumin, and fennel.

"I do not always know what I want, but I do know what I don't want."

– Stanley Kubrick

THE

SINGAPORE & STRAITS SLING

PINK SLINGS FOR PALE PEOPLE.

SPECS

SINGAPORE SLING AKA STRAITS SLING

GIN
40ML (1½ OZ)

CHERRY HEERING
10ML (2 TSP)

BENEDICTINE
10ML (2 TSP)

LEMON JUICE
10ML (2 TSP)

ANGOSTURA BITTERS
2 DASHES

ORANGE BITTERS
2 DASHES

SODA
TO TOP

METHOD

1. Shake and strain over cubed ice into a highball, top with soda.

2. Garnish with a lemon slice and cherry.

The history of the *Singapore Sling* is another case of the official party line not quite standing up to scrutiny...

The story according to the Raffles Hotel, Singapore is that it was invented there in 1915, by bartender Ngiam Tong Boon at the hotel's 'Long Bar'. The specs on the cards distributed by the hotel are said to be true to Boon's original, transcribed onto a bar-chit by a visitor in 1936 who asked the bartender for the formula.

Now, everyone agrees it was indeed invented by Ngiam Tong Boon at Raffles, but it couldn't have been in 1915 – drinks writer/sleuth Simon Difford informs us that Boon died that year, shortly after leaving the hotel to return home to Hainan, China. Difford suggests a more realistic invention window; sometime between 1899 (when Boon started working there), and 1915 ...when he died.

The most significant point of contention regarding the provenance of the *Singapore Sling* is determining what guise and constitution it had in its infancy. Raffles insists the recipe on their handout cards is as Boon invented it; consensus opinion, however, says it started off as a very different drink, and its original moniker was the *Straits Sling* (as printed in Robert Vermeire's *Cocktails and How to Mix Them, 1922*).

Singapore at the time was part of the 'Straits Settlements' – a group of four Southeast Asian provinces under British Colonial rule; Singapore, Malacca, Penang and Dinding.

Vermeire notes next to the recipe that it was a "well-known Singapore drink": *Straits Sling, ½ gill of Gin, 1/8 gill of Benedictine, 1/8 gill of Dry Cherry Brandy, The juice of half a lemon, 2 dashes of Angostura bitters, 2 dashes of Orange bitters. Shaken and served in a tumbler, topped up with soda.*

Vermeire's recipe is a much simpler drink, and more in line with the classical definition of a *Sling.* We know that *Gin Slings* were a popular drink in Singapore at the end of the 19th century – there's mention of *Slings* being regularly consumed in the region in an 1897 article from the *Straits Times*, found by David Wondrich. A few years later in 1903, there is the first mention of "pink slings for pale people." Could this *'Pink Sling'* be Ngiam Tong Boon's original *Singapore Sling* i.e. the *Straits Sling?*... Or, could it be that *Pink Slings* were commonplace at the start of the 20th century and Boon just made his own twist on an established cocktail popular locally?

Continued on next page...

S

SINGAPORE & STRAITS SLING

SPECS

RAFFLES SINGAPORE SLING

GIN
30ML (1 OZ)

CHERRY HEERING
15ML (½ OZ)

LIME JUICE
15ML (½ OZ)

GRENADINE
10ML (2 TSP)

COINTREAU
7.5ML (¼ OZ)

BENEDICTINE
7.5ML (¼ OZ)

PINEAPPLE JUICE
60ML (2 OZ)

ANGOSTURA BITTERS
1 DASH

METHOD

1. Shake and strain into a highball or sling glass over cubed ice.

2. Garnish with a cherry and a pineapple wedge.

EARLY PRINT APPEARANCES

Looking at early cocktail book appearances we see similarities to Vermeire's spec:

Harry Craddock's *The Savoy Cocktail Book (1930)* – Craddock's *Strait Sling* is identical to Vermeire's, and his *Singapore Sling* is even simpler: ½ cherry brandy, ¼ dry gin, the juice of ¼ lemon and soda.

Sloppy Joe's *Cocktails Manual (1932)* – Listed simply as a *Singapore*, the recipe is: one third each of Gordon's gin, Benedictine and cherry brandy, with a peel of lemon (they mean lime) and topped with mineral water.

Charles H. Baker *The Gentleman's Companion (1939)* – His Singapore Sling is the same as Sloppy Joe's: one third each of gin, cherry brandy and Benedictine, topped with club soda with a lime peel.

David Embury *The Fine Art of Mixing Drinks (1948)* – Listed as a *Singapore Gin Sling:* 1 ½ jiggers gin, 1 pony cherry brandy (Kirsch), juice of ¼ large lemon or ½ large lime, 1 tsp sugar syrup and 1 dash Angostura, topped with soda and garnished with a lemon peel. Embury prefaces his recipe by saying that he's never seen two recipes for a *Singapore Sling* that are the same, and that it's essentially a *Gin Sling* with cherry brandy. He also adds that some recipes call for a pony of Benedictine.

All of these early print recipes share broadly the same DNA and are vastly different from the Tiki-style drink served at Raffles. Simon Difford notes on his website that sceptics believe the pineapple and grenadine were added to the recipe only when the hotel re-launched in the 1970s – a period when such Tiki-style drinks were in fashion.

WHAT KIND OF CHERRY BRANDY?

Another offshoot debate concerns the type of cherry brandy used... It used to be thought, based on Vermeire's use of the term 'dry cherry brandy', that the original called for a cherry eau de vie, such as Kirschwasser.

However, David Wondrich explains (in his *Imbibe* magazine article from 2011) that this is probably incorrect – it was likely a red cherry brandy, such as Heering or Bols, as those were the only brands being advertised in Singapore at the time. Confusion may further stem from David Embury specifically putting "Cherry Brandy (Kirsch)" in his spec; perhaps similarly misinterpreting Vermeire's recipe.

Further corroboration that Vermeire intended a red cherry brandy (such as Heering or Bols) is that elsewhere in his book he specifically calls for 'Kirsch' when he means cherry eau de vie, as seen in the recipe:

"Polichinelle or Cassis-Kirsch, ½ gill of Cassis de Dijon, 1/6 gill of Kirsch."

THE

SOUTHSIDE FIZZ

A MINTY VARIANT OF THE FIZZ.

SOUTH SIDE FIZZ
Made same as Gin Fizz, adding fresh mint leaves

Recipes for Mixed Drinks, *Hugo R. Ensslin, 1917 (2nd Edition)*

The *Southside Fizz* is a variant of the Gin Fizz, with the addition of mint. Most people will have come across this drink as a result of Harry Craddock's *The Savoy Cocktail Book (1930)*.

IN TERMS OF ITS ORIGIN, THE THREE MOST COMMON STORIES ARE:

- It was invented during Prohibition, at a speakeasy in New York called Jack & Charlie's (later renamed the 21 Club).
- It was invented during Prohibition, somewhere on the South Side of Chicago during the mob days. It was created by gangsters to cover the rough taste of bathtub gin.
- It was invented at the turn of the century at the Southside Sportsmen's Club on Long Island, where *Mint Juleps* were very popular.

S

SOUTHSIDE FIZZ

SOUTH SIDE COCKTAIL.	The Juice of ½ Lemon. ½ Tablespoonful of Powdered Sugar. 2 Sprigs Fresh Mint. 1 Glass Dry Gin. *Shake well and strain into medium size glass. Add dash of siphon soda water.*

The Savoy Cocktail Book, *Harry Craddock, 1930*

The first printed recipe is found in Hugo R. Ensslin's *Recipes for Mixed Drinks (1917, 2nd Edition).* As this predates Prohibition, it rules out the 21 Club and Chicago mobster tales, making the Sportsmen's Club the most likely of the three by default.

VARIATIONS

Southside: Same ingredients, shaken and served straight up in a cocktail glass; no soda.

Southside Royale: Same as a *Southside;* just add champagne instead of soda.

SPECS

GIN
50ML (2 OZ)

LEMON JUICE
25ML (¾ OZ)

SUGAR SYRUP (2:1)
15ML (½ OZ)

MINT LEAVES
3-4

SODA
TO TOP

METHOD

1. Muddle mint in the bottom of a shaker, add other ingredients, shake and strain into a highball glass over ice, top with soda. Or serve without ice as with a traditional Fizz.

2. Garnish with a mint sprig.

"No. It's for me."

– Hauptmann Gerd Wiesler

THE

SOYER AU CHAMPAGNE

I GOT SOME ICE CREAM! I GOT SOME ICE CREAM!

Soyer au Champagne is as much a dessert as it is a cocktail.

According to Jared Brown and Anistasia Miller in *Spirituous Journey (Book Two),* this drink was created in the mid 19th century by French chef Alexis Benoît Soyer. It makes an early appearance in Louis Fouquet's *Bariana (1896).* The brandy is missing from Fouquet's recipe, which is just curaçao and maraschino with the obligatory ice cream and champagne.

Later on in Harry McElhone and Harry Craddock's books, as well as the 1949 Esquire's *Handbook for Hosts* the brandy has been included. McElhone notes that it was 'a very popular beverage on the continent'.

Note: It's important not to stir the cognac, curaçao and maraschino with ice; they work better undiluted. You can just pour them individually over the vanilla ice cream before topping up with champagne if desired.

SPECS

COGNAC
15ML (½ OZ)

ORANGE CURAÇAO (PIERRE FERRAND)
15ML (½ OZ)

MARASCHINO
15ML (½ OZ)

VANILLA ICE CREAM
1 SCOOP

CHAMPAGNE
TO TOP

METHOD

1. Add a small scoop of vanilla ice cream to a large coupette, stir the first three ingredients without ice and pour over the ice cream. Pour champagne over the top, and serve with a teaspoon.

T H E

STINGER

THE STINGER HOLDS ITS OWN AS GOOD AS ANY.

155. The Judge.

A mixing-glass ⅔ full of ice,
3 dashes of gum,
⅓ of crême de menthe,
⅔ of brandy.

Shake to the freezing-point; strain, and serve in a cocktail glass.

The Flowing Bowl, *A. William Schmidt, 1892*

As with the *Grasshopper,* a lot of people poo-poo the *Stinger* because it contains creme de menthe, a liqueur saddled with negative connotations due to featuring in so many horrendous cocktails and shots from the 1970s-90s (...the darkest time in cocktail history).

But forget that – when made using a high-quality brand of creme de menthe, the Stinger holds its own as good as any, and it's no spring chicken either.

The first we see of the *Stinger,* albeit under a different name is A. William Schmidt's *The Flowing Bowl (1892);* here it's listed as ***The Judge.***

George J. Kappeler adds Angostura bitters and rebrands it the ***Brant*** in *Modern American Drinks (1895).* Finally, by 1913 it appears as the Stinger in Jacque Straub's *Manual of Mixed Drinks.*

STINGER

STINGER
½ Jigger Brandy.
½ Jigger Creme de Menthe White.
1 Lemon Peel.
Shake, strain into Cocktail Glass.

Manual of Mixed Drinks, *Jacques Straub, 1913*

In the 2005 updated edition of his book *Imbibe!,* David Wondrich says that if the rumours are true it may have been invented by Reginald Claypoole Vanderbilt (of the Vanderbilts) father of fashion designer Gloria Vanderbilt (who incidentally is the mother of present-day TV personality Anderson Cooper).

Its popularity over the years has been cemented by numerous cultural nods – from James Bond drinking it in Ian Fleming's novel *Diamonds are Forever (1956)* to appearances in such notable films as Bing Crosby and Frank Sinatra's *High Society (1956), Kiss Them for Me (1957)* with Cary Grant and Jayne Mansfield, and Billy Wilder's *The Apartment (1960)* starring Jack Lemmon and Shirley MacLaine.

SPECS

COGNAC
50ML (2 OZ)

WHITE CREME DE MENTHE
25ML (1 OZ)

METHOD

1. Shake and strain into a cocktail glass.

2. No garnish.

THE

STONE FENCE

NOT UNLIKE THAT PRODUCED BY RUNNING DOWNHILL INTO ONE.

209. Stone Fence.

(Use large bar glass.)

1 wine-glass of whiskey (Bourbon).
2 or 3 small lumps of ice.
Fill up the glass with sweet cider.

The Bon Vivant's Guide or How to Mix Drinks,
Jerry Thomas, 1862

The *Stone Fence* is a very old American drink – around since at least the late 1700s. It had been a mainstay in bars and taverns for a long while by the time Jerry Thomas included it in *The Bon Vivant's Guide or How to Mix Drinks (1862)*. It was originally made with rum, but at an unknown point, whiskey became the fortifying spirit of choice.

STONE FENCE

98. STONE FENCE.
(Use a whiskey glass.)
1 wine glass full of whiskey;
2 or 3 lumps of broken ice;
fill up the glass with cider, stir up well with a spoon, and serve.

Bartender's Manual, *Harry Johnson, 1882*

The name could come from the "fact that a man who drank it was likely to seek the lea of a stone fence to sleep off his potation", *Farm Journal, Volume 37 (1913)*. Or, as David Wondrich puts it:

"a name which hints at the effect produced by getting outside too many of these, which is not unlike that produced by running downhill into one."

SPECS

BOURBON
60ML (2 OZ)

CIDER (BRETON)
TO TOP

METHOD

1. Pour cider into beer mug or highball, add a few cubes of ice and pour bourbon on top.

TI' PUNCH

TO

TWENTIETH CENTURY

CO-SPECS

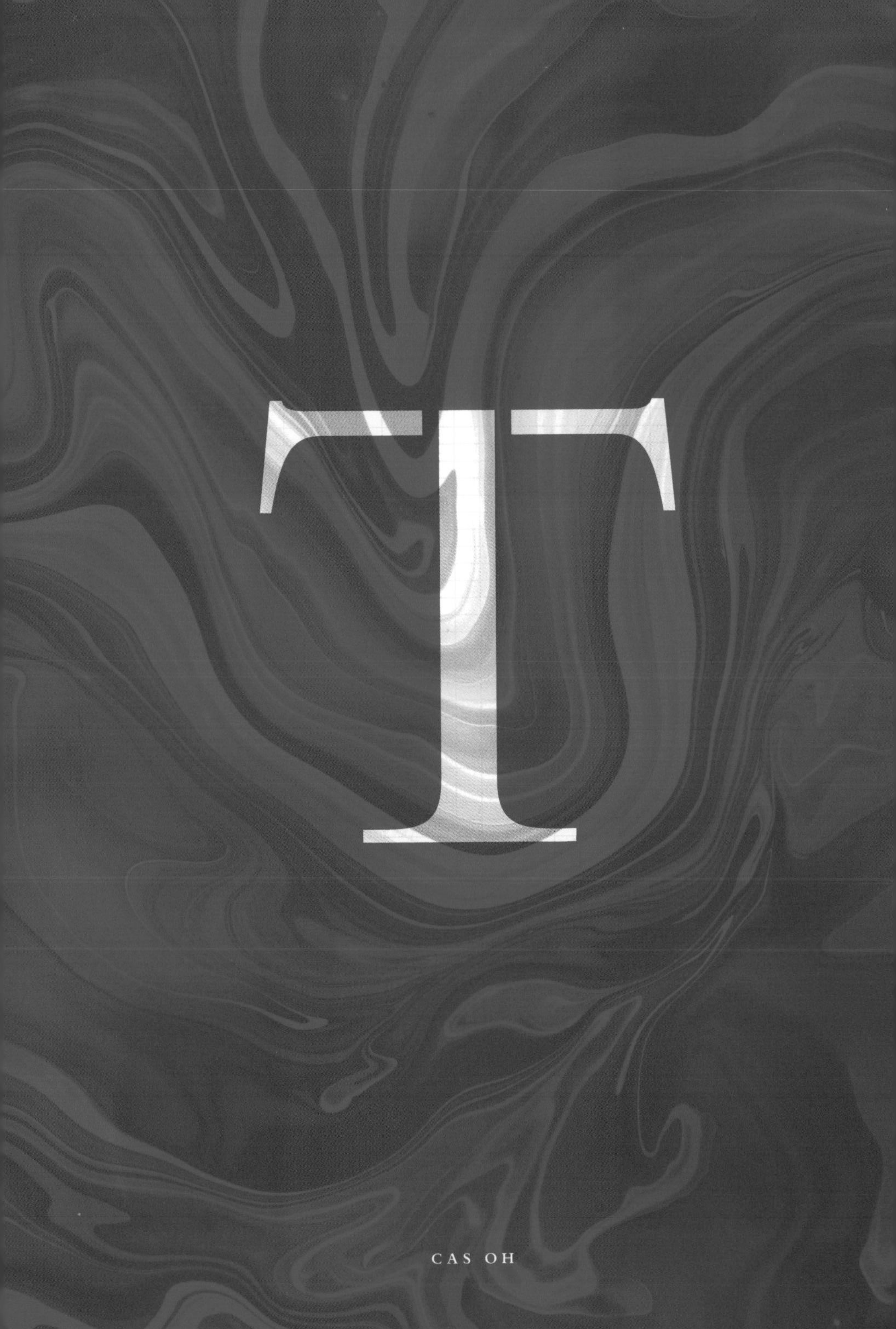
T
CAS OH

TI' PUNCH

T

THE

TI' PUNCH

'EACH PREPARES HIS OWN DEATH.'

SPECS

WHITE RHUM AGRICOLE
60ML (2 OZ)

DEMERARA SYRUP (2:1)
5ML (1 TSP)

LIME
1 SMALL DISC OF LIME WITH A BIT OF FLESH

METHOD

1. Add the sugar and rum to a rocks glass and swizzle with a traditional le bois lélé Martinique swizzle stick (if you have it, otherwise stir with a spoon). Cut a coin-sized slice from the side of a lime, so there's a bit of pulp; squeeze this into the drink and place into the glass.

2. Garnish with the disc of lime.

Ti' Punch (pronounced tee-paunch) means 'petit' or 'little' punch. It is the national drink of Martinique and is pretty much exclusively how agricole rhum is consumed on the island.

It is usually served in a do-it-yourself manner, where you're presented with a small plate of granulated sugar, a spoon, a circular piece of lime, a swizzle stick, a tumbler glass, and a bottle of rum. This tradition is referred to with the fantastic French expression 'chacun prépare sa propre mort' which translates as 'each prepares his own death'.

In his book *Potions of the Caribbean (2013),* Jeff Berry says the first mention of this drink is by Lafcadio Hearn – the English travel writer – in his 1890 book *Two Years in the West Indies*. To keep with tradition serve this neat. You can use granulated sugar, but if so, make sure you swizzle/stir it for long enough to dissolve all the sugar.

THE

TIPPERARY

IT'S A LONG WAY TO TIPPERARY

TIPPERARY COCKTAIL
⅓ Bushmills Irish Whiskey
⅓ Chartreuse
⅓ Italian Vermouth
Shake well in a mixing glass with cracked ice, strain and serve.

Recipes for Mixed Drinks, *Hugo R. Ensslin, 1917*

We're not sure how this cocktail was named, but an educated guess would be that it was referencing the famous World War I song *'It's a Long Way to Tipperary'*.

Tipperary is a county in Ireland, and the eponymous song was written in 1912 by duo Henry James 'Harry' Williams and Jack Judge. It became closely associated with the war after a *Daily Mail* news reporter, George Curnock witnessed an Irish regiment singing the song as they marched through Boulogne, a coastal city in Northern France in 1914. After Curnock reported this, it was soon adopted by all of the British Army and became part of the soundtrack to the First World War. The song would have been well known by the time the *Tipperary* cocktail makes its first print appearance in Hugo R. Ensslin's *Recipes for Mixed Drinks (1917)*. Harry MacElhone also included a Tipperary in his 1922 book *ABC of Mixing Cocktails,* however that's a very different drink consisting of gin, orange juice, grenadine, dry vermouth, and sprigs of mint. That version later appears in Harry Craddock's *The Savoy Cocktail Book (1930)* under the name *Tipperary No.2.*

SPECS

IRISH WHISKEY (SINGLE POT STILL)
30ML (1 OZ)

SWEET VERMOUTH
30ML (1 OZ)

GREEN CHARTREUSE
15ML (½ OZ)

METHOD

1. Stir and strain into a cocktail glass.

NOTES

As with all Irish whiskey cocktails, best to use a single pot still style.

The equal parts ratio in Ensslin's 1917 specs has the Chartreuse dominating the other flavours, so a 1:1:½ ratio lends itself to a better balance of the three.

REDBREAST
21

“Everything we hear is an opinion, not a fact. Everything we see is a perspective, not the truth.”

– Marcus Aurelius

T H E

TOM & JERRY

A POPULAR WINTER WARMER IN AMERICA DURING THE 19TH CENTURY, WITH ITS OWN SIGNATURE SERVING BOWL AND CUPS.

METHOD

1. Divide the egg yolks and whites into two separate bowls. Whisk the egg yolks, then add the sugar, rum, spices and further whisk until well mixed.

In the other bowl, whisk the whites until stiff peaks are formed. Gently fold the whites into the yolks until well integrated. Spoon this batter into a mug, filling it about halfway.

Add the cognac, and top up with hot frothed milk (as you would a cappuccino).

2. Garnish with grated nutmeg.

Similar to an *Eggnog* but served hot, the *Tom & Jerry* was a highly popular drink in America in the 19th century, especially towards the end – it was a staple of the winter season.

174. Tom and Jerry.

(Use punch-bowl for the mixture.)

5 lbs. sugar.
12 eggs.
½ small glass of Jamaica rum.
1½ teaspoonful of ground cinnamon.
½ do. do. cloves.
½ do. do allspice.

Beat the whites of the eggs to a stiff froth, and the yolks until they are as thin as water, then mix together and add the spice and rum, thicken with sugar until the mixture attains the consistence of a light batter.

To deal out Tom and Jerry to customers:

Take a small bar glass, and to one table-spoonful of the above mixture, add one wine-glass of brandy, and fill the glass with boiling water, grate a little nutmeg on top.

Adepts at the bar, in serving Tom and Jerry, sometimes adopt a mixture of ½ brandy, ¼ Jamaica rum, and ¼ Santa Cruz rum, instead of brandy plain. This compound is usually mixed and kept in a bottle, and a wine-glassful is used to each tumbler of Tom and Jerry.

N. B.—A tea-spoonful of cream of tartar, or about as much carbonate of soda as you can get on a dime, will prevent the sugar from settling to the bottom of the mixture.

This drink is sometimes called Copenhagen, and sometimes *Jerry Thomas.*

The Bon Vivant's Guide or How to Mix Drinks,
Jerry Thomas, 1862

T TOM & JERRY

The batter would be served in a communal *'Tom & Jerry* bowl' and ladled individually into mugs, topped up with hot water or milk.

Jerry Thomas claimed to have invented this drink in 1847, naming it after himself, but this can't be true: David Wondrich cites a reference to the drink in the *Salem (Massachusetts) Gazette* from 20th March 1827 (Thomas was born in 1830). While he may not be the creator of the drink, Jerry Thomas was a least a great ambassador for it, spreading the word and contributing to its popularity with its inclusion in his cocktail book *The Bon Vivant's Guide or How to Mix Drinks (1862).*

It is also sometimes miscredited to English writer Pierce Egan, who wrote a stage play in 1821 called Tom and Jerry, or Life in London. It's possible the name stems from Egan's characters, though he's certainly not responsible for the drink.

SPECS

BATTER

EGGS 8

ICING SUGAR
2 CUPS

DARK RUM
30ML (1 OZ)

VANILLA EXTRACT
1 TSP

GROUND CINNAMON
1 1/2 TSP

GROUND CLOVES
1/2 TSP

GROUND ALLSPICE
1/2 TSP

CREAM OF TARTAR
1/2 TSP

PER MUG

BATTER
1/2 MUG (6 OZ)

COGNAC
45ML (1 ½ OZ)

HOT FROTHED MILK
TO TOP

THE

TOM COLLINS

A DRINK THAT FINDS ITS ROOTS IN 19TH CENTURY GIN PUNCHES.

David Wondrich covers the history of this drink in great detail in his books *Imbibe! (2007)* and *Punch (2010)*; a lot of what we know about the Tom Collins stems from his research.

Wondrich says the ***Collins*** finds its roots in the ***Gin Punches*** made in the early 19th century, starting at the Garrick Club and leading onto Limmer's Hotel, before crossing the ocean and taking on its current form.

RICHARD PRICE AND THE GARRICK CLUB

The story begins with a New Yorker named Richard Price, who managed the famous Park Theatre for 18 years, before moving to London in 1826 to take over the Covent Garden Theatre. Things didn't go so well for him in London – he only lasted a couple of years – but luckily for him, when the Garrick members club opened in 1831 (which is still going today), he swung a job as the manager.

Price was described as a rather rough-and-ready fellow, lacking in polish and decorum – starkly in contrast to the club's aristocratic and thespian client base. His saving grace was the ***Gin Punch*** he brought with him from New York; a mix of gin and iced soda water (a pioneering combination at the time). Punches back then were traditionally served with ice, whereas his had none.

T

TOM COLLINS

Instead, it was chilled by the soda water. Other signature touches included soaking the lemon peel in gin to take on the oils, as well as adding maraschino. The gin he used in his punch would most likely have been genever (Price being a New Yorker), as that was the predominant style in America during this period.

A mention of Price's Garrick *Club Punch* can be seen in the *London Quarterly in 1835: "Pour half a pint of gin on the outer peel of a lemon, then a little lemon juice, sugar, a glass of maraschino, about a pint and a quarter of water, and two bottles of iced soda water. The result will be three pints of the punch in question."*

TOM COLLINS WHISKEY

(Use large bar glass) 5 or 6 dashes of gum syrup. Juice of a small lemon. 1 large wineglass of whiskey. Fill the glass half full of shaved ice, shake up well and strain into a large bar glass. Fill up the glass with plain soda water and imbibe while it is lively.

TOM COLLINS BRANDY

The same as *Tom Collins Whiskey,* substituting brandy for whiskey.

TOM COLLINS GIN

The same as *Tom Collins Whiskey,* substituting gin for whiskey.

– Bar-Tender's Guide, Jerry Thomas, 1876

Continued on next page...

SPECS

GIN
60ML (2 OZ)

LEMON JUICE
25ML (¾ OZ)

SUGAR SYRUP (2:1)
15ML (½ OZ)

SODA
TO TOP

METHOD

1. Build in a large highball glass. Stir and serve. As with all mixers in cocktails, make sure you use them cold from the fridge.

2. Garnish with a lemon wedge.

NOTE

In America, the *Tom Collins* is commonly garnished with an orange slice and cherry; in Europe, with a lemon or orange wedge.

JOHN COLLINS AND LIMMER'S HOTEL

As Price's cocktail spread around London, soon John Collin – head waiter of Limmer's Hotel, on Conduit Street in London – was making his own version, substituting the genever for Old Tom, and switching the maraschino for capillaire (a thick sugar syrup gently flavoured with orange flower water). Mentions of *Limmer's Gin Punch* can be found from the 1830s, and over the next two decades its fame grew, quickly surpassing that of the Garrick version. John Collin's fame also grew in parallel, and the drink eventually became known as the *John Collins*. By 1864 the *John Collins* cocktail had made its way to Canada (served at Dolly's Tavern in Montreal). It then crossed the border to the United States where, by the 1870s, it had spread to bars in many of the major cities.

FROM JOHN TO TOM

Somewhere in transit it morphed into a tall single-serve drink, and split into two separate drinks: the *John Collins* made with genever, and the *Tom Collins,* (mostly) made with Old Tom gin. That being said, in its first cocktail book appearance in *Jerry Thomas' Bar-Tender's Guide (1876),* Thomas lists the *Tom Collins* as a drink that can be made with either whiskey, brandy or gin. As genever disappeared from the American landscape, the *John Collins* would eventually become a bourbon drink. Why the name changed from *John Collins* to *Tom Collins* is an interesting question; it could be because Old Tom gin had gained traction, and people were using it instead of genever. Or, it could be due to the *'Tom Collins hoax'* of 1874, in New York.

This was a popular but short-lived prank that involved the prankster going to a bar, and worriedly telling a chosen 'mark' that a man named 'Tom Collins' was saying provocative or disparaging things about the mark. The idea was to whip the mark into a frenzy and send him off to another bar in search of the offender slandering his name. Upon arrival, the bartender of the establishment (very much in on the joke) would let the mark know he'd "just missed him!", and then send him on to the next venue also in on the game. On and on this would go until the mark finally cottoned onto the ruse. Sounds about as fun as binge-watching Hannah Montana, but this joke was apparently a big deal for a short while – songs were written, and even the newspapers got in on it.

DIFFERENTIATING A FIZZ AND A COLLINS

The main difference between a *Gin Fizz* and a *Tom Collins* (as they share the same ingredients) is that a *Fizz* is served without ice, and in a much smaller glass (around 6-8 oz) and was meant to be consumed quickly. The *Collins*, by contrast, had larger amounts of the ingredients and was served in a bigger glass (around 16 oz, which ended up being called a Collins glass). Both drinks are shaken and served without ice in Jerry Thomas' book, but the *Collins* soon included ice as standard. If you want to further differentiate the two, you could say that traditionally a *Fizz* is shaken, and a *Collins* is built in the glass.

TOMMY'S MARGARITA

T

THE

TOMMY'S MARGARITA

JULIO BERMEJO'S MODERN CLASSIC.

SPECS

TEQUILA REPOSADO
50ML (2 OZ)

LIME JUICE
25ML (1 OZ)

AGAVE MIX
(1 PART AGAVE SYRUP TO 1 PART WATER)
25ML (1 OZ)

METHOD

1. Shake and strain over ice in a rocks glass.

2. No garnish.

A modern classic that has justifiably spread to every corner of the earth, the *Tommy's Margarita* was invented by Julio Bermejo in the early 1990s, at his family-owned 'Tommy's Mexican Restaurant' in San Francisco.

Bermejo has long been a champion and spokesman for 100% agave tequila. At a time when everyone was using cheap mixto tequilas, he was the first to exclusively stock 100% agave, and even put one (Herradura) in the speed rail. He also insisted on using freshly squeezed lime juice when elsewhere sour-mix was the norm – his restaurant has probably gone through enough limes to have saved everyone who has died of scurvy in human history.

At Tommy's they make the drink in the jug of a Hamilton Beach blender, which they shake with ice and pour directly into a rocks glass, making up to five at a time. It goes without saying that for this – and all tequila-based cocktails – only use 100% agave tequila.

Note: It's scientifically impossible to be in a bad mood while drinking a Tommy's Margarita.

THE TOREADOR

AN APRICOT VARIATION OF A MARGARITA.

When you get all dressed up and your bull cancels on you.

The *Toreador* can be thought of as a variation of the *Margarita,* with apricot brandy in place of triple sec. It comes from W.J. Tarling's *Café Royal Cocktail Book (1937): "½ Tequila, ¼ Apricot Brandy, ¼ Fresh Lime or Lemon Juice, Shake."* Toreador means bullfighter and is often used interchangeably with matador, the difference being that a matador kills the bull at the end.

Note: A reposado tequila works well in this drink, and lime is better than lemon.

SPECS

TEQUILA REPOSADO
50ML (2 OZ)

LIME JUICE
25ML (1 OZ)

APRICOT BRANDY
25ML (1 OZ)

METHOD

1. Shake and strain into a cocktail glass.

"The first draft of anything is shit."

– Ernest Hemingway

THE

TORONTO

A SUPERB RYE AND FERNET COCKTAIL.

The first appearance of the *Toronto* cocktail is in David Embury's 1948 book *The Fine Art of Mixing Drinks,* and is listed as: *"6 parts Canadian whisky, 2 parts Fernet Branca, 1 part sugar syrup, Optional dash of Angostura bitters, Garnished with an orange twist."* Embury says it can be made in an Old Fashioned glass, or stirred with ice and served straight up (in a cocktail glass).

Prior to that though, a drink appears in Robert Vermeire's 1922 *Cocktails - How to Mix Them* called a Fernet Cocktail which shares the same ingredients: *"¼ gill Cognac or Rye, ¼ gill Fernet Branca, 2 dashes sugar or gum syrup, 1 dash of Angostura bitters. Stirred and served in a cocktail glass, and garnished with a lemon peel."*

Vermeire adds the notation: *"This cocktail is much appreciated by the Canadians of Toronto"*. It seems likely that this was the original incarnation, and that sometime between the two books the name was changed to *Toronto.*

SPECS

RYE WHISKEY
60ML (2 OZ)

FERNET-BRANCA
10ML (2 TSP)

SUGAR SYRUP (2:1)
5ML (1 TSP)

ANGOSTURA BITTERS
1 DASH

METHOD

1. Stir and strain into a cocktail glass.
2. Garnish with an orange twist.

THE
TURF CLUB

ONE OF THE FIRST TIMES GIN AND VERMOUTH WERE MIXED TOGETHER IN A COCKTAIL.

TURF COCKTAIL.

(Use a large bar glass.)

¾ full of fine shaved ice;
2 or 3 dashes of orange bitters;
2 or 3 dashes of maraschino;
2 dashes of absinthe;
½ wine glass of French vermouth;
½ wine glass of Plymouth gin;
Stir up well with a spoon, strain into a cocktail glass, putting in a medium size olive; and serve.

Bartender's Manual, *Harry Johnson, 1900*

The *Turf Club* cocktail (sometimes referred to as *Turf Cocktail)* is a relative of the *Martinez* and the *Martini,* and was one of the first times gin and vermouth were mixed together in a cocktail.

T TURF CLUB

SPECS

TURF CLUB
GEORGE WINTERS

OLD TOM GIN
45ML (1½ OZ)

SWEET VERMOUTH
45ML (1½ OZ)

PERUVIAN BITTERS (SUB. ANGOSTURA BITTERS)
2 DASHES

METHOD

1. Stir and strain into a cocktail glass.

SPECS

TURF COCKTAIL
HARRY JOHNSON

PLYMOUTH GIN
45ML (1½ OZ)

DRY VERMOUTH
45ML (1½ OZ)

MARASCHINO
5ML (1 TSP)

ABSINTHE
2 DASHES

ORANGE BITTERS
2 DASHES

METHOD

1. Stir and strain into a cocktail glass.

SPECS

TURF COCKTAIL
JACQUES STRAUB

GENEVER
60ML (2 OZ)

SWEET VERMOUTH
30ML (1 OZ)

ANGOSTURA BITTERS
2 DASHES

METHOD

1. Stir and strain into a cocktail glass.

Continued on next page...

TURF CLUB COCKTAIL.

Two or three dashes of Peruvian Bitters;
One-half wine glass of Tom gin;
One-half wine glass of Italian Vermouth;
Fill glass three-quarters full of fine ice, stir well with spoon and strain in fancy cocktail glass, then serve.

TURF COCKTAIL NO. 1
2 Dashes Orange Bitters.
2 Dashes Maraschino.
1 Dash Absinthe.
½ Jigger French Vermouth.
½ Jigger Dry Gin.

TURF COCKTAIL NO. 2
2 Dashes Angostura Bitters.
⅓ Jigger Italian Vermouth.
⅔ Jigger Holland Gin.
Stir.

How to Mix Drinks: Bar Keeper Handbook, *George Winter 1884*
Straub's Manual of Mixed Drinks, *Jacques Straub, 1913*

Turf clubs were venues set up in the latter part of the 19th century by wealthy gentlemen, as a place they could fraternise, drink and gamble on the ponies. Turf clubs were ubiquitous, though the most famous was the one by Madison Square Park in New York – it's posited the drink may have originated there.

Today, turf clubs are a generic term for any horse racing clubs, of which there are several across Asia and Australia, regions known for gambling. The term 'turf accountant' refers to a bookmaker.

We find a myriad of recipes for the *Turf Club* in cocktail books, but we'll focus on the three most common versions...

NOTABLE COCKTAIL BOOK APPEARANCES: **VERSION ONE**

The first version (and the first time it appears in print) is in George Winter's *How to Mix Drinks: Bar Keeper Handbook (1884)*. His recipe is equal parts Old Tom gin and sweet vermouth, with two or three dashes of Peruvian bitters.

Note: You can use Amargo Chuncho Peruvian bitters but Angostura bitters make a better drink.

NOTABLE COCKTAIL BOOK APPEARANCES: **VERSION TWO**

The second version is the *Turf Cocktail* found in the 1900 edition of *Harry Johnson's Bartenders Manual*. He changes the sweet vermouth to dry, and the gin from Old Tom to Plymouth (a sign of the shift in tastes at the beginning of the new century), as well as adding dashes of absinthe, maraschino and orange bitters.

Note: Johnson's Turf Cocktail is pretty much identical to his Tuxedo – the only difference being the use of Old Tom gin for his Tuxedo.

Johnson's version was the most widely adopted and is copied pretty much verbatim in many cocktail books that followed, including:

- J.A.Grohusko, Jack's Manual *(1908)*
- Jacques Straub, Drinks *(1914)*
  (Listed as Turf Cocktail No.1 – Plymouth is changed to dry gin)
- Robert Vermeire, Cocktails: How to Mix Them *(1922)*
- Harry MacElhone, ABC of Mixing Cocktails *(1922)*
- Harry MacElhone, Barflies and Cocktails *(1927)*
- Harry Craddock, The Savoy Cocktail Book *(1930)*

NOTABLE COCKTAIL BOOK APPEARANCES: **VERSION THREE**

The third version, a simple 2:1 ratio of genever to sweet vermouth, with Angostura bitters, was for a long time attributed to Albert Stevens Crockett's *Old Waldorf Bar Days (1931),* but this recipe actually precedes the Waldorf and can be found in Jacque Straub's two books, *Straub's Manual of Mixed Drinks (1913)* and *Drinks (1914),* listed as a *Turf Cocktail No.2.*

The first genever and sweet vermouth combo appears even earlier than that in William Boothby's *American Bartender (1891),* where his *Turf Cocktail* is equal parts genever and sweet vermouth, with dashes of Angostura, orange bitters and sugar syrup, garnished with a lemon twist.

Note: The main decision when making a Turf Club is whether to go for sweet vermouth (à la Winters and Straub) or dry vermouth (à la Johnson), and then to use the corresponding gin. The earliest recipe called for sweet vermouth, however, the most prevalent version is Harry Johnson's made with dry vermouth and Plymouth gin, which moves it one step closer to the Dry Martini.

“Sometimes nothin’ can be a real cool hand.”

– *Paul Newman*

THE

TUXEDO

...MANY DIFFERENT DRINKS UNDER THE TUXEDO MONIKER.

TUXEDO COCKTAIL.
(Use a large bar glass.)

¾ glass full of fine-shaved ice;
1 or 2 dashes of maraschino;
1 dash of absinthe;
2 or 3 dashes of orange bitters;
½ wine glass of French vermouth;
½ wine glass Sir Burnett's Tom gin;
Stir up well with a spoon, strain into a cocktail glass, putting in cherry, squeeze a piece of lemon peel on top and serve.

Harry Johnson's Bartender's Manual, *1900*

This drink is believed to have taken its name from the Tuxedo Club, a country club founded in 1886 in Tuxedo Park, New York. There are many different drinks under the *Tuxedo* moniker, but we can delineate them into two main classifications... The first and most predominant type are all iterations of the earliest *Tuxedo* recipe found, in the 1900 edition of *Harry Johnson's Bartender's Manual*. They have a gin (Old Tom or dry) and dry vermouth base, with maraschino, absinthe, and (either) orange or Angostura bitters. The second type is a much simpler cocktail made up of gin, sherry and orange bitters. This combination is first listed as a *Tussetto* in Jacques Straub's *Manual of Mixed Drinks (1913): "⅓ Sherry, ⅔ Dry gin, 2 dashes orange bitters, Stir."* He does include a *Tuxedo* as well, which is again like Harry Johnson's, but with the unusual addition of a spoon of sherry.

Note: Johnson's recipe is almost identical to the recipe for his Turf Club cocktail.

T TUXEDO

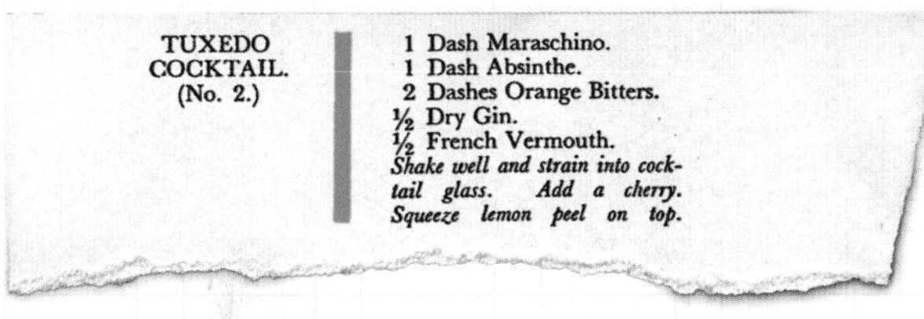

TUXEDO COCKTAIL. (No. 2.)

1 Dash Maraschino.
1 Dash Absinthe.
2 Dashes Orange Bitters.
½ Dry Gin.
½ French Vermouth.
Shake well and strain into cocktail glass. Add a cherry. Squeeze lemon peel on top.

TUXEDO COCKTAIL

1 Dash Maraschino.
3 Dashes Angostura Bitters.
1 Dash Absinthe.
⅔ Jigger Dry Gin.
⅓ Jigger French Vermouth.
1 Barspoon of Sherry Wine.
Stir well.

The Savoy Cocktail Book, *Harry Craddock, 1930*
Straub's Manual of Mixed Drinks, *Jacques Straub, 1913*

Albert Stevens Crockett features the same recipe as Straub's Tussetto, minus one dash of orange bitters, and calls it a plain *Tuxedo* in *Old Waldorf Bar Days (1931).*

Above his recipe, he includes a note saying *"After a settlement on the Erie R.R. where many customers of the Bar had country places."* The Erie R.R. is a reference to the Erie Railroad, and this settlement is where the Tuxedo Club was located. Based on this note, and the reputation of the Waldorf Astoria (and indeed Crockett's book), there are those who say this version of the cocktail was likely invented at the hotel.

The Savoy Cocktail Book (1930) adds some confusing nomenclature to the mix by printing two versions, a *Tuxedo Cocktail No.2,* which is similar to Johnson's and a *Tuxedo Cocktail No.1* which is a stripped down version without the maraschino and orange bitters.

SPECS

OLD TOM GIN
45ML (1½ OZ)

DRY VERMOUTH
45ML (1½ OZ)

MARASCHINO
2.5ML (½ TSP)

ABSINTHE
1 DASH

ORANGE BITTERS
2 DASHES

METHOD

1. Stir and strain into a cocktail glass.
2. Garnish with a cherry and lemon twist.

TWENTIETH CENTURY

T

THE

TWENTIETH CENTURY

NAMED AFTER A TRAIN THAT LOOKS LIKE A...

SPECS

GIN
40ML (1½ OZ)

WHITE CRÈME DE CACAO
20ML (¾ OZ)

COCCHI AMERICANO
20ML (¾ OZ)

LEMON JUICE
20ML (¾ OZ)

METHOD

1. Shake and strain into a cocktail glass.

2. No garnish.

Invented in the 30s by C. A. Tuck, the *Twentieth Century* cocktail first appeared in W. J. Tarling's *Café Royal Cocktail Book in 1937: "⅖ Booth's Dry Gin, ⅕ Crème de Cacao, ⅕ Lillet, ⅕ Lemon Juice, Shake."*

Jim Meehan, in his *Bartender's Manual (2017),* adds additional details about Tuck, noting that he was the head bartender at London's Piccadilly Hotel for 17 years, and that he published his own book in 1967 titled *Cocktails and Mixed Drinks.*

Named after the famous passenger train – the most advanced of its time – it travelled from New York to Chicago in 16 hours. The train was famous for its elegant and luxurious Art Deco design; the term 'red carpet treatment' actually originates from here – passengers were greeted with a red carpet, literally rolled out for them.

A wonderfully balanced cocktail. If you're a gin drinker and haven't tried this yet, don't waste another second.

THE

VESPER

VESPER

"IN HIS MIND HE FINGERED THE NECKLACE OF THE DAYS TO COME." - IAN FLEMING, CASINO ROYALE

The *Vesper* is named after the character 'Vesper Lynd', from Ian Fleming's first James Bond novel Casino Royale. In chapter seven, Bond orders a *Dry Martini* from the barman, saying: *"Just a moment. Three measures of Gordon's, one of vodka, half a measure of Kina Lillet. Shake it very well until it's ice-cold, then add a large slice of lemon peel. Got it?"*

Gilberto Preti is often credited with inventing the *Vesper* for Fleming at Dukes Hotel in London, (which can't be true as Preti started at Dukes 23 years after Fleming died). Dukes was one of Fleming's favourite haunts, and the *Vesper* will forever be associated with the iconic hotel bar, but the real creator of the *Vesper* may have been Fleming's good friend Ivar Bryce, to whom he gave a copy of *Casino Royale* with the inscription *"For Ivar, who mixed the first Vesper and said the good word."* Kina Lillet - as mentioned in the recipe - is no longer available, as it was sadly reformulated in 1986 with less quinine, in an attempt to make it more appealing to the masses after decades of declining sales. The closest modern-day substitute would be Cocchi Americano.

A *Vesper* (or *Dry Martini)* at Dukes Hotel, made by the hand of Alessandro Palazzi, is a must for anyone passing through London.

SPECS

GIN
60ML (3 OZ)

VODKA
20ML (1 OZ)

COCCHI AMERICANO
10ML (½ OZ)

METHOD

1. Shake and strain into a cocktail glass.
2. Garnish with a lemon twist.

VIEUX CARRÉ

V

THE VIEUX CARRÉ

A QUINTESSENTIALLY NEW ORLEANS COCKTAIL.

SPECS

RYE WHISKEY
30ML (1 OZ)

COGNAC
30ML (1 OZ)

SWEET VERMOUTH
30ML (1 OZ)

BENEDICTINE
5ML (1 TSP)

ANGOSTURA BITTERS
2 DASHES

PEYCHAUD'S BITTERS
2 DASHES

METHOD

1. Stir and strain over ice into a rocks glass.

2. Garnish with a lemon twist.

The *Vieux Carré* is said to have been invented in the mid to late 1930s by Walter Bergeron, at the Hotel Monteleone, New Orleans.

Vieux Carré literally translates to 'old square', one of the early French names for the French Quarter. It first appears in Stanley Clisby Arthur's Famous *New Orleans Drinks and How to Mix 'Em (1937)* listed as: *"⅓ jigger rye whiskey, ⅓ jigger cognac, ⅓ jigger Italian vermouth, ½ teaspoon Benedictine, 1 dash Peychaud's bitters, 1 dash Angostura bitters."*

Clisby Arthur suggests the optional garnishes of cherry and pineapple, however just a lemon twist will suffice.

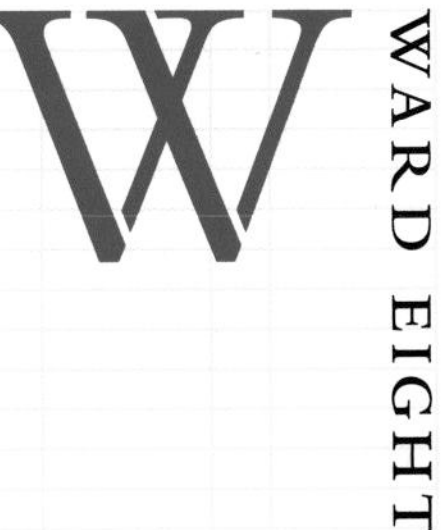

WARD EIGHT

THE WARD EIGHT

NAMED AFTER BOSTON'S EIGHTH WARD.

The *Ward Eight* is said to have been created in 1898 by bartender Tom Hussion, at the Locke-Ober – the second oldest restaurant in Boston.

It was made to celebrate the victory (potentially with the help of some dirty tricks) of politician Martin Lomasney's campaign to take control of the Senate seat representing Boston's Eighth Ward.

It makes its first cocktail book appearance in Robert Vermeire's *Cocktails: How to Mix Them, 1922:* *"1 teaspoon of Grenadine, ⅛ gill of Orange juice, ⅛ gill of Lemon juice, ¼ gill of Rye whiskey."*

SPECS

RYE WHISKEY
45ML (1½ OZ)

LEMON JUICE
15ML (½ OZ)

ORANGE JUICE
15ML (½ OZ)

GRENADINE
10ML (2 TSP)

METHOD

1. Shake and strain into a cocktail glass.

2. No garnish.

THE

WHISKEY SOUR

THE MOST POPULAR SOUR.

142. Brandy Sour.

(Use small bar glass.)

The brandy sour is made with the same ingredients as the brandy fix, omitting all fruits except a small piece of lemon, the juice of which must be pressed in the glass.

143. Gin Sour.

(Use small bar glass.)

The gin sour is made with the same ingredients as the gin fix, omitting all fruits, except a small piece of lemon, the juice of which must be pressed in the glass.†

* The Santa Cruz fix is made by substituting Santa Cruz rum instead of brandy.

† The Santa Cruz sour is made by substituting Santa Cruz rum instead of gin. In making fixes and sours be careful and put the lemon skin in the glass.

The Bon Vivant's Guide or How to Mix Drinks,
Jerry Thomas, 1862

Sours are a family of drinks where you can substitute the base spirit for your preferred tipple.

W WHISKEY SOUR

SPECS

BOURBON
50ML (2 OZ)

LEMON JUICE
25ML (¾ OZ)

SUGAR SYRUP (2:1)
15ML (½ OZ)

EGG WHITE
1

METHOD

1. Dry shake, then shake with ice and strain into a rocks glass over one large block of ice.
2. No garnish.

The first cocktail book it appears in is Jerry Thomas' *The Bon Vivant's Guide or How to Mix Drinks (1862)*. Thomas lists three *Sours:* Brandy, Gin and Santa Cruz rum.

He says to make it the same as a *Fix,* but replace the seasonal fruit garnish with a squeezed piece of lemon instead. At this early stage the *Brandy Sour* was the most popular, but soon the *Whiskey Sour* – made with bourbon (and sometimes rye) – took over, and remains the best known *Sour* today.

The addition of egg white is first mentioned in Robert Vermeire's *Cocktails and How to Mix Them (1922)*. He says *"A few drops of white of egg improve all Sours"*. Indeed they do. Over time, egg white has become a requisite addition to all varieties.

Sours can be served straight up in a coupe, or in a sour glass. Garnishes range from Angostura bitters (in the drink, or dashed on top) to cherries and orange slices, depending on which part of the world you're in.

WHISKY MAC

W

THE

WHISKY MAC

THE MAIN USE FOR GINGER WINE.

SPECS

SCOTCH
50ML (2 OZ)

STONE'S GREEN GINGER WINE
25ML (1 OZ)

METHOD

1. Build over ice in a rocks glass.
2. No garnish.

Whisky Mac is short for Whisky MacDonald; the drink is named after Colonel Hector MacDonald, who is said to have invented it during the days of the British Raj in India. Apparently, it was first made with Crabbie's ginger wine, although these days it's usually Stone's.

Stone's ginger wine is a fortified wine invented in 1740 by a grocer from High Holborn, London, named Joseph Stone. It is made with a fermented blend of ginger root, raisins, and pepper (amongst other things) and is fortified with brandy.

Originally poured in a glass and served neat, nowadays it is commonly built over ice, or stirred and strained.

"I'm very happy by myself — I'm lucky in that way. If I have enough to read and something to write about, and a bit of alcohol for me to add an edge, not to dull it."

– *Christopher Hitchens*

THE

WHITE LADY

HARRY CRADDOCK'S SIGNATURE COCKTAIL.

¼ Lemon Juice.
¼ Cointreau.
½ Dry Gin.
Shake well and strain into cocktail glass.

WHITE LADY COCKTAIL.

The Savoy Cocktail Book, *Harry Craddock, 1930*

The *White Lady* is an iconic cocktail, and the signature drink of legendary bartender Harry Craddock of The American Bar at The Savoy, London.

There is actually another Harry who lays claim to this cocktail – Harry MacElhone. MacElhone did, it seems, invent a drink called a *White Lady* in 1919, at Ciro's in London. This cocktail consisted of: Cointreau, white creme de menthe and lemon juice. Obviously that's not the *White Lady* we know – out of the three ingredients, only the Cointreau is a match.

It does get one ingredient closer a few years later in *ABC of Mixing Cocktails (1922)* where the recipe is: brandy, creme de menthe and Cointreau. However, it's still a very different animal.

MacElhone may have been the first to christen a cocktail the *White Lady,* but smart money is on Craddock as the creator of what we recognise as a *White Lady* today. It was certainly Craddock who made the drink famous, during his tenure at The Savoy, including the cocktail in his magnum opus *The Savoy Cocktail Book (1930).*

W WHITE LADY

That White Lady just got zested son!

By the end of the 1930s, he had firmly established it as a future classic, and the *White Lady* would forever be the cocktail most associated with Craddock. When the bar at The Savoy was remodelled in 1927, Craddock placed a three-piece shaker with the ingredients for a *White Lady* inside a wall of the building. Although not specified in Craddock's recipe, egg white is now a common (and recommended) addition.

Note: MacElhone did later claim to have changed his brandy, menthe, Cointreau version White Lady to the recognizable gin, Cointreau and lemon juice version in 1929, after opening Harry's New York Bar in Paris, though this was already two years after Craddock buried the shaker (as mentioned above).

SPECS

GIN
50ML (1½ OZ)

COINTREAU
25ML (¾ OZ)

LEMON JUICE
25ML (¾ OZ)

EGG WHITE
1

METHOD

1. Dry shake, then shake with ice and strain into a cocktail glass.

2. No garnish.

Photo of Nathan Merriman courtesy of Jesús del Toro García.

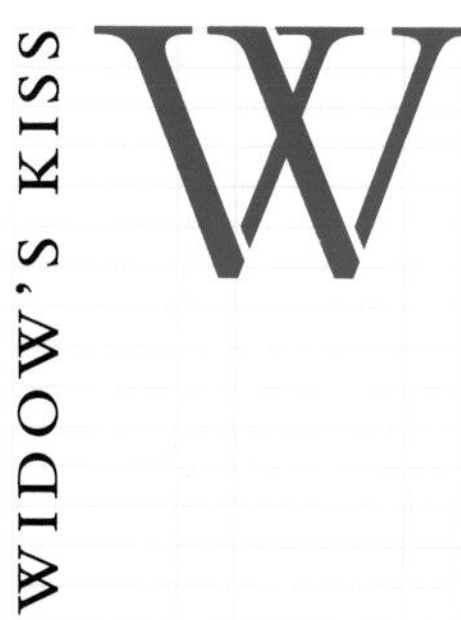

THE

WIDOW'S KISS

SWEET YET COMPLEX.

SPECS

CALVADOS
40ML (1½ OZ)

YELLOW CHARTREUSE
20ML (¾ OZ)

BENEDICTINE
20ML (¾ OZ)

ANGOSTURA BITTERS
2 DASHES

METHOD

1. Stir and strain into a cocktail glass.
2. No garnish.

> **Widow's Kiss.**
>
> **A mixing-glass half-full fine ice, two dashes Angostura bitters, one-half a pony yellow chartreuse, one-half a pony benedictine, one pony of apple brandy; shake well, strain into a fancy cocktail-glass, and serve.**

Modern American Drinks, *George J. Kappeler, 1895*

The *Widow's Kiss* was invented by a German fellow named George J. Kappeler – head bartender of the Holland House Hotel in New York. He came up with it sometime before he published *Modern American Drinks,* in 1895.

A sweet yet complex cocktail – Chartreuse and Benedictine share many of the same herbs and spices, and both play well with brandy.

"I made the wrong mistakes."

– *Thelonious Monk*

ZOMBIE

CO-SPECS

CAS OH

THE ZOMBIE

A MENDER OF BROKEN DREAMS.

We have Jeff Berry to thank for finding the lost recipe for this legendary drink. Invented by Donn Beach (Don The Beachcomber) at his Hollywood bar in 1934, no one knew the recipe for the ***Zombie*** – not even the bartenders who worked in his venue.

Donn was famously secretive about what went into his drinks, he would mark the bottles containing various recipe ingredients with coded letters and numbers, such as 'Don's Mix' or 'Don's spices #4'. The drink's reputation grew rapidly, and word spread that any visitors to Hollywood had to stop by The Beachcomber's to try one. Donn would wisely allow just two per customer.

The drink was imitated across the country in numerous bars, with bartenders guessing the formula to try and approximate Donn's secret recipe, usually with lacklustre results. Incredibly, in 2005 Jeff Berry came upon a drinks recipe notebook from 1937 owned by Dick Santiago, a bartender at Don the Beachcombers. Santiago had carried it around in his shirt pocket for 15 years while working there, and finally the original recipe was discovered at long last.

Z ZOMBIE

Zombie Punch 'old': ¾ oz lime, ½ oz Don's Mix [see below], ½ oz swizzle or falernum, 1½ oz Lownes Jamaica, 1½ oz Puerto Rican Dk., 1 oz Demerara 151, Dashes angostura, grenadine & absinthe. – *Dick Santiago's notebook from Jeff Berry's Sippin Safari, 2007.*

Listed as ***Zombie Punch*** 'old', it had the signature coded reference of 'Don's Mix' as one of the ingredients, which Berry discovered after some sleuthing was: two parts white grapefruit juice to one part cinnamon syrup.

With as many ingredients as original members of the Wu-Tang Clan, it seems like everything and the kitchen sink was thrown in... but the ***Zombie*** – when made to the original specs – is a blinder (and could also make you blind). Donn poetically referred to this drink as *'a mender of broken dreams'*.

DON'S MIX

2 parts white grapefruit juice
1 part "Don's spices #4" *i.e. cinnamon syrup*

Note: For the overproof demerara rum Lemon Hart 151 works well; if you can't find it, Goslings 151 works fine.

SPECS

GOLD RUM
45ML (1½ OZ)

JAMAICAN RUM
45ML (1½ OZ)

151 PROOF DEMERARA RUM
30ML (1 OZ)

LIME JUICE
22.5ML (¾ OZ)

DON'S MIX
15ML (½ OZ)

FALERNUM
15ML (½ OZ)

ABSINTHE
6 DASHES

ANGOSTURA BITTERS
1 DASH

GRENADINE
5ML (1 TSP)

METHOD

1. Blend with crushed ice and serve in a large highball.

2. Garnish with a mint sprig.

Please drink
responsibly.

Cas Oh

Take 2 dashes Angostura bitters.
1 pony of brandy.
1 pony of whiskey.
1 pony of Vermouth.

Shake up well with two small lumps of ice; strain into a claret glass, and serve with a quarter of a slice of lemon.

2 or 3 dashes of Bitters; (Boker's genuine only.)
1 dash of Curaçoa;
1/2 wine glassful of Old Tom Gin;
1/2 " " " Vermouth;
stir up well with a spoon, strain it into a fancy cocktail glass, squeeze a piece of lemon peel on top, and serve. (See Illustration, Plate No. 13.)

½ Dry Gin.
Shake well and strain into cocktail gl

, one dash orange bitters, half a jigger , half a jigger French vermouth, a mixing-half-full fine ice. Mix, strain into cocktail-

Old-Fashioned Whiskey Cocktail.

Dissolve a small lump of sugar with a little water in a whiskey-glass; add two dashes Angostura bitters, a small piece ice, a piece lemon-peel, one jigger whiskey. Mix with small bar-spoon and serve, leaving spoon in the glass.

TUXEDO COCKTAIL. (No. 2.)
1 Dash Maraschino.
1 Dash Absinthe.
2 Dashes Orange Bitters.
½ Dry Gin.
½ French Vermouth.
Shake well and strain into cocktail glass. Add a cherry. Squeeze lemon peel on top.

BEE'S KNEES
½ jigger Orange
1 spoon Honey
into chilled cocktail glass a

(A small wine-glass.)

. Mix, take out the ice, add a small d lemon-peel.

¼ pony brandy.
1 " French vermouth.
3 dashes Angostura bitters.
3 " gum syrup.

In m the jell tact wi assume

aschino.

SATAN'S WHISKERS COCKTAIL. (STRAIGHT)
Of Italian Vermouth, French Vermouth, Gin and Orange Juice, two parts each; of Grand Marnier one part; Orange Bitters, a dash.
Shake well and strain into cocktail glass.

SATAN'S WHISKERS COCKTAIL. (CURLED)
For the Grand Marnier in the foregoing Cocktail, substitute the same quantity of Orange Curaçao.
Shake well and strain into cocktail glass.

1/6 jus de citron
1/6 Miel
faire ce mélange avant

Neg sorts of be mad togethe

Manhattan Cocktail.

(Use small bar-glass.)

dashes of Curaçoa or Maraschino.
pony of rye whiskey.
wine-glass of vermouth.
ashes of Boker's bitters.
mall lumps of ice.
well, and strain into a claret glass. Put a quarter of a slice of lemon in the glass and serve. If the customer prefers it very sweet use also two dashes of gum syrup.

Mint J

e pulverized sugar.
r, mix well with a spoon.
s of fresh mint, and press them r, until the flavor of the mint is half wine-glass of Cognac bran- fine shaved ice, then draw out sert them in the ice with the he leaves will be above, in ge berries, and small piec asty manner, dash with Jar gar on top. Place a stra d you have a julep that is f

Prepared in th tuting whiskey f

stimulant and drying than pure wine.

61. MANHATTAN COCKTAIL.

bar glass.)

98. STONE FENCE.

(Use a whiskey glass.)

1 wine glass full of whiskey;
2 or 3 lumps of broken ice;
fill up the glass with cider, stir up well with a spoon, and serve.

rup;
(Boker's genuine o
absinthe if required);
key.
mouth;
to a fancy cocktail
squeeze lemon peel on the top, and serve, leave it for the customer to decide whether to use Absinthe or not. This drink is very popular at

Juic
Juic
4 Stra
1 teas
1 drin
1 pony
Made and served as directe

TIPPERARY COCKTAIL
Bushmills Irish Whiskey
Chartreuse
Italian Vermouth
glass with cracked ice, strain and serve.

SILVER BULLET COCKTAIL.
½ Gin.
¼ Lemon Juice.
¼ Kummel.
Shake well and strain into cocktail glass.

mon, or orange, add 2 tablespoonfuls of syrup, 1 wine-glass of Jamaica rum, table- of Curaçoa; mix in soda-water glass; add with shaven ice.

Knickerbocker à la Madame.—½ pint lemon-water ice, ½ pint sherry or Madeira, 1 bottle seltzer water, ¼ pint shaven ice.

107. Brand
(Use small
hes of gum syrup
bitters (B
lass of brand
Cur
peel

ss of whi
ll lumps of ice.
e glass with sweet cider.

ER
Jigger Brandy.
Jigger Creme de Menthe White.
Lemon Peel.
hake, strain into Cocktail Glass.

1/8 Absinthe.
Teaspoonful powdered Sugar.
3 dashes Raspberry Syrup.
Shake and strain off into coloured glass. Put a slice of lemon on top.

one ; or cut ely thin, and o lemons into calves-feet jelly antities of cinna- all-spice. Put the r one quarter of boiling cover the jug close, let it quarter of an hour, and then add bottle of boiling hot white wine. Grate

Brad
e bar-g
1
1/3
2/3

New Orleans Style

dashes of Boker's, Angostura or Peychaud bitters—either will make a fine cocktail. One lump of sugar, one piece of lemon peel, one tablespoonful of water, one wineglassful of liquor, etc., with plenty of ice. Stir well and strain into a cocktail glass.

LIBERAL
⅓ Jig
⅔ Jig
1 Das
Stir.

ANOTHER WAY—SPOON COCKTAIL

One lump of sugar, two dashes Angostura bitters, one piece of lemon peel, one lump of ice. Serve plain

RATTLE-SNAKE COCKTAIL.* (6 people)
4 Glasses Rye Whisky.
The Whites of 2 Eggs.
1 Glass Sweetened Lemon Juice.
A Few Dashes Absinthe.

57-
tumbl
ful of
syr